KATHARINE HEPBURN

Grace Carter

INTRODUCTION

In a film and stage career that spanned the better part of a century, Katharine Houghton Hepburn lived life just as she wanted. The list of adjectives used to describe her – bold, stubborn, self-sufficient, witty, beautiful – only begin to hint at the complex woman who entranced audiences around the world, exerted a singular influence on American popular culture, and challenged assumptions about how women ought to behave – on screen and off.

Her acting achievements alone earned Hepburn a place among the brightest stars of the twentieth century. During a marathon career that lasted sixty-six years, she appeared in a staggering forty-four feature films, thirty-three plays, and eight television movies – everything from screwball comedies to period dramas. She was nominated for twelve Academy Awards for Best Actress, winning a record four times, and was inducted into the American Theater Hall of Fame. Many of her movies have become classics, including four – *The African Queen*, *The Philadelphia Story*, *Bringing Up Baby*, and *Guess Who's Coming to Dinner* – that rank among the American Film Institute's 100 Greatest American Films of all time. Two others, *Adam's Rib* and *Woman of the Year*, were included in the AFI's list of the Greatest American Comedies Ever.

Yet, Hepburn was far more than a successful actress. With her distinctive, aristocratic voice and forceful personality, she proved to generations of fans that women could be as assertive, razor sharp, and successful as any man. "What she brought us was a new kind of heroine – modern and independent," wrote film historian Jeanine Basinger. Her insistence on wearing pants wherever she went changed the way women dressed. To commemorate her influence on women's fashion, the Council of Fashion Designers of America in 1986 presented her a lifetime achievement award.

In spite of her many accomplishments and awards, Hepburn was often criticized as not being a particularly versatile actor. "Picture Katharine Hepburn in every movie she ever starred in and ask yourself if she's not playing, essentially, the same part over and over," said the playwright and author David Macaray.

Hepburn did not disagree. "I think I'm always the same," she told a journalist in 1991. "I had a very definite personality, and I liked material that showed that personality." A more pointed appraisal came from Dorothy Parker, who attended one of Hepburn's early stage appearances and famously proclaimed that her performance ran "the gamut of emotion from A to B."

Despite her reputation as a proto-feminist, Hepburn later in life was sharply critical of women's sexual freedom and lamented the loss of the virile male hero. Critics noticed that many of her characters ended up in subservient roles – "restored to a safe position within the status quo," as film scholar Andrew Britton put it. "The dire or merely domestic outcomes of so many of her movies can be easily dismissed as the requirements of a less enlightened age," wrote Claudia Roth Pierpont in *The New Yorker*, "or as a sign of the ongoing bewilderment about how a truly 'modern' woman's story might conclude."

Off screen, Hepburn was fiercely private, and for many years rarely gave interviews or rubbed shoulders with fans. She rejected Hollywood society and attended the Academy Awards just once – to present an award to a friend, producer Lawrence Weingarten, in 1974. Friends and family said she could be controlling, selfish, and self-righteous – but always, they would quickly add, filled with an almost Herculean zest for life.

Hepburn was married, briefly, in her twenties. She had an affair with aviation tycoon Howard Hughes and, it was whispered, with several women. Most famously, she maintained a secret twenty-six-year relationship with her frequent co-star Spencer Tracy, who remained married to someone else. Most of this we know from Hepburn's 1991 autobiography, *Me: Stories of My Life*, which some critics complained showed a lack of introspection and empathy and shrewdly evaded or revised important biographical details. But the book was an enormous hit, staying at the top of bestseller lists for more than a year.

How did Hepburn develop into such a powerful, enigmatic woman who, even today, remains so deeply embedded in the American psyche? Her love affairs and life-long friendships certainly played a crucial role, but her biggest influence, without a doubt, was her parents, passionate and determined people who diligently instilled in her many of the qualities that would later make her world famous.

1
"WOMEN ARE
AS GOOD AS MEN"

Both of Katharine Hepburn's parents were progressive New Englanders in an age of stodgy conservatism. Thomas Norval Hepburn, known as Tom, born in 1879 outside Richmond, Virginia, met his future wife, Katharine Martha Houghton - "Kit" - in 1901 when she visited her sister Edith at Johns Hopkins University in Baltimore, Maryland, where they were both attending medical school. Kit, Edith, and their younger sister Marion came from a prosperous lineage: Their grandfather, Amory Houghton Sr., was the founder of Corning Glass Works. Kit was immediately enchanted by Tom, a tall, brawny redhead. When her sister pointed out that he had little money, Kit exclaimed, "I'd marry him even if I knew it meant I'd die in a year – and go to hell!"

At the turn of the century, it was rare for women to go to college, but Kit's mother, Caroline Garlinghouse Houghton, insisted that her three daughters do so; she wanted them to be educated and independent. Caroline and her husband, Alfred Houghton, both amateur musicians in Buffalo, New York, raised their girls to be agnostic free-thinkers, making them heretics in the eyes of the rest of the conservative, Episcopalian Houghton clan.

Alfred, who suffered frequent bouts of depression, was fired from the Corning glass factory, run by his older brother, Amory Jr., for chronic lateness. One day, he was found dead on railway tracks, killed by a self-inflicted gunshot to the head.

To add to the tragedy, not long afterward, Caroline was diagnosed with stomach cancer. Knowing she did not have long to live, she told her daughters they must go to college.

She drove sixteen-year-old Kit, the oldest, to Pennsylvania to visit Bryn Mawr College.

When Caroline died, the girls' Uncle Amory suggested they skip college and go to finishing school to learn to be ladies. Anticipating interference from her conservative family, Caroline purposely had not named legal guardians. When Kit was old enough to appoint her own, she threatened to name an adversary of her uncle's unless he allowed her to attend Bryn Mawr.

Grudgingly, Amory relented. But he used his control over Kit's finances to make her life difficult. At one point he sent her a letter berating her for borrowing money from a friend in an attempt to free herself from his influence. ". . . you are an extravagant, deceitful, dishonest, worthless person," he wrote, signing it, "Disgusted, your affectionate uncle, A. Houghton, Jr."

Clearly, Kate Hepburn was the product of a dramatic family, with, on her mother's side, two generations of smart, strong-willed women who carved a wide path for her to follow. "When Caroline Garlinghouse died, she was thirty-four years old," Kate wrote in her memoir. "She must have been a very strong character. My mother talked a lot about her: her beauty, her strength of character – her determination that the daughters get an education . . . I can see Mother to this day as she described herself sitting next to her mother. Her mother was lovely-looking. And I felt the enormous effect she must have had on my mother . . ."

Kate also cherished a quote from George Bernard Shaw that her grandmother had passed down to her three daughters: "This is the true joy in life, the being used for a purpose recognized by yourself as a mighty one; the being thoroughly worn out before you are thrown on the scrap heap; the being a force of nature instead of a feverish selfish little clod of ailments and grievances complaining that the world will not devote itself to making you happy. Don't give in. Fight for your future. Independence is the only solution. Women are as good as men. Onward!"

In 1899, Kit fulfilled her mother's dream by graduating from Bryn Mawr with a degree in history and political science. The following year, she earned her master's degree in chemistry and physics from Radcliffe (though some Hepburn biographers say the degree was in art history). Her sister Edith was studying medicine at Johns Hopkins, where she often exercised by fencing with a classmate, the handsome Tom Hepburn.

Tom was the youngest of five children born to an Episcopal minister, the Reverend Sewell Snowden Hepburn, and Selina Lloyd Powell. The family lived in Virginia and owned a farm near Chestertown, Maryland, but had been hurt financially by the Civil War. Like Kit, Tom's mother was a strong, independent woman. "Dad really loved his mother," Kate wrote later. "They were very close, and he developed a high regard for the female sex through her. She was his ideal – a fighter with the highest standards. She believed in education."

After meeting Tom at Edith's apartment, Kit was so taken with him that she took a teaching job at Johns Hopkins just to be near him. Tom was smitten, too, but took his time in proposing, leaving Kit to question his commitment. Finally, in an effort to shake him off the fence, she said, "You know, the great thing about our relationship is that whenever one of us marries, it won't hurt our relationship at all."

Tom was shocked. "I don't know how you can say such a thing," he said. "If I don't marry you, I shall never marry anyone."

"May I take this as a proposal?" Kit replied.

Tom informed her that he had been proposing to her for six months, but she never noticed: "Where's your common sense!"

In 1904, the couple married, just after Tom returned from a surgical internship in Germany to continue his residency at Hartford Hospital in Connecticut. They moved into a small red house on 22 Hudson Street in Hartford, across from the hospital's entrance.

Before the year was out, Kit gave birth to Thomas Houghton Hepburn, the first of their six children. Tom Sr. finished his residency and opened an office on High Street, specializing in surgical urology – a field almost unheard of at the time. It would take several years before the hospital would put Dr. Hepburn on its staff, but once he was hired, his reputation as a surgeon grew.

On May 12, 1907, the Hepburns had their second child, Katharine Houghton Hepburn. Kit was thrilled about her newborn daughter's red hair and asked the nurse to "hold her up to the window" so Tom could see it. "Yes, it's red!" she shouted to Tom. The proud father called the infant "Redtop"; everyone else called her Kathy, though, for most of her life, she would be known simply as Kate.

In the early 1900s, Hartford was a small, industrial city run by conservative men from its business establishment, which was founded on three insurance dynasties: Aetna, Phoenix, and Travelers. The town's manufacturers included Royal and Underwood, makers of typewriters, Pratt & Whitney, which tooled machine parts, and Colt, a gun maker. The wives of these businessmen struggled to mix beauty and culture into the fabric of the city, but it was a drab, blue-collar town.

Though the Hepburns were not considered wealthy by Hartford's standards, they owned their own home, employed servants, and were among the first families to get a car. Kit Hepburn was a true New Englander – wary of strangers and inclined toward clannishness – but soon began to feel restless with her comfortable life and narrow role as a homemaker.

One day, as she was walking through the park, pushing baby Kate in a stroller with Tom walking by her side, she thought, "Here I am, these two adorable children, a handsome, brilliant husband looking forward to his brilliant career. But me, what of me, what of me? Is this all that I'm here for? There must be something. I have a Bachelor's degree, I have a Master's degree."

When she returned home, her husband held up the newspaper and said, "Look here . . . a woman named Emmeline Pankhurst is speaking about women and the vote tonight." That evening, Kit went downtown to hear Pankhurst, a political activist and suffragist who had founded the Woman's Social and Political Union, a militant suffrage organization in the United Kingdom.

Interested in Pankhurst and her cause, but concerned about

the possible repercussions of joining such a group, Kit asked her husband if being an activist would cause problems for him. Yes, he replied, but added, "If I haven't enough brains to succeed in spite of it, why, we'll take the penalty."

Kit adopted her new cause with ferocity, marching and carrying banners painted by her husband that read: EQUALITY FOR WOMEN. She became such a fervent suffragist that Dr. Hepburn's colleagues stopped speaking to him except about work-related matters. One editorial in the *Hartford Courant* was so scathing that a friend suggested Kit sue for libel. She was unfazed. "Silly, isn't it?" Kit said. "They must have needed something to print."

Consumed with her new avocation, Kit took her daughter to suffragist meetings and lectures, where Kate would sit on the dais or in the first row and listen to her mother rally attendees to her cause. During one campaign that Kit spearheaded for birth control, she caused a stir by appearing in public obviously pregnant. In 1911, her third child, Richard "Dick" Hepburn, was born, and six weeks later, Kit was back at her meetings, bringing a nurse along to hold the baby and breast-feed him in a back room.

Two years after Dick arrived, when Tom was eight and Kate was six, the Hepburns had their fourth child, Robert ("Bob"). The closest in age, Tom and Kate were also emotionally close, as were the two youngest brothers, who often played together. Five years after Bob, in 1918, Kate's sister Marion was born, followed by Margaret ("Peg") two years later. Her sisters were so much younger than her, Kate recalled, that "to them, I was really another grown-up."

In her memoir, Kate says little about her siblings except to note that after she moved to New York, they would visit her and she would dress them up and take them to the theater, movies, and museums. "I was a sort of rich aunt, and we had great fun together," she recalls. "I'm sure that this was why I never had children of my own . . . I sort of had the experience of motherhood without the obligations."

When their parents died, the siblings remained close. "Their problems are my problems and vice versa," Kate wrote. "We're sort of a 'group' going through the world together. Isn't that wonderful? I feel so lucky. I feel cared for, and I have always felt cared for. . . . I cannot say anything in detail about my sisters and brothers. They are so much a part of me that I simply know that I could not have been me without them. They are my 'box' – my protection."

Tom and Kit raised the Hepburn children to be athletic as well as strong-minded; Dr. Hepburn touted exercise as the surest path to wellness. Tom Jr., afflicted with a form of rheumatic fever that occasionally left him confused and depressed, would perform rigorous activities in an attempt to overcome his illness. Dr. Hepburn led the children in daily calisthenics, taught wrestling holds, and included them in touch football games with his friends. Both the Hepburns encouraged their children to be adventurous and take risks, something Kate embraced with enthusiasm.

A natural athlete, by the time she turned eight, Kate had become a skilled wrestler, tumbler, and trapeze artist. She loved to climb trees, especially a hemlock on their property. Once a worried neighbor called to say, "Kit! Kathy is in the top of the hemlock!" Her mother replied, "Yes, I know. Don't scare her. She doesn't know that it's dangerous."

The Hepburn children were not permitted to complain. Once, Peg burst out crying because Marion and her friend wouldn't play with her. "I don't blame them," her mother said. "You're a moaner." At the dinner table, Kit engaged her children in lively debates and expected them to intelligently discuss the day's events; she had no patience for lazy thinking.

Despite Kit's rebellious nature and dynamic personality, the Hepburn household was clearly a patriarchy, and Dr. Hepburn had no reservations about spanking his children – mostly for disobedience and thoughtless behavior. Kit later recalled that Kate was "cuffed around a good deal" by her father, who loathed a cry-baby. By nine, Kate had stopped crying, and the spanking stopped, but her stubbornness increased.

Dr. Hepburn required all the children to take cold baths, which he believed stimulated the brain and body. Kate would splash into the icy water, then leap out and race naked to the fireplace, where her mother would wrap her in a red Navaho blanket. She later said the experience "gave me the impression that the bitterer the medicine, the better it was for you."

Kate viewed her father as "a real intellectual – a thinker – not just a memorizer." She once said, "There are men of action and men of thought, and if you ever get a combination of the two – well, that's the top – you've got someone like Dad."

In the Hepburn household, the children were never asked to go elsewhere to prevent them from listening to adult conversation. Little Kate listened as Emmeline Pankhurst,

Charlotte Gilman, and Emma Goldman – all revolutionary women with radical ideas – discussed venereal disease, prostitution, and contraceptives, and often heard her father discuss the specifics of his medical cases.

Kit believed that being frank about sex encouraged children to confide in their parents. When Kate asked her mother about the details surrounding her own birth, Kit described it "scientifically and specifically." Delighted to hear that no husband was required, Kate replied, "Oh, then I can have a baby without getting married. That's what I shall do!"

Shortly after Kate was born, the Hepburns had moved to 133 Hawthorne Street in Hartford, an early Victorian house made of red brick painted with a black lace trim. By 1917, with four children and needing more space, the family moved to a larger home at 352 North Laurel and hired more servants. As Dr. Hepburn's practice grew, he built a vacation home in the Fenwick borough of Old Saybrook, Connecticut, located on the waterfront where the Connecticut River flows into Long Island Sound. The Hepburns called their new summer home "Fenwick."

Tom Jr.'s health improved significantly by the end of their first summer at Fenwick, and when the family returned to West Hartford, he entered the Kingswood School, situated in a house once owned by Mark Twain. By then, Dr. Hepburn was already encouraging his son to follow him into the medical profession.

In 1918, just before she turned eleven, Kate enrolled in the coed Oxford School, where she took sewing and cooking classes. Of her school days, Kate would later say, "I was never a member of the club. I never knew what other girls were talking about."

At home, Kate depended on her big brother for companionship and devoted her non-academic hours to playing sports with her father. "I was freckled - wore my hair like a boy's," Kate recalled later. "In fact, with one brother Tom older and my two younger, Dick and Bob, being a girl was a torment. I'd always wanted to be a boy. Jimmy was my name, if you want to know."

When her school moved to the old Ensworth House, an elegant home on Farmington Avenue, Kate eventually made a few friends, but she didn't fit in or enjoy her classes. She longed for summer, when she could run barefoot along the waterfront at Fenwick, dive off the pier, and dig for clams. She and Tom sometimes swam two or three miles down the channel from their house.

One day, when Kate and Tom were swimming in the Sound, they were nearly swept out into the ocean by a gale. A local fisherman named William Ingham rescued them. After that, Kate haunted Ingham's fish shed. He taught her to fish, clean her catch, and row a boat. She persuaded her father to buy her a small boat – christened the *Tiger* – but it was ravaged by a storm its first summer while Kate was at the helm; she saved herself by swimming to shore clinging to the board sporting the boat's name.

In addition to athletics and the outdoors, Kate's passions were theater and films. She adored cowboy star William S. Hart and would cut grass and shovel snow to earn enough money to attend his movies and buy fan magazines. When she was eight, she staged *Uncle Tom's Cabin* in a little theater her parents built for her behind their Laurel Street house, casting kids from the neighborhood. "I wouldn't play Eva because Eva was too good," Katharine recalled. "I played Topsy – and as there was a little girl in the neighborhood who I wanted to get even with – I chose her for Eva – as Topsy played all the mean tricks on her." Later she would add, "I was never willing to watch any other girl being wonderful."

At Fenwick, Kate and her brothers staged theatrical productions using fruit boxes, pillows, and furniture as props. Their crowning achievement was *Beauty and the Beast,* which they performed for a large crowd of neighbors, raising $75 for the Navaho Indians in New Mexico, one of Mrs. Hepburn's favorite charities.

The single most important character in Kate's theatrical productions – indeed in her life to that point – was her beloved brother Tom, who played the banjo, sang, and wrote songs. At fifteen, he had earned a letter playing football at Kingswood School's football team and displayed academic prowess as well. Dr. Hepburn wanted Tom Jr. to enter Yale Medical School in the fall of 1921, but Tom was undecided and had difficulty changing Dr. Hepburn's mind.

Not long after Peg was born, in April 1921, Tom and Kate accompanied their mother on a train trip to New York that would change their lives forever. They were visiting Mary Towle, the friend of Kit's from Bryn Mawr who had loaned her the money that had infuriated her Uncle Amory so many years before.

Kate and Tom were delighted by the dynamic "Auntie Mary" and her friend "Auntie Bertie" who lived next door in the bohemian Greenwich Village neighborhood. Tom, fifteen, and Kate, fourteen, were enthralled by the non-stop hustle of the big city. Knowing their mother planned to leave on Thursday, they begged her to let them stay until Sunday morning when they could take the train back home. Kit said yes and went home to Connecticut.

It was a fateful decision. Years later, Kate told of returning home to Auntie Mary's place one night after going to the theater. Tom looked at her and said, "You're my girl, aren't you? You're my favorite girl in the whole world." It was almost as if he had a troubling premonition and wanted Kate to know how much he loved her – though later, she realized she was not sure he really said it. "Was it true?" she wondered. "I mean, did Tom really say it? I don't know any longer."

2
"YOU CRY – BUT INSIDE I WAS FROZEN"

For Tom and Kate, it was an exciting weekend in Manhattan. They explored the Village, Fifth Avenue, and Central Park, and on Friday night, April 1, they saw William Fox's film *A Connecticut Yankee in King Arthur's Court* at the Selwyn Theatre. On Saturday night, Tom played his banjo for Auntie Mary and some of her young friends, and around 10:00 p.m., Kate and Tom went to their rooms, Kate's on the first floor and Tom's in the attic. Tom's room, Kate would recall, was "full of junk and trucks and had no ceiling – just roof and rafters. His bed was a cot next to the wall."

At 8:30 on Sunday morning, after eating breakfast, Mary told Kate to go upstairs and get Tom; if they waited any longer, they might not catch the 10:20 train to Hartford. When Kate yelled for him and got no answer, she climbed up the stairs and rapped on his door. When he didn't respond, she opened the door and walked inside. The bed had been slept in, but the room appeared empty. Tom's pants were laid out flat on a table; she didn't see his suitcase.

As Kate walked further into the room, she brushed against something heavy hanging between the doorway and the corner. She looked up and saw Tom, still in his pajamas, hanging from a torn bedsheet strung from one of the rafters. Although he had apparently climbed onto his suitcase to reach the noose, his feet were touching the floor, his knees bent.

What happened next is the subject of some dispute. "In a state of numb shock, I cut him down and laid him on the bed," Kate wrote in her memoir. "Tom was dead. He was just plain dead. Yes. I touched him. Cold. He was dead."

Confused about what to do next – "Auntie [Mary] was too

emotional – she would be frantic," Kate said - she ran out the door and across the street, where she had seen a doctor sign on one of the houses, and rang the bell. A woman peered out.

"Yes?"

"My brother's dead."

"What?" she said.

"My brother – he's dead."

"Then the doctor can't help him, can he?" the woman replied, shutting the door.

"I stood for a moment," Kate recalled, thinking, "No – yes, it's too late for the doctor. Yes, she is right. The doctor – too late for the doctor to help."

Still afraid to tell her Auntie Mary, she rang the bell at Auntie Bertha's house. "Tom is dead," she said when Bertha answered the door, bursting into tears. "This is what I thought I should do. People die – you cry – but inside I was frozen."

Auntie Bertha told Auntie Mary, who called Kit. Kate's brother Bob, who was there when Kit received the call, watched his usually stoic mother slump over on the kitchen table as she learned the news.

Kate's recollection of the event, however, is inconsistent with the police report and other accounts that claimed she screamed upon discovering the body, causing Mary Towle to race upstairs, where the two frantically tried to undo the noose. When they couldn't, Mary ran for help. Since the torn bedsheet was so long, Tom had to pull it hard to strangle himself – he apparently deliberately tried to choke off the air.

So for Kate, it actually wasn't a matter of cutting the body down but raising it up. Kate grabbed the lower part of Tom's body and lifted it so the noose would not pull at his neck. Fifteen minutes later, when Dr. Gonzales from nearby St. Vincent's Hospital arrived, Kate was still holding her brother's suspended body above the floor. The doctor estimated that Tom had been dead about five hours.

The Hepburns immediately came to New York, where reporters had gathered in front of Mary Towle's house, waiting for a statement. "My son was normal in mind and body," Dr. Hepburn told the press. "The taking of his own life can be accounted for only from a medical point, that he was suddenly afflicted with adolescent insanity."

Dr. Hepburn returned to Hartford the next day, while Kit and Kate waited for the coroner to release the body on Monday. On April 4, 1921, the story ran on page six of *The New York Times* under the headline: MYSTERY IN SUICIDE OF SURGEON'S SON." The newspaper was only doing its job, but from that moment on, Kate would have little affection for the press.

The following day, Dr. Hepburn offered the newspapers an alternate explanation for his son's death: "I am now convinced that the boy was the victim of an accident as the result of a foolish stunt," he told *The New York Times*. All suggestions that Tom had committed suicide were subsequently rejected by the family.

Dr. Hepburn arrived at his "foolish stunt" theory after remembering a story he used to tell his children about pretending to hang himself when he was a kid. By holding his neck in a certain position, he could hang from a noose without cutting off his air supply. "Dangerous sport," Kate recalled later. "Could it be that Tom was practicing this using sheeting instead of a rope – the noose was slippery and he could not control it? Dad felt this was a reasonable possibility. And how this must have tortured Dad, but we never talked about it."

Those who believed it was suicide pointed to the rheumatic fever Tom had as a child that often left him despondent. Depression and suicide ran in both families – Kit's father had killed himself, and so did Dr. Hepburn's brother, two days after getting word of Tom's death, by leaving his car running with the garage door closed. Some speculated that Tom Jr. was gay and knew his family would disapprove, making him guilt-ridden and ashamed. "There seemed to be a sort of feeling at the time that he might have made a pass at his girl, and maybe it didn't work out," causing him to sink into despair, Kate later said.

But to Tom's family and friends, it was inconceivable that he would take his own life. He was getting good grades in school, excelled in athletics, and was popular with his classmates. He seemed fine the night before when he played the banjo for Auntie Mary and her friends, and he left no suicide note. He had even purchased two parlor-car seats on the morning train in preparation for their return home the next day.

To some Hepburn scholars, the most plausible explanation was a phenomenon rarely acknowledged in public at the time: auto-erotic asphyxia, the practice of deliberately restricting oxygen to the brain to enhance sexual arousal. "Until recently, deaths resulting from auto-erotic asphyxia were often misidentified as suicides by hanging," wrote William J. Mann in his biography, *Kate: The Woman Who Was Hepburn.*

"If Tom wanted to kill himself, why choose a process in which he wasn't assured of success?" Mann wrote. "He was a bright boy, after all; he would have clearly seen that the beam was too low for him to hang, at least not with that extra-long length of muslin sheet he'd fashioned. As described in the reports, his determined efforts to cut off his breath are identical to the mechanics used during auto-erotic asphyxia. And the fact he was doing all this at three o'clock in the morning (as estimated by [Dr.] Gonzales) has always been a jarring detail of the 'accidental' theory. Why would a boy get up at that hour to practice a stunt?"

As Mann points out, mistaking auto-erotic asphyxia for suicide was not documented in medical literature until 1927, six years after Tom's death, so it's doubtful the medical examiner would have considered the possibility. And even if the family had suspicions, it's unlikely they would have wanted to discuss it publicly.

"Anyway," Kate said later, "we'll never know."

When Tom's body was released, the family crossed the Hudson River to a crematorium in New Jersey. Kate, standing on the bow of the ferry, gazed at her mother, a woman who knew something about sorrow, having lost her father to suicide and her mother to cancer before she was sixteen. "I looked across at Mother," Kate recalled later. "She was crying. My mother was crying. Oh dear. What can I do? I'd never seen my mother cry before. And I never saw her cry again. Never. She was stalwart."

"My father," she added, "didn't cry either."

After Tom's death, Kate's parents never mentioned him again, nor did they visit the cemetery where his ashes were buried. "They simply did not believe in moaning about anything," Kate later said. "The important thing was that Tom was dead. In the first terrible shock, Mother cried. Yes. But she never allowed the fact of his death to dominate the atmosphere. We were not a sad household."

It was an attitude Kate and her siblings absorbed deeply. One day decades later when Peg lost a son in the Vietnam War, his twin sister was talking about him to her younger siblings. "Don't do that!" Peg said to her daughter. "He's dead. We all love him, but he's gone. Don't moan. It does no good."

Kate agreed with this approach – "She's right, of course" – but found other ways to remain bound to her brother. When she shaved years off her age – a common practice among actresses – she also changed her birthday to November 8, Tom's birthday.

Her brother's death affected Kate deeply and for a long time. She became depressed, let her grades slip, and avoided her peers. As she put it, "This incident seemed to sort of separate me from the world as I'd known it . . . I knew something that the girls did not know: tragedy. They were curious, and I would not, did not, want to talk or to discuss it." Her parents rarely left her by herself. "Whenever I needed them, they were there," she later remembered. Her brother's death, she said, "threw my mother and father and me very close together. Very close."

In June, with Kate still fragile, the Hepburns began home-schooling. Now the eldest, Kate took on much of the responsibility for her two brothers and two sisters as Kit went back to working with Margaret Sanger in the crusade for birth-control legislation, and Dr. Hepburn continued his surgical practice.

To occupy herself in the wake of Tom's death, Kate became serious about golf. As a young girl, she had loved playing at courses near Fenwick in the summers; now that she was not in school, she wanted to play every day. She began taking daily lessons with a pro named Jack Stait, and at age fifteen, took second place in the Connecticut Women's Open. In the winter, she passed the time by taking walks with her father; ever the stoic Yankees, they wore scarves and gloves but no coats. Their close relationship partly eased the pain of Tom's death.

Kate had grown into a beautiful, boyish teenager. Tall and lean, she had brick-red hair, blue-gray eyes, and proud, sharp features that made a dramatic impression.

When she was fifteen, boys started lining up at the Hepburns' door. Her father would stand at the top of their curved staircase, glaring down at his daughter's guests. Once, Kate brought home a Catholic boy. "Oh, with what chill politeness my father made him welcome," she later remembered. "Some days I'd go with him to mass – not that I'd go inside his church – I wasn't that brave. I'd sit on the steps outside and wait for him. Somehow my father would just happen to drive by every time I was sitting on those Catholic steps waiting, and he'd smile at me and keep on driving. Pretty soon that boy and I just seemed to drift apart."

When Kate accused her father of prejudice against Catholics, Dr. Hepburn replied, "Your beaux are the dullest I have ever known!" To his wife, he said, "If she marries any of them, it's going to be hell!"

But marriage was the last thing on Kate's mind. She had few friends and spent most of her time taking care of her younger siblings or joining her parents in political arguments - one so heated that the usually dignified Kit once hurled a full coffeepot at Dr. Hepburn.

Summers at Fenwick were still the highlight of Kate's year. Tanned and freckled, she swam, fished, and boated down the Connecticut River into Long Island Sound. But at the end of the summer of 1924, she left for college in Philadelphia, her first time living away from her family.

Kate was seventeen when she arrived at Bryn Mawr. As always, she did things her way, without the slightest regard for convention. Other girls in her class found her difficult to relate to: She took showers after midnight when everyone else was in bed, waded in the fountain outside the library, rolling herself dry on the grass, and fell behind on her classwork, getting poor grades. She posed for nude photographs in her dorm room, then mocked the drug-store owner when he wouldn't print the pictures.

Kate shunned collegiate activities and made no effort to make friends during her freshman and sophomore years. She dressed in rumpled clothes, and her moods became "exhaustingly intense," as she put it. As her grades continued to plummet, the dean finally told Dr. Hepburn that his daughter might do better elsewhere. The doctor responded, "If I had a patient in the hospital, and the patient grew worse, I should not discharge him, but try to work out a more efficacious treatment."

At some point in her first two years at Bryn Mawr, still emotionally guarded after her brother's death, Kate decided she would become an actress. "It was there that she decided to make a career out of expressing emotion in front of as many people as she could get to watch," wrote Claudia Roth Pierpont in *The New Yorker*.

Aware that she wouldn't qualify for campus dramatics without a vast improvement in her grades, she changed her major from history to English at the beginning of her junior year and studied night and day. That year, she earned leading roles in two plays – A. A. Milne's *The Truth about Bladys* and *The Cradle Song*. No one made note of her talent, but she finally made friends with a small group who, for reasons unknown, called themselves The Tenement.

In the summer of 1927, before her senior year, Kate and a Tenement friend named Alice Palache planned a trip to Europe. Alice already had the $500 needed for the trip, but Kate, with no source of income, was ready to sell her bedroom furniture until her father relented and gave her the money. The girls bought round-trip tickets in steerage for $210 each, rented bicycles when they disembarked in Plymouth, England, then took a train to London.

Unwilling to walk or bike around the city, they bought an automobile for £95. With living expenses draining their pocketbooks, they later sold the car back to the gentleman and took a train to Paris. They stayed at the Hotel Cayré on the Boulevard Raspail and ate at a little restaurant across the street where Kate, to Alice's annoyance, would study herself and her facial expressions in a mirror near their table. They traveled all over the city and went home without a penny to their name.

Back at Bryn Mawr, a young man Kate had met the year before at a dance at Yale, Robert J. "Bob" McKnight, was showing more interest in her. McKnight, an Ohio native, wanted to be a sculptor.

While dancing with McKnight, Kate asked him, "What are you going to be?"

"I'm going to be the greatest sculptor in the world," McKnight replied. "What about you?"

"I'm going to be the greatest actress in the world," she declared.

McKnight visited the Hepburns during Easter break, sharing a room with Kate's younger brothers Dick and Bob, then in their early teens. The Hepburns were a new experience for the conservative young man, who couldn't believe the children were permitted to ask questions about sex or their parents' work, and actually received explicit answers.

Dr. Hepburn got along well with McKnight and persuaded him that if he really wanted to be a sculptor, he should go to medical school to study anatomy. Kate had invited him over but paid little attention to him – though one morning she woke him with a kiss before racing out of the room. McKnight took this to mean that she was in love with him, as he was with her.

McKnight later asked her to marry him. While she did not say yes, he was left with the impression that she was undecided. Kate later called McKnight "my great friend" and said that a year after she graduated from college, they lived together briefly in Rome, where he went to study in 1929 after winning the Prix de Rome as one of the top sculptors in America. "It was all very innocent," she recalled. "We were both wildly ambitious and thrilled with life and its possibilities. We weren't wasting our strength rolling around. It was all or nothing for . . . each of us . . . We protected each other."

Much later, in 1941, Kate posed for McKnight, who created a fourteen-inch, white-marble bust for her as a gift. She loved the sculpture so much that she used it in her film *Woman of the Year* (the bust can be seen in her character's living room).

Too busy for relationships, Kate found her passion in the theater. She was, of course, still an inexperienced actor. But she landed the lead role in John Lyly's *The Woman in the Moon*, and a friend of hers named Jack Clarke was so impressed with her performance that he gave her a letter of introduction to Edward H. Knopf, a young screenwriter who was co-producing a season of summer stock in Baltimore. Concerned that her father would disapprove, Kate called McKnight in New Haven and asked him to send her gas money so she could drive to Baltimore to see Knopf.

Once in Baltimore, Kate was not subtle. Over the objections of his assistant, she burst into Knopf's office above the Auditorium Theatre. He later recalled how uneasy she seemed. "Her forehead was wet. Her nose shone," he said. "She was tremendously sincere, but awkward, green, freaky-looking. I told her that my plans for the season were already made, and there was no place for her, especially since I only hired professional actors. Then I rose in the hope this would indicate to her that the interview was over. Her parting shot from the door was, 'Thanks Mr. Knopf, I'll be back as soon as school is finished.'"

Days before her graduation in June of 1928, she returned, and during a rehearsal, snuck in and sat down directly behind Knopf. In the dark theater, she whispered to him, "You see, I've kept my promise." When he failed at first to recognize her, she reminded him that she had promised to return. He reminded her that he had no part for her and didn't hire amateurs.

Unfazed, Kate replied, "Oh, that's all right. I'll just stay here and watch," then came back every day for the next three days.

Worn down by her persistence, on the Wednesday before she was to graduate, Knopf called to her from the stage. "There are four ladies-in-waiting in *The Czarina*. Report Monday morning for rehearsal."

On Saturday, Kate went back to Bryn Mawr for graduation, and her parents took the train to the college, expecting her to drive them back to Hartford after the ceremony. Fearing her father's reaction to her acting job in Baltimore, Kate waited until they were already in the car heading home before she blurted out the news.

Furious, Dr. Hepburn bellowed, "You want to be an actress only because it is the easiest and most conspicuous way to show off!" Then he insisted she stop the car so he could take a train the rest of the way home. Kate managed to convince him to stay in the car, and they argued all the way to Hartford.

The next day, Dr. Hepburn yielded and gave his daughter $50 to cover her expenses for a few weeks, until she recovered "from this madness," as he called it, adding "that's the last penny you'll get from me until you do something respectable."

Money in hand, Kate packed her suitcase and waved goodbye to her family as she drove away. No matter what happened in Baltimore, she decided, she would not return home defeated. Hepburns were many things, but they were not quitters.

3
"WELL, THAT'S THAT - I'M A STAR"

In Baltimore, Eddie Knopf gave Kate a small role in *The Czarina*, a three-act play about Catherine the Great. After rehearsals started on June 11, 1928, he fully expected her to give up quickly and go home.

An established actor with aspirations of becoming a director in Hollywood, Knopf had little patience with Kate, who did not take instruction well. But when she walked on stage in costume and curtsied deeply to Catherine the Great, played by Knopf's star Mary Boland, he and the rest of the Auditorium Theatre Players - including future film star Robert Montgomery - were taken aback at her transformation and her command of the stage.

Kate even rattled Boland, who complained that the newcomer was staring at her from the wings and making her uneasy. Still, Boland confessed that she had "never seen anyone more beautiful than that eager girl, so proud to walk across a stage that she and the costume seemed borne up by light."

Kate's parents did not attend Kate's debut in *The Czarina*, but her Aunt Edith did, as did some of Dr. Hepburn's associates from Johns Hopkins. Word of her captivating performance made it back to Hartford, and Kate began receiving letters from her father, saying he'd won some money at bridge or golf, so here it is.

Following her appearance in *The Czarina*, Kate was given a small role as a flapper in Russell Medcraft and Norma Kenneth Mitchell's *The Cradle Snatchers*, sharing the stage with Kenneth MacKenna, a silent film star who worried about making the transition to the talking pictures that were shaking up the movie business.

In her memoir, Kate remembered the play as being *The Torch Bearers*, but whichever version is correct, everyone agreed she struggled in this show. "When I got nervous, my voice would shoot up into the top of my head," she recalled later. "I didn't really know how to control this." MacKenna recommended she contact Frances Robinson-Duff, a highly regarded acting and voice coach in New York whose students had included stars such as Helen Hayes, Clark Gable, and Mary Pickford.

MacKenna's advice was to get coaching after she left the company, but Kate, unwilling to wait, quit instead and headed to New York immediately. Needing money for the lessons – $200 for three months of twice-weekly appointments – she wrote to her father, who continued to be "disgusted and heartsick" about her decision to go into acting. "Thought it a silly profession closely allied to street-walking. That I had developed into a cheap show-off and that I was entering a shabby profession which was based on youth and looks. Definitely a foundation of sand for a silly life," she remembered.

Her mother, on the other hand, was all for it – anything to avoid the trap of being a stay-at-home wife or mother. "She thought women should give life a whirl. See if they could swing it so that they could be more independent of the male sex. Dad was for this, too. He just didn't care for the road I'd chosen."

In her letters to her father, Kate stressed the importance of training for the career she had chosen. "I knew that with a small push he would be on my side," she recalled. In one of his letters back to her, he wrote, ". . . remember only that I would love to kiss you 21 times and give you a million dollars" and signed it, "Your hopeless Dad."

Kate stayed with her Aunt Betty Hepburn – the widow of her dad's brother Charles – in a spare room in a brownstone in the East Sixties, not far from Robinson-Duff's home. It was raining the morning of her first lesson, so Kate arrived at her new teacher's townhouse soaking wet. A French butler led her to Robinson-Duff's fourth-floor studio, where she burst into the room and announced, "I want to be an actress. I want to learn everything."

Rain was running in rivulets down Kate's face from her messy, drenched hair, and her coat was dripping all over the floor. "Sometimes we have an inward vision, a flash," Robinson-Duff later said. "I looked at her, huddled there, bedraggled and wet - at the terrific intensity of that face - and something inside whispered, 'Duse. She looks like Duse.'" She was referring to Eleanora Duse, the celebrated Italian actress who had died a few years earlier and was regarded as one of the greatest of all time.

"Darling," Robinson-Duff said, "we will begin immediately. "First you must learn the proper use of your diaphragm and the control of your breathing. Before learning to act, one must first learn to breathe . . . put down your coat and come nearer." She asked her new student to put her hand on the older woman's diaphragm.

"Now I can call 'HEY!' straight from the diaphragm," Kate said later. "But my lack of success with really connecting my voice and volume to the diaphragm cost me great worries in my career. I lost my voice and would get very hoarse whenever I played a part which was fast and loud. It was an agony

. . . I think that I was so excited by life and living and my future that I was simply wound up so tight I didn't - couldn't - relax."

Robinson-Duff also took issue with Kate's unusual attire. One of her other acting students, Laura Harding, remembered that Kate wore her long hair pulled back in a knot, a man's sweater pinned at the back with a big safety pin, and a tweed skirt. After months of frustration with Kate's unkempt appearance, Robinson-Duff finally said, "You won't wear clothes fit for a decent scarecrow, but will you do me a favor [and] . . . throw away that old felt hat and get one without a hole in it."

"Good Lord!" Kate replied. "What's the matter with people? Can't their imaginations supply enough cloth for that little hole?"

Kate's outward self-confidence, however, concealed fears and insecurities. Professional acting was harder than she had imagined. Auditions were torture; she consistently arrived sweaty, disheveled, and late. Her odd wardrobe of men's sweaters and pants - entirely too big for her slender five-foot-eight-inch frame – was considered eccentric.

Theresa Helburn, a casting director at the time, remembered Kate walking into her first audition "carelessly groomed . . . an odd-looking child. But when she opened the office door it was as though someone had turned on a dynamo. The air vibrated with the electric force of her personality."

Though Kate was focused on her acting career, she found time for men, particularly H. Phelps Putnam, a poet she had met at Bryn Mawr. "I took one look at him and I was stricken with whatever it is that strickens one at once and for no reason when one looks at a member of the opposite sex," she remembers. "He absolutely fascinated me."

During their close association, Putnam wrote a poem, "The Daughters of the Sun," that Kate was convinced was about her: "She was my nourishment, my sister and my child," he wrote, "My lust, my liberty, my discipline/And she laid fair, awkward hands upon my head."

When Kate arrived in New York, "Phelpie," as she called him, was living in a railroad flat on East Fifty-Fourth Street near the East river that was owned by Russell Davenport, son of a wealthy industrialist and a future managing editor of *Fortune* magazine. Kate loved the place so much – sitting on the fire escape watching the boats go by – that she decided to move in, too.

"I had no intention of living in sin with Phelpie," she recalled later. "I just wanted living. Sin could wait. Living itself was a sort of ecstasy . . . the opportunities . . . the hopes. I was on my own in a high state of excitement. I did not need anything else."

Phelps knew everyone, including the humorist Robert Benchley of Algonquin Round Table fame, and escorted Kate to the "in" spots of the city, where they drank and dined well. Phelpie, unfortunately, was married and constantly broke. "I had a lot of common sense and I could clearly see that until and only if I could support him, it had better be a glorious friendship," Kate recalled. "And so it was."

What she didn't know at the time was that her father had

delivered a stern message to the penurious poet: "Look here
. . . I hope you are aware that my daughter Kath has her eye
on you. You are a fascinating fellow. Hence I cannot blame
her. But you are married and you are considerably older
than she is. Now . . . she will make every effort to seduce
you. I can only compare her to a young bull about to charge.
So . . . you had better look out. Because if you lay hands on
her, I shall shoot you."

Taking Dr. Hepburn's admonition to heart, Phelpie decided
to move out of the railroad flat and take an extended trip
to Nova Scotia. When he left and Davenport returned, Kate
moved out, too – into a roomy apartment on Park Avenue
belonging to the family of a college friend who was out of
town for the summer.

After Phelpie left, Kate began seeing a man she had been
introduced to at Bryn Mawr named Ludlow Ogden Smith,
whom she called "Luddy." Luddy was wealthy, a graduate
of the University of Grenoble in France. Though his degree
was in industrial engineering, he had decided to pursue a
career as an insurance broker instead.

Luddy and Jack Clarke, the man who had given Kate the letter of introduction to Edwin Knopf, had shared Clarke's tiny
house in the country, not far from Bryn Mawr. When Kate
was still in college, the men would invite her and her college
friends over for picnics. "We were all about eighteen, nine-
teen to twenty, and full of joy and innocence," she recalls.

Not so these men, who were nearly a decade older. "Jack
and Luddy were looking for trouble," she recalled later. "But
as far as they got was taking naked pictures. Photographs of
me lying on a big sofa which they had in the living room. I

posed with total confidence, as I rather fancied myself."

When Kate arrived in New York, Luddy and Clarke had already moved there, too. Kate was attracted to Luddy's charm and air of sophistication. Tall and lean with a striking profile, the twenty-nine-year-old dressed impeccably, wearing blazers with imported silk ties and paisley ascots. Urbane and amusing, he spoke fluent French and seemed to have a quotation for every occasion. He also had a car and would drive Kate up to Fenwick on weekends. He was an attentive, sympathetic friend who enthusiastically supported Kate's acting career.

For Kate, the turning point of their relationship was the moment at Clarke's apartment when she found herself alone with Luddy. "I guess that I knew that Luddy was in love with me," she recalls. "But you see my hitch was that I was in love with myself . . . I wanted to be a big star . . . Anyway, Luddy and I were alone in the apartment and there was the bed and there didn't seem to be any reason not

to . . . Luddy knew what he was doing - and I didn't object. So we did it. And that was the end of my virtue. He was my beau from then on."

While spending time with Luddy, Kate got her first big career break: The Knopf Stock Company asked her to understudy for Lucile Nikolas, the star of its New York production of *The Big Pond*, which they had tried out successfully in Baltimore. Kate was thrilled. Watching Nikolas rehearse, she was confident that she was a much better actress than the leading lady. "She was a very competent actress who did not have the advantage of being very young and absolutely outrageous and full of a sort of wild confidence based on nothing but energy and ego," Kate said later.

Just before the show was scheduled to open, Kate was told she would be replacing Nikolas as leading lady. Though some of her biographers say Nikolas quit, Kate says Nikolas was fired. "One lunch hour, after the play had been in rehearsal a week, they asked me to stay and play a scene," she recalls. "Pushed by a sort of frenetic boiling-over, I must have read it very well. They fired the leading lady and took me."

Kate was not surprised that her superior talent had finally been recognized: "I took this change in my status as a matter of course. I was the leading lady. I had been in the theater about four weeks. This was happening just as I had imagined it would . . . it should. I was arriving."

Excited, Kate rehearsed her lines over and over. On opening night, she wanted to arrive at the theater as late as possible – it was "too terrifying" to get there early, she said – and showed up only fifteen minutes before curtain "to the fury of everyone." During the rushed make-up job, she got mascara in her eye, and at the last minute, realized that the elastic on her lace panties was loose, so she took them off and handed them to a stagehand.

When the audience applauded after her opening scene, it threw her timing off and she raced through her delivery, her vocal pitch rising higher and higher and her body stiff. She mixed up her lines and tripped over her feet. By the end, the audience was laughing *at* her, though she was unaware of it. "Naturally I thought, Well . . . that's that - I'm a star," she recalled later. When the play was over, however, she couldn't help but notice that nobody was approaching her to tell her how amazing she was.

The play's producers decided to fire Kate immediately but lacked the heart to tell her themselves. So they asked Robinson-Duff to do it. The next morning, as Kate was about to leave for rehearsal, her teacher asked to come to her house. When she protested that she would be late, Robinson-Duff said, "They won't mind."

"They won't mind?" Kate thought. "What does that mean?"

When she arrived, her teacher's long, serious face said it all. "I've been fired," Kate said.

"Yes," Robinson-Duff said.

"Well . . ." At a loss for words, Kate said, "I'm not crying . . . aren't you proud of me!"

"No," she said, "I'd be prouder if you were. That was the trouble with your performance last night. Too self-contained."

Kate wanted to know who would be taking her place. "Lucile Nikolas," her teacher replied. A disappointed Kate headed back to the theater, where she congratulated the leading lady for getting her job back and politely declined the chance to resume her role as understudy. In her memoir, Kate does not reveal how embarrassed and humiliated she must have felt; that's not how Hepburns react to a crisis. Luddy drove her to Hartford so she could tell her parents, who joked that they would never again miss one of her opening nights because that might be her only performance. Ignoring the pain, everyone had a good laugh.

Back in New York the next day, Kate was surprised but

delighted to receive phone calls from two producers – J. J. Shubert and Arthur Hopkins – who saw potential in Kate's performance. She went first to see Shubert. "They were fools to let you go," he said, and offered her a five-year contract with a beginning salary of $250 per year – just $3,400 in today's dollars – increasing over time to $1,500 ($20,500 today). Kate, unhappy with the low starting pay and unwilling to be tied down for five years, declined immediately – stunning the producer – and went to see Hopkins.

"Hello, dear. I saw you the other night. You were good," Hopkins said when she arrived. Handing her a script, he said, "I'd like to have you work for me. Read this . . . the part of Veronica. We go into rehearsals next week. Monday - eleven o'clock." There was no discussion of salary, but Kate accepted on the spot.

The role of Veronica, a schoolgirl in the play *These Days* by Katharine Clugston, was not a large one; regardless, she would be paid $125 a week, a sizable sum for an unknown actress in 1928, the equivalent of $1,700 today.

During rehearsals at the Plymouth Theatre in New York, Hopkins and the actors sat around a big table and read and reread the play until everyone knew it backward and forward. Only then did they ditch the script and add physical life to the characters.

"This seemed to me then and now a very sensible way of doing it," Kate said later. "Jumping up immediately with a script in one's hand and wandering about before you know the part, I could never understand . . . if I know the play before I rehearse, I'm in a better position to feel where I'd like to be to play a scene . . . and in a better position to argue with the director."

Kate worked daily with Robinson-Duff and took ballet lessons from the Russian dancer Mikhail Mordkin. *These Days* opened first in New Haven, then her hometown of Hartford, and finally, on November 12, 1928, premiered at the Cort Theatre in New York. Though the overall reviews were scathing, Kate got raves. John Anderson of the *New York Evening Journal* wrote that "a perfect passage of repressed deviltry is done gorgeously by Miss Katharine Hepburn."

The next night, the cast was despondent. "Not I, of course," Kate recalled. "I had been praised and that was the only part of the review which anyone with any sense would [read] ... certainly it was the only part that I read. To me it was a hit."

The show closed after only eight performances. Fortunately, within days, Hopkins asked her to understudy for Hope Williams, the star of a play called *Holiday*, a comedy by Philip Barry.

Kate watched rehearsals from the top of the stagehands' thirty-foot ladder, teetering back and forth, until Hopkins threatened to fire her if she didn't get down. After the show opened, Kate watched Williams from the wings, making her exceedingly nervous.

The show was a big hit, but Kate was restless waiting in the wings; she knew her chances to replace Williams were slim. And she and Luddy were getting more deeply involved by the day. After about two weeks, she shocked Hopkins by suddenly handing him her uncashed salary checks and telling him she was getting married - to Luddy.

Just about everyone who knew them – from Robinson-Duff

to the cast – was astonished, having assumed that Kate and Luddy were just good friends. But on December 12, 1928, they were married in a small ceremony in the living room of her parents' home at 201 Bloomfield Avenue in West Hartford. Kate was twenty-one, eight years younger than the groom. Presiding was her grandfather, Reverend Sewell Snowden Hepburn. The house was the fourth and last home owned by Kate's parents – a large, twenty-two-room brick structure filled with early American antiques in cherry and brass and oversized chairs with plush cushions.

Kate wore a dress by the Middle Eastern fashion designer Vitaldi Babani, whose clients included the legendary actress Eleonora Duse. It was white and made of crushed velvet with antiqued gold embroidery around the neck and sleeves. To forestall any questions regarding her acting career, no marriage announcements were published in the newspapers.

After their wedding, Kate and Luddy went to Bermuda for a brief honeymoon, then returned to Philadelphia to shop for houses and begin the process of settling down. "Luddy was always an angel of understanding," she said later. "I said, 'Oh yes - we'll live in Strafford, Pennsylvania,' and we began looking for a house. Well, my enthusiasm lasted about two weeks."

As they looked at houses on the Main Line, Kate kept asking herself, "What am I doing? I couldn't live here!"

Realizing her mistake, Kate quickly reversed direction, moving into a small walk-up on East Thirty-Ninth Street, where her husband joined her on weekends. Luddy, ever loyal and understanding, "was swell about it," she said. Few people in New York were even aware that Kate had married; she had kept her maiden name and her independence.

Later, she would say, "I wasn't fit to be married. He was a nice man and no nice man should marry an actress or anyone else whose mind is always on herself. I know if I were a man I wouldn't be dumb enough to marry someone who couldn't pass a mirror without looking into it."

The marriage would not last long, and for the rest of her life, she would never rebmarry. For Katharine Hepburn, the goal was always clear: to become a movie star. Being obligated to a husband – never mind children – would be nothing more than an obstacle to her one great desire.

4
"THE KID HAS SOMETHING"

When Kate returned to New York after her hastily arranged wedding, she paid a visit to Hopkins to ask for her old job back as understudy to Hope Williams in *Holiday*. Hopkins seemed to know her better than she knew herself. "Yes, of course," he said. "I expected you."

After about three months, Hopkins came to watch Kate in rehearsal. Though she was convinced that she was much better than Williams in some of the emotional scenes, she still had a lot to learn, especially about the common trap of descending into self-pity. Afterward, Hopkins came up onto the stage. "Fine," he said, patting her. "Just don't ever be sorry for yourself."

"A keen criticism of an overemotional youngster," she realized later.

In all, Kate spent six months watching Williams perform. There was something about the way the star carried herself that appealed to Kate: Her forthright manner. Her slim figure and boy's haircut. The way she walked – an arms-swinging stride, like a cowboy about to mount a horse. She was stylish and original.

Few knew it at the time, but Williams was on the vanguard of a new look and attitude for women, one that Kate recognized immediately. "Hope Williams obviously had a tremendous influence on my career," she wrote later. "Vocally, walk-wise, I incorporated a lot of Hope into my so-called personality. It was in the air, that boy-woman. My arrival in the big city was well timed."

In the summer of 1929, *Holiday* closed on Broadway – before Kate had a chance to stand in for Williams – and she decided to travel to France for a vacation with Luddy. Kate was sick for most of the trip and bickered often with Luddy, so they cut the trip short and returned to New York after less than two weeks.

Holiday reopened in the Riviera Theatre at Ninety-Seventh Street and Broadway, and Kate finally got a chance to play the lead for a single night when Williams got sick. "It was there and then that I found out how very good Hope was," Kate recalled later. "And how I had to find my own personality in the part. Not imitate her. It was a baptism by fire. Places where she had got roars of laughter, I got nothing. But by the third act I had found my way a bit."

When *Holiday* went on the road, Kate stayed in New York and went back to auditioning. She read for the part of the ingénue in Sam Behrman's play *Meteor*, produced by the Theatre Guild, and got the part, at $225 a week.

Then Kate got another call, to read for the female lead in *Death Takes a Holiday*. She already had a job, but this script excited her – her character gets romantically involved with the human embodiment of Death, played by Philip Merivale (later, the play was adapted into a successful film starring Fredric March). She was sensational in the audition and landed the part. She backed out of *Meteor* and felt bad about it, but feelings of loyalty were no match for her ambition.

Throughout rehearsals and five weeks of performances on the road – during which she got mixed reviews – Kate battled the play's director, Lawrence Marston, who disagreed with her vision of the heroine. This did not sit well with the play's producer, J.J. Shubert, whose five-year contract she had turned down the previous year. Shubert and his older brother Lee were well on their way to establishing a Broadway dynasty – by 1924, they had eighty-six theaters in the United States - and were not to be trifled with. Ever the self-involved diva, Kate was in her own world, oblivious. "I had not the vaguest suspicion that anything was dangerously wrong," she said later.

Three days before the New York opening, Shubert asked for her resignation. "Resign hell!" Kate told Marston. "If he wants me out of the cast, he can fire me." Shubert did, then fired Marston, too. Her mother had already seen the show in Washington, so Dr. Hepburn drove in from West Hartford to Philadelphia to watch her last performance. When it was over, he stormed backstage. "They're absolutely right! . . . You are galumphing there like a maniac," he yelled at his daughter. "Who's going to believe that my daughter, a big healthy girl like you, could fall in love with death. With death, for God's sakes!"

It was a difficult time. Kate spent Christmas 1929 in West Hartford with Luddy and her family. The stock market had crashed in October and Luddy's new career as an insurance broker was in trouble. Dr. Hepburn was doing better, having made some shrewd investments, but the financial crisis cast a pall over the holidays. Kate knew that meant fewer plays in production and tougher competition for roles. As always, Dr. Hepburn looked on the bright side, saying the need for excellence was even greater during hard times. And Kate had fully absorbed her family's dictum to never, ever moan. "I'd better get something – anything – fast," she told herself. "Don't wallow about, being sorry for yourself."

In New York, she resumed her studies with Robinson-Duff

and humbly returned to the Theatre Guild to see if she could still accept their original offer for *Meteor*; the Guild declined but suggested she see Rouben Mamoulian, the show's director, who had adapted Ivan Turgenev's *A Month in the Country* to be performed in the spring. By the time Kate auditioned for the role of the ingénue, Mamoulian was at his wit's end trying to find the right actress, having endured nearly fifty auditions.

When Kate arrived in his office, shaking and sweaty, her hair askew, Mamoulian gave her a scene to read and ten minutes to prepare. After the audition, Mamoulian told her that while he did not think she was ready for such a difficult role, he would consider her for a smaller part if the opportunity arose. He told the casting director to take down Kate's name, saying, "The kid has something."

"There was something about her - it's very difficult to describe in words," Mamoulian later recalled. "You can't describe music. There was - is - a kind of luminosity . . . some faces that project the light. Hers does."

The director offered Kate the role of understudy to Eunice Stoddart - chosen to play the ingénue - for $25 a week, far less than the $225 the Guild had previously offered her for *Meteor*. Desperate, she grabbed it. Five weeks after *A Month in the Country* opened in March 1930, to mediocre reviews, Kate replaced Hortense Alden as Katia, the maid. She continued to understudy for Stoddart, but when she was refused a $5-per-week raise, her dissatisfaction showed and she silently vowed to get even with her producers. She stayed on, but Stoddart never missed a performance.

By this time, Kate had gotten to be good friends with Laura

Harding, her fellow Robinson-Duff student, and they decided to join the Berkshire Playhouse, a summer-stock theater in Stockbridge, Massachusetts, where Harding had apprenticed the year before. All twenty-one company members stayed in an old eighteen-room house owned by a minister and his family; Kate and Harding shared a room.

All the actors shared a single bathroom and were frequently annoyed by Kate's bathing several times a day and late at night while shouting out French poetry. Luddy, who took a room in the local hotel, washed her hair for her on the weekends and brought her ice cream from the village.

Living and working with such a diverse group, and being exposed to differing political and artistic opinions, Kate fought with everyone but Harding. The two got to know each other well that summer, Harding said, and "laughed an awful lot" as she coaxed Kate into playing pranks on fellow company members.

Kate and Harding constantly battled with a member of the theater company, George Coulouris, who later ridiculed Kate as this "skinny red-haired girl [who] ran in saying, 'I've come all the way from Hartford with a golf tee between my teeth!' in a high, squeaky voice." She drove an expensive LaSalle convertible, dressed in pants, and put her knees nearly up to her face while eating. "She played the prima donna from the time of her arrival," Coulouris complained.

Kate loved baiting Coulouris at dinner, and Coulouris once got so angry he left the table. Kate followed him through the house, each threatening the other with silverware. Finally, Coulouris turned around and wagged his fork at her, shouting, "You're a fool, Katharine Hepburn! You're a fool! You'll never be a star. You'll never be important in the theater. You don't make any sense at all."

Kate responded, "You're the fool! I will be a star before you're ever heard of!"

The Berkshire Playhouse had hired her for five weeks, with an option for an additional five if she performed well. In the first play of the season, Sir James Barrie's *The Admirable Crichton*, Kate's role was no larger than Harding's, which irked her; for Harding, a wealthy heiress, acting was a mere diversion, a fun way to pass the time. For Kate, it was an obsession and a blood sport.

Frustrated, Kate ignored the director's instructions and was rude to him. Kate and Harding portrayed the ridiculous Lady Agatha and Lady Catherine, and the two were on-stage together much of the time. In one scene, when Kate was supposed to call out, "Catherine? Lady Catherine?" she instead yelled, "Lau-au-ra! Lau-au-ra Ha-a-rding!" The director, Alexander Kirkland, had had enough.

"Miss Hepburn, you just can't do that!"

"No? Who's going to stop me?" she asked.

The production, starring Richard Hale and June Walker – who later became known on Broadway as Lorelei Lee in *Gentlemen Prefer Blondes* – opened on June 30 to good reviews, though neither Kate nor Harding was mentioned.

Kate tried desperately to win the lead in the company's second production, *The Romantic Young Lady*, but the part went to Edith Barrett, who had starred in *Michael and Mary* on Broadway the previous season. Given a lesser role, Kate made conspicuous efforts to attract attention, including wearing her dress backward and her hat reversed; again, she failed to garner any reviews.

After obtaining a minor role in *Romeo and Juliet* – and failing to win a part in the next production, *The Torch Bearers* – Kate left Stockbridge. She had completed only three weeks of her five-week contract.

Some members of the company blamed what one called her "disruptive perverseness" for her abrupt departure, and said her behavior was so out-of-control that Kirkland would never have invited her to stay for another five weeks. Most were happy to see her leave and did not believe she would be missed.

Kate disagreed. "I asked for decent parts and they gave me strictly mediocre," she later explained. "I just don't like to be half good. It drives me insane . . . I think perfection is the only standard for . . . stars."

By the fall of 1930, Kate Hepburn was not a star and her ideas about perfection had alienated her from many of her theater colleagues. She didn't enjoy being part of an ensemble; her driving passion was to be always at center stage, in the limelight.

With Luddy and her parents' support and her self-confidence growing, she approached theatrical agents, who told her she looked too aristocratic to play anything but a society girl. So she bypassed them and visited producers herself. When she heard that the British playwright Benn W. Levy needed a young woman to play the daughter of the leading lady in his upcoming Broadway production of *Art and Mrs.*

Bottle, she abandoned what little restraint she had.

Wearing her usual unorthodox attire, Kate burst into Levy's office – the same way she had Edwin Knopf's in Baltimore – and announced she would take the part. Levy found her arrogance amusing. Kate was too lanky, bony, and freckled for the role, but because Jane Cowl, his star, didn't want someone too pretty to play her daughter, he permitted Kate to audition and hired her.

Levy's enthusiasm waned, however, when Kate showed up for rehearsals wearing men's faded, silk pajamas, a Chinese coat, and scruffy slippers; she also refused to obey instructions. Levy fired her, but after fourteen unsuccessful interviews with other applicants, Cowl insisted that he rehire her. He did, even agreeing to Kate's demand to increase her pay from $125 per week to $150.

The play opened on November 18, and Cowl told Kate she must wear makeup for the premiere. Kate did so grudgingly, but splashed alcohol on her face - a habit she developed to give herself a healthy glow – which streaked her makeup and made her look harsh. She also left a garish lipstick mark on Ms. Cowl after kissing her cheek in the first act when she came on stage. Ms. Cowl demanded Kate use smudge-proof lipstick, but Kate did exactly the same thing the next night.

"Didn't I ask you to get some indelible lipstick?" Cowl asked her.

Kate replied, "Well, I just thought I mightn't like it."

Despite her idiosyncratic behavior, Kate was attracting attention as a blossoming talent. "An uncommonly refreshing performance was given by Katharine Hepburn as the young daughter," Alison Smith wrote in the *New York World*. Theater legend Noel Coward – one of the most successful playwrights of that period – climbed five flights of stairs to her dressing room to tell her how much he enjoyed the show.

Despite Kate's rudeness to Jane Cowl, the star was so impressed with Kate's "promise of power" that she later said, "I don't think anything that child could have done could have turned me against her."

In the summer of 1931, Kate and Laura Harding headed to Ivoryton, Connecticut, for another summer of stock theater. Kate's marriage to Luddy did not interfere with her desire to run off for the summer like that; she and Luddy never acted like a married couple, despite their obvious affection for each other.

Harding, who had no need to work and by then had given up on an acting career, followed Kate around, living vicariously through her friend's achievements. At Ivoryton, Kate was given the option to play major roles in three plays: *Just Married, The Man Who Came Back* (opposite Henry Hull), and *The Cat and the Canary*. The latter play was a supreme challenge – she had to play a sophisticated woman of forty. "How did I dare?" Kate asked herself. Terrified, she called her father, who calmed her down, and she got through it. "Ivoryton is where I learned a lot," she said later.

After seeing her perform in Ivoryton, producer Gilbert Miller offered her a sizeable role in *The Animal Kingdom*, a play he and actor Leslie Howard were bringing to New York that fall. Kate was ecstatic. When summer stock ended, Luddy joined her and Harding at the Hardings' Pennsylvania mountain retreat for three weeks and helped her learn her lines.

At rehearsals, Kate and Leslie Howard found each other impossible from the start. Howard, who would become best known for playing Ashley Wilkes in *Gone with the Wind*, loathed Kate's "outrageous posturings" and her "insufferable bossiness." But to anyone who knew her, it was just Kate being Kate. "Try as hard as I could to be subservient . . . sweet . . . feminine . . . anything which would tame down my too vivid personality, I struggled," she recalled later. "Nothing worked."

Communication between the two leading actors broke down. While rehearsing one scene, Kate said, "What would you like me to do here, Mr. Howard?" Her co-star replied, "I really don't give a damn what you do, my dear."

The Animal Kingdom's author, Philip Barry, remembered Kate from his previous play, *Holiday*, and liked her; he even added lines Kate had ad-libbed during rehearsals. But Howard insisted on a new leading lady and asked Miller to fire Kate. It wasn't that simple: Actors' Equity rules stipulated that members who had rehearsed for six days must receive two-weeks' notice and severance pay; so when Kate showed up to work on her fifth day, a Friday, she was told they were not rehearsing her scenes that day. She decided to drive home to West Hartford for the weekend.

When she got to her parents' house, she sat cross-legged on the living room floor and chatted excitedly about her first week to her sisters Marion and Peggy, brothers Bob and Dick, and Dick's Harvard friends. Kit did not like the script, describing it as a "la-de-da commercial" play with little "to do with what really mattered in the world." But her dour opinion didn't dampen Kate's excitement.

The next day, Kate was playing tennis with Dick and his friends when a registered letter arrived from Miller, the producer. It read in part: "Pursuant to clause C-1 in your contract, you are hereby given notice of the termination thereof."

Kate was devastated. She stomped through the house, blaming Leslie Howard, then called Barry. "But why . . . why should I be fired?" she demanded.

"Well, to be brutally frank," he replied, "you weren't very good."

Kate castigated Barry with what he later called "a fishwife tirade." After a few minutes of her abuse, he shouted, "They're right about you! Nobody with your vicious disposition could possibly play light comedy! You're totally unsuited to the part! I'm glad they threw you out!"

In her memoir, Kate still sounded befuddled and mystified about why she was let go: "I'd been fired because I wasn't any good. But I was good, wasn't I? I was doing my best. The part was just my dish. What was wrong?" She claims to have tried hard to get along with Howard. "I had watched my p's and q's. Tried to be soft and sweet. Why in hell did they fire me? I wasn't bad in that part. Some things I've been fired out of I've understood. But that one - no. That was my part! Why . . . ?"

But Kate tried not to wallow, repeating her mantra, "Get busy - get busy." A few weeks later, she got one of the biggest breaks of her career when she was cast as Antiope, an Amazon queen in Julien Thompson's farce, *The Warrior's*

Husband.

The play was loosely based on Aristophanes's comedy *Lysistrata,* about the women of Greece banding together to withhold sex until their men stop their warring ways. Though she was perfectly suited for the part, the producers decided they wanted a star and replaced her with Jean Dixon, who was beginning to establish a film career that would later include *My Man Godfrey* and *Holiday* (appearing with Kate). A few days later, they changed their minds again and put Kate back in.

The play opened at the Morosco Theatre on March 11, 1932. Kate appeared onstage in a short-skirted Greek costume carrying a fake deer around her shoulders, then bounded down a large staircase, three steps at a time, threw the deer to the ground, and wrestled with leading man Colin Keith-Johnston. "I didn't mind risking my life for fame," she said later. "I was just full of the joy of life and opportunity and a wild desire to be absolutely fascinating."

Richard Garland of the *New York World-Telegram* gave her a rave review: "Miss Katharine Hepburn comes into her own as Antiope. Ever since she supported Miss Jane Cowl in *Art and Mrs. Bottle* I've been waiting for Miss Hepburn to fall heir to a role worthy of her talent and her beauty. Antiope is that role and Miss Hepburn makes the most of it, bringing out its tenderness, its humor, its bite. It's been many a night since so glowing a performance has brightened the Broadway scene."

"In *The Warrior's Husband,*" Kate said later, "I began to feel for the first time like a real actress."

The play ran for eighty-three performances. Suddenly, Harding had to help Kate fend off reporters and talent scouts. She was earning $76 a week, a solid wage during the Depression, and with assistance from her parents, rented a four-story brownstone on East Forty-Ninth Street in a Manhattan neighborhood called Turtle Bay for $100 a month. (The basement rooms were converted into a comfortable and charming apartment for Luddy). It would remain her New York home for the next sixty years.

Kate still went to West Hartford on the weekends, leaving after the Saturday night performance and returning Monday morning, sometimes bringing Harding, Luddy, and members of the cast along. Despite the late hour, she would throw open the door and shout, "Hello, everybody! Here I am!" Within minutes, the entire family would gather around her and exchange gifts, as if it had been months since they last saw each other.

Colin Keith-Johnston remembered his first of these visits. "Kate had some little present for everybody, and everybody had a present for her," he said. "I remember that two presents were made by the givers' hands. The children stood around. We grownups sat where we could - the room was her mother's combination bathroom and dressing room. We all ate bananas and milk, and all talked at once, and it was all bewildering and warming."

Halfway through the run of *The Warrior's Husband,* a Hollywood agent named Leland Hayward began pursuing Kate as a client.

Hayward, a friend of Harding's since her debutante days, was charming and good looking, but Kate thought him "rather horrible and rather awful." Hayward, however, saw star potential in Kate and thought her personality and appearance would shine on film.

Though she had loved films since childhood, to go to Hollywood as a low-paid contract player was not enough. She told Hayward to set her price at $1,500 a week ($20,500 in today's dollars) - any studio that agreed to pay an ingénue that well, she figured, would work hard to make her an important player. When RKO Pictures asked her to take a screen test in New York, she chose a scene from *Holiday* and asked Alan Campbell, who was also appearing in *The Warrior's Husband,* to play opposite her. Refusing Hayward's advice, Kate kept her back to the camera throughout most of the test, except in one scene when she picked a champagne glass off the floor and turned toward the camera with misty but defiant eyes.

Meanwhile, George Cukor, set to direct RKO's *A Bill of Divorcement*, with John Barrymore in the father role, was undecided about who should play the pivotal role of the daughter. Until he saw Kate's screen test, that is. Cukor later recalled, "She had this very definite knowledge and feeling [of the camera]. She was quite unlike anybody I'd ever seen . . . I thought, I suppose right away, 'She's too odd. It won't work.' But at one moment in a very emotional scene, she picked up a glass. The camera focused on her back. There was an *enormous* feeling, a *weight* about the manner in which she picked up the glass."

Cukor, who at age thirty-three was just starting to make a name for himself in Hollywood, wanted Kate badly. When he could not convince RKO executive David O. Selznick to look at the test, he went to screenwriter Adela Rogers St. Johns and begged for her help. "She's too marvelous," Cukor told her. "She'll be greater than Garbo. Nobody wants her but me so come and help me fight for her. You don't need to see the test. It's a foul test anyway. She looks like a boa constrictor on a fast, but she's great."

Dragging St. Johns across the studio lawn to Selznick's office, he coached her. "Just say you think she's great. Start raving. Don't go too strong. Just say she'll be better in the part than Katharine Cornell."

Meanwhile, *The Warrior's Husband* had closed and Kate was working summer stock at the Croton Playhouse in Ossining, New York, playing the role of Psyche Marbury in Will Cotton's *The Bride the Sun Shines On*. On June 30, during a Thursday night performance, she received a telegram from Hayward telling her that not only would RKO pay her $1,500 a week but that she had to get on a train bound for Hollywood on Sunday to appear opposite John Barrymore in *A Bill of Divorcement*. She was so excited she raced through her lines that night, forcing her struggling co-star to keep up.

It would be 1938 before Kate saw that RKO screen test, at a party celebrating the end of filming the big screen version of *Holiday*. She recalled the experience for *The New York Times* in 1948: "The company laughed themselves sick. I didn't think it was so awfully funny. It's true, I looked terrible in it. But there was something awfully heartbreaking about the girl I was in those days, I was trying so hard - too hard. I was so eager - too eager."

Before Kate left for Hollywood, the Croton Playhouse company threw a picnic supper on the playhouse terrace in her honor. As she was nervously accepting congratulations, the legendary theater producer Jed Harris, for whom she had once auditioned and been turned down, approached her and said, teasingly, "Not bad for an amateur."

On Sunday morning, Kate and Luddy arrived at the train station in Croton-on-Hudson, New York and searched for Harding, who had decided to come along for the ride. There she was, sticking her head out the window, already on the train with her two dogs – Jamie, a Scottie, and Twig, a Shelburne terrier. Kate scrambled to get her luggage aboard as the engine started. Finally, the train pulled away as Luddy waved from the platform, shouting, "Good luck!"

At long last, Kate Hepburn was ready for Hollywood. But to those who knew her well, the question was: Is Hollywood ready for Kate?

5
"MADE FOR THE SCREEN"

As they rode the train to Hollywood in the summer of 1932, Kate and Laura Harding were beside themselves with excitement – especially Kate, who had not traveled much domestically. She had been to Europe several times, and made many trips between Pennsylvania, New York, and Connecticut, but she had never been out West. So they decided to do some sightseeing along the way; while changing trains in Chicago, they enjoyed the venerable Art Institute of Chicago and stayed at the Blackstone Hotel.

With so much at stake in her first film role, Kate was grateful to be accompanied by Harding, who was five years older than Kate and came from a wealthy family. "She knew all the sort of highbrow customs of the time and I learned the way," Kate recalled. "The Vuitton luggage - the clothes - where to shop - what to buy."

As they rode the train together, they discovered there were other luminaries aboard: Adolph Zukor, head of Paramount Pictures, and actress Billie Burke with her husband, the Broadway producer Florenz Ziegfeld (Kate didn't know that Burke was about to play her mother in *A Bill of Divorcements*). Though the country was still being wracked by the Great Depression – 15 million people out of work; 30 million living on welfare and charity; bread lines and soup kitchens everywhere – Kate, Harding, and the other entertainment industry figures were living in a rarified world mostly untouched by the social and economic upheaval taking place around them.

At one point during the trip, Kate caught a glimpse of Burke and Ziegfeld's private car. "It was hung with special slipcovers which covered the walls, the chairs - every object in the room," she recalled. "This seemed quite an extraordinary luxury to me. But it was really 'the thing to do'. . . The baby pillows and blanket to make the drawing room cozy . . . This was way beyond anything that I knew about. I had come from a small town - well, Hartford - a medium-sized town. But sophisticated in the luxuries I certainly was not."

The trip was an unpleasant one, however, as a heat wave gripped the Midwest. With no air-conditioning, Kate and Harding spent much of their time on the train's sooty observation platform, where, just past Albuquerque, a freak accident occurred. A tiny fleck of steel that probably chipped off the railroad track pierced Kate's eye. Trying to remove it only forced it deeper, painfully swelling her eye shut.

When the train finally arrived in Pasadena, California, however, Kate had gathered herself and was determined to make a good impression. She had gone to Elizabeth Hawes, New York's highest-priced designer, to have a special outfit to wear when she got off the train. It was a Quaker gray-blue silk grosgrain suit, with a very long, flared skirt. The blouse was a turtleneck with a ruffle around the top. Over that, she wore a nineteenth-century riding coat with tails.

And the hat? "Well, the hat was a sort of gray-blue straw dish upside down on my head," she recalled. "I had long hair, screwed up tight . . . The dishpan sat on top of this - a bit formal and more than a little eccentric. But it had been very expensive, the whole costume, and I had great faith in it."

Kate disembarked feeling elegant, if a little puffy in the eye. They were met at the station by Leland Hayward and Myron Selznick, who ran the Hollywood office of Hayward's New

York talent agency. When they saw Kate, they were aghast. Her outfit was not so much stylish as it was bizarre. And her eye was swollen and red.

"It was, I realize now, hardly an appropriate costume to arrive in, in Pasadena on July 4th with a temperature of ninety-odd," she said later. "A sweatshirt and an old pair of white pants would have been more appropriate."

"Which one?" asked Myron Selznick as the train pulled in.

"The one with the funny hat."

"You're kidding - we got fifteen hundred dollars for *that*?"

"She's an original," said Hayward.

"Very. What does she drink? Get a load of those eyes."

After introductions, they got into the car - a gray Rolls Royce – and another driver took their bags to the Château Élysée Hotel, where they would stay until other arrangements were made.

Kate asked Hayward for a doctor to look at her eye but he did not want to keep her new bosses waiting. They drove straight to RKO Pictures to meet George Cukor, who would be directing *A Bill of Divorcements*, and Myron Selznick's younger brother David O. Selznick, the thirty-two-year-old boy wonder who was the studio's head of production. When they arrived, Kate stared at the actors parading around the RKO lot, making for a glorious sight: Western gunmen, gypsies, men in tuxedos, and women in gowns filled the streets.

Seeing Kate for the first time, Cukor felt faint. Fearing he had made a terrible mistake - and worried what David Selznick would do when he saw this unconventional creature – he had to pretend all was well as they headed down to the commissary for lunch.

The screenwriter Adela Rogers St. John later said, "As long as I live, I will never forget the first day she appeared on the lot. Everybody was in the commissary at lunch when she walked in with Mr. Cukor."

Studio executives were stunned. David Selznick nearly choked on his chicken wing. "We beheld a tall, skinny girl entirely covered with freckles and wearing the most appalling and incredible clothes I have ever seen in my life," he recalled. "They looked like something Lee Tracy [an actor] would design for the Mexican army to go ski-jumping in - yet you could tell they were supposed to be the last word. George Cukor looked across at us. He was a little pale . . ."

After lunch, in Selznick's office, the studio executive greeted his new star with apprehension as he debated whether to send her straight back to New York. Trying to make the best of the situation, Cukor escorted Kate to his office to show her sketches of the costume designs they had planned for her to wear in the film.

It was the beginning of a long, warm, and highly productive relationship between Cukor and Kate that would last through eight films over the next twenty years. "He was really fat," Kate recalled about their first meeting. "About five feet eight inches and over 220 pounds. He was very energetic, full of laughter and vitality. He summed me up very accurately for what I was: a lady, so-called - a sort of a snob - and totally insecure. I summed him up too. Very bright -

sharp as a tack and a good sense of humor."

Once Cukor had Kate alone, his dismay turned to wonder. As he watched her sort through the costume designs - rejecting one dress after another - he was fascinated by her Garboesque quality and imperious attitude.

"I'm sure Miss De Lima is very talented," Kate said, referring to the designer Josette De Lima as she wiped tears from her swollen eye, "but I want my clothes designed by someone like Chanel or Schiaparelli."

"Considering the way you look," Cukor retorted, "I can hardly take your judgment seriously."

Shocked by his response, Kate defended her attire. "I thought these clothes were pretty fancy," she said. "I paid a great deal for them."

"Well, they're terrible," Cukor said. "You look ghastly. I think any woman who would wear such an outfit outside a bathroom wouldn't know what clothes are. Now, what do you think of that?"

In the awkward silence, Kate eyed the heavy, dark-eyed man. Though only seven years older than Kate, he seemed intelligent and astute beyond his years.

"You win," she said. "Pick out the clothes you want."

Cukor could plainly see that Kate was difficult – but that made her just right for the part she would play, a strong-willed woman named Sydney Fairfield. For the first time since her arrival, he was certain he had made the right choice.

Co-star John Barrymore, meeting her for the first time that day, was the only one who seemed concerned enough about her eye to offer help. The aging matinee idol studied her puffy eye, then handed her a bottle of eye drops, saying, "I also hit the bottle occasionally, my dear."

When the day's meetings were over, Kate and Harding walked out of the studio and saw a man standing on the street. "I beg your pardon," Kate said. "Do you happen to know an eye doctor? I have something in my eye."

By chance, the man was a surgeon named Sam Hirschfeld, who immediately drove them to his office. He tried but failed to remove the steel bits, saying he didn't have the right instruments. So he called around and found a doctor downtown who was still open. The kindly Hirschfeld drove them there, and the eye surgeon went to work. "Three steel filings embedded," Kate recalled. "I could hear them click against her knife. She got them out. Dug them out. Flick flick went the white of my eye, like celluloid. Then she put a patch over my eye. Gave me some pills."

It was a tumultuous first day in Hollywood. By the time Hirschfeld dropped them at their hotel, Kate and Harding were too late for room service, so they sent out for chicken-salad sandwiches and fell into bed, exhausted.

The next morning, Kate headed to the studio with a patch over her eye. She thought it would be funny to tell her limousine chauffeur to park under Cukor's office window and honk loudly as she got out. The director was not pleased – and his anxiety about RKO's new star only intensified as the day wore on.

The studio was taking a huge chance on this unknown actress. RKO had a complex history, including a close call with bankruptcy, several mergers, and some acquisitions (in 1928, the Kennedy patriarch Joseph P. Kennedy had merged several of his Hollywood acquisitions to form Radio-Keith-Orpheum, shortened to RKO). Despite the success of *Cimarron*, its Academy Award-winning Western, the studio was on shaky financial ground when David Selznick took a gamble on Kate despite her arrogant behavior and demands for $1,500 a week.

Her conduct upon arrival didn't help matters. Kate's first appointment with the studio's press department was brief. Her private life was her own, she said, and she did not like or want publicity; in fact, the department would not know she was married until much later. Her meetings with the make-up and hairdressing departments did not go much better. Cukor finally agreed to Kate's demand to keep her natural, intelligent good looks - minus the freckles and frizzy hair.

At lunch, a studio photographer shot pictures of Kate with Billie Burke and Barrymore, giving copies to Kate to autograph and send to out-of-town executives. The young diva refused, which incensed Cukor. "You! Do you really think anyone would want your autograph alongside Barrymore's and Miss Burke's?" he said. "Those two are actors! If you study for twenty-five years, maybe your signature will be worthy to go with theirs!"

After she and Harding moved from the Château Élysée to a small cottage in Franklin Canyon, Kate immersed herself in the script for *A Bill of Divorcement*. She had plenty of time for it, since she and Harding had managed to alienate most of RKO with their antics. Invited to a formal tea at a studio executive's home, Kate wore overalls, a fireman's shirt, and beat-up tennis shoes and sent Harding inside while she stayed in the front yard. No one in Hollywood knew what to make of her. Kate demanded privacy but was always making a scene.

Many found her masculine clothing, her apparent disinterest in men, and her relationship with Harding an intriguing topic of conversation. As she worked on the film, word began to spread that Kate and Harding were lovers. This assertion has also been made by some of Kate's biographers, who quote friends saying that Harding was "the great love of her life." In her memoir, Kate did not confirm or deny such speculation, though she did offer a possible explanation for how the rumors started. A director named Mark Sandrich was getting his hair cut, according to Kate, when he heard Harding calling Kate on a pay telephone. When the person on the other end kept saying, "Who is this?" Harding finally said, "Oh, tell her it's her husband!"

Sandrich "heard this and was absolutely shocked," Kate wrote. "He told me years later he thought that he could have been the one who was responsible for the very strong rumor that we were lesbians. Anyway, the rumor certainly started and even New York was buzzing with it." Beyond that, all Kate said about Harding is that "We all had a very good time together. She's been a good friend for all my life."

Though Kate was still married, Harding had long since replaced Luddy as Kate's confidant and friend, something Kate later attributed to the fundamental differences between men and women. "I think women are more interested in the same things," she said. "Two women can live together as friends. It's more difficult for a man and a woman to be friends and not leap into bed. Of course, it depends on the individual but I've always thought that men and women are not too well suited to each other. It's inevitable that they should come together, but, again, how well suited are they to live together in the same house?"

Kate and Harding did have their differences. Harding was more open and enthusiastic while Kate found most people troubling and exhausting. Still, their home life was relaxed and peaceful; after work, Kate would head home, eat supper, study her lines, wrap her feet in cold cloths, and go to bed about nine. She didn't date and refused to be photographed with a man or to bring an escort to studio events, maintaining that her private life was nobody's business.

Filming began barely two weeks after Kate's arrival. Harding usually stayed on the set with her during the shoots, but afterward, made the rounds with her West Coast friends while Kate stayed at home. Kate called her parents almost daily. When she told her father that she'd spent all the money she'd earned, Dr. Hepburn was furious. He insisted that she send her checks to him; he would forward her an allowance that met her needs. Kate agreed, an odd decision for an otherwise independent - and married - woman. Clearly, she didn't trust her own judgment.

With the help of Cukor and Barrymore, Kate devoted herself to honing her skills. Barrymore said years later that he remembered "every hour" they spent working together. "Something about her recalled my mother, Georgiana Drew, the best actress who ever lived," Barrymore said. "Miss Hepburn's talent was so clearly perceptible, and she was so intelligent in learning, that working with her was all pleasure. But Lord, she was innocent! I'd have to punch her black and blue to force her upstage in front of the camera. You have to knock most actresses practically unconscious before you can get yourself into the picture."

Kate said Barrymore was exceedingly helpful. "I learned a tremendous lot from Barrymore," she recalled. "One thing in particular has been invaluable to me - when you're in the same cast with people who know nothing about acting, you can't criticize them, because they go to pieces. He never criticized me. He just shoved me into what I ought to do. He taught me all that he could pour into one greenhorn in that short time."

While she initially thought Barrymore's first scene seemed phony, she soon changed her opinion. "When we had the scene together in which I said, 'I think you are my father,' and he came over to me and took my face in his hands . . . he was absolutely shattering."

At the time, Barrymore was an aging star and years of drinking had left their mark. His womanizing was legendary, and most of his leading ladies made easy prey. Later, Barrymore confessed that he had ulterior motives when he invited Kate to rehearse some scenes in his dressing room one day. She jumped at the invitation, but when he removed his robe, Kate was stupefied.

"My first thought was to get out, but I simply couldn't move," she said later. "I was petrified - couldn't speak."

Barrymore was quite open about what happened next. "She

didn't move, so I did and started to grab her, but she backed away and practically plastered herself against the wall," he said. "I've never been so damn flabbergasted. I said to her, 'Why not?' and what do you think she said? 'My father doesn't want me to have any babies!' and she edged over to the door and made a quick exit."

Barrymore was angry for a few days, but his admiration for Kate's talent eventually overcame his damaged pride. Kate possessed a special spark, he thought, even though he considered her "a nut." In a weak joke, he added, "She must come from Brazil, where the nuts come from."

George Cukor's doubts about Kate dissolved when she performed before the camera. Her impatience and directness were perfect for the role of Sydney Fairfield, the daughter of a shell-shocked World War I veteran who escapes from a mental hospital and returns home the day his ex-wife is set to remarry. Sydney also has plans to marry but breaks off the engagement when she realizes that his psychiatric affliction is not war-related but genetic and that she risks passing the condition on to her children.

Cukor was hard on Kate. Once during the shooting, she responded with an insult: "Just because you don't know what you're doing don't take it out on me!" she snapped. Still, it didn't take long for him to appreciate her acting instincts.

Kate was an early riser and went to bed early, so the

ten- and twelve-hour days were not a problem for her; she and Harding were up at six-thirty and at the studio an hour later. Kate's dressing room became her second home. She preferred to eat her lunch there rather than joining her co-workers in the studio commissary. Her strict regime impressed those on the set, and she made friends with the crew, telling jokes and handing out candy. Some of the unconventional behavior that had marked her stage work had dissipated. Cukor saw that Kate's face was "made for the screen," adding that her "odd awkwardness, her odd shifts of emphasis" brought her performance alive. "She wasn't too smooth, she was fresh," he said.

Barrymore was easier for Kate to relate to than Billie Burke. Now forty-seven, the beautiful Ms. Burke had been the toast of Broadway in her younger years. She was intent on keeping her sixty-five-year-old husband, the producer Florenz Ziegfeld, but Ziegfeld found monogamy almost impossible. It didn't help matters that his Ziegfeld Follies featured the most beautiful women of the day. Burke's advice to younger women in her position was simple: "It's your job to creep out of bed early - ten minutes early will do, five in a pinch - brush your hair and your teeth, put on something crisp, use some scent, and - no matter how tired you are, no matter how your head aches, no matter how late you were up last night - look kissable!"

While this subservient attitude rankled Kate, she soon gained respect for Burke, who maintained her professionalism even when her husband died of pleurisy midway through filming. Three days after Ziegfeld's death, Burke returned to the set and gave a top-notch performance.

Near the end of Kate's first week on the film, reporters started visiting the set – and, to their delight, the young actress showed up between scenes in her old blue jeans. The studio threatened to steal the pants unless Kate stopped wearing them, but she refused to give them up. One day, when she returned to her dressing room to find them gone, she threatened to walk "practically naked through the RKO lot" if they were not returned.

"So I did it," Kate recalled. "Of course I did it. I walked through the lot in my underpants." Barrymore thought it was hilarious, but no one else was laughing. Executives confiscated the pictures taken of the embarrassing scene and gave Kate back her pants.

Harding was often an accomplice in Kate's antics. Once, they stowed away in the trunk of director William Wellman's limousine. When it reached his house, they jumped out and made faces at him. Occasionally, they sneaked through the window of a Hollywood home while the owners were away and left unsigned notes. "I could look over a place and get in faster than any teenager in Juvenile Court," Kate bragged.

But she always required an accomplice. "We're going in here," Harding would say, and Kate would reply, "Oh, do you think we ought to?" Harding would say, "Yes, you go up and drop through that skylight." On the way back out, Kate would throw a rope down and pull her friend back up. "I don't have too much nerve on my own," Kate said, "but I have great ability when I am prodded."

The press didn't catch wind of these antics, but Kate's eccentricity still made news. She bought a pet monkey and walked around with it on her shoulder. She wore pants almost exclusively while off the set, citing indigestion. When Cukor complained about her wardrobe and her refusals of all dinner invitations, she explained that she would not make a very polite guest: "If my feet are as high as my seat, I digest my dinner, if they aren't, I don't," she said.

One social event she did attend was Cukor's private Sunday afternoon gatherings, a festive meeting ground for the city's gay subculture (it was an open secret that Cukor was gay, though in keeping with the times, he was discreet about it). Calling Kate "the tigress," Cukor warned his intellectual friends they should put on their boxing gloves when she was around.

Kate's idiosyncrasies could be charming, however, and she was well versed in subjects ranging from atomic energy to growing beans in the backyard. Greta Garbo, an actress Kate idolized, also attended Cukor's soirees on occasion. One Sunday, Kate was skinny dipping in Cukor's pool, and as she was getting out of the water, he and Garbo appeared. Horrified, Kate frantically grabbed a towel to cover herself and sputtered a greeting, leaving Garbo speechless.

Kate's peculiar behavior off the set did not seem to affect her work on *A Bill of Divorcement*, which she took very seriously. Filming took only four weeks. When it was over, she and Harding took a train back to New York.

By then, it was clear there was not much left of the marriage between Kate and Luddy – but they decided to travel to Europe before the film previewed to see if they could revive the spark. After all, she had just earned $6,000 for less than a month's work – $82,000 in today's dollars – so why not splurge a bit? It didn't work. Kate insisted on booking tickets in steerage, the cheapest fare, which caused friction between them, and the trip was unpleasant.

As the film's release date approached, studio executives were nervous. "The world knows that startling Hepburn face now, but when she first appeared on the RKO lot there was consternation," David Selznick explained. "'Ye Gods, that horse face!' they cried, and when the first rushes were shown, the gloom around the studio was so heavy you could cut it with a knife."

While Kate and Luddy were still in Europe, the film opened in New York. When glowing reviews began to appear, the studio breathed a sigh of relief. Kate's performance, in particular, was heralded as a harbinger of great things to come. "Katharine Hepburn . . . seems definitely established for an important cinema career," wrote Richard Watts of the *New York Herald Tribune*. Thornton Delehanty of the *New York Evening Post* wrote that with her "dignity and an instinct for underplaying an emotion . . . Miss Hepburn has the makings of a star . . ." The *Journal-American* raved that she "flamed like an opal, half-demon and half-Madonna."

Some critics insisted that the acclaim was due to the role, not the actress; although her performance was genuinely touching, they said, a number of talented performers could have played it just as well.

Still, this new starlet had a magnetism that resonated with the audience. She certainly had an intriguing face, but it was more than that; the camera amplified her already powerful personality, providing an immediacy and intimacy that viewers longed for. And as "talkies" replaced silent films in the early 1930s, Hollywood was desperate for performers who could speak distinctly; many silent-screen stars simply did not have the voice to make the transition. Kate, with a rare combination of brains, beauty, and highly distinct vocal mannerisms, was precisely the kind of actress the new medium demanded. *Bill of Divorcement* was a box-office hit, earning a profit of $110,000 for RKO in its first year of release.

When Kate and Luddy finally arrived in New York, photographers were waiting for her and snapped a photo as she stood on the deck of the French liner, her lean figure etched against the Statue of Liberty in the background. Luddy discreetly got off the ship later; because Kate was registered on the ship as Mrs. Ludlow Smith, a reporter asked if she was married. She denied she was; later, when a fan magazine writer asked if she had any children, she responded, jokingly, "Yes, two white and three colored."

It was the kind of mocking, mischievous remark that the press would criticize her for later. But to her audiences, Kate Hepburn could do no wrong. Selznick says he could feel it right away, in the first few minutes of *Bill of Divorcement*: "During the first few feet, you could feel the audience's bewilderment at this completely new type, and also feel they weren't quite used to this kind of a face," Selznick said. "But very early in the picture there was a scene in which Hepburn just walked across the room, stretched her arms, and then lay out on the floor before the fireplace. It sounds very simple, but you could almost feel, and you could definitely hear, the excitement in the audience."

Clearly, something had changed in the world of cinema. Selznick, who would later win Academy Awards for producing *Gone with the Wind* (1939) and *Rebecca* (1940), was sure of it. "It was one of the greatest experiences I've ever had,"

Selznick said. "In those few simple feet of film, a new star was born."

6
"AN ARISTOCRATIC
AMERICAN GARBO"

After the smashing success of Kate's first film, her agents and RKO's executives – who had picked up the option on her contract – were eager to start another project. But the film they had agreed on, *Three Came Unarmed*, had to be abandoned because of difficulties in trying to adapt E. Arno Robertson's novel to the screen. Also, RKO producer David Selznick didn't like the idea of Kate playing a missionary's daughter in Borneo, feeling that she was miscast.

The role Selznick had in mind for her was Cynthia Darlington, the aristocratic, daredevil aviator in the film adaptation of Gilbert Frankau's novel, *Christopher Strong*. Selznick had hired one of America's few female directors, Dorothy Arzner, to make the film.

Now in her thirties, Arzner started out waiting tables in her father's Hollywood cafe before working her way up the Hollywood ladder, first as a secretary, then as a script clerk, film cutter, and editor. She had edited dramatic bullfight scenes in Rudolph Valentino's *Blood and Sand* and the silent-screen classic *The Covered Wagon* before graduating to script writing.

In 1927, Arzner, then twenty-seven, directed her first film. She was one of the few directors who had weathered the transition from the silent era to the new Hollywood, and all her films featured independent women. Even so, her relationship with Kate was a rivalry from their first meeting.

Adding yet another woman to the mix, Selznick hired the author and playwright Zoë Akins to work on the script. Although Kate gradually developed a grudging respect for Arzner – who was unpretentious and proud of her working-class roots – Akins was nouveau riche, and Kate despised her manner.

Because Akins's husband was terminally ill, she refused to leave him to go to the studio and insisted they meet at her posh stucco home in Pasadena. Kate, who was adamantly opposed to exposing one's personal tragedies to outsiders, was offended by the experience. She also felt that Akins's script was dull.

Christopher Strong was plagued with problems from the start. Kate came down with the flu during production and had to be hospitalized for several days; her father wanted to fly her home to West Hartford, but she refused to go. Meanwhile, Arzner told David Selznick that she would quit if Miss Hepburn didn't stop interfering with her direction. Selznick didn't budge, however, and all three women stayed on to finish the film.

In the end, *Christopher Strong* was a major disappointment. Despite generous funding, delightful sets, striking costumes, and a stellar cast, the lackluster script and Arzner's heavy-handed direction kept all the other elements from shining.

The film opened on March 10, 1933, at Radio City Music Hall to mixed reviews. Of Kate, Jack S. Cohen Jr. of the *New York Sun* wrote, "She resembles somewhat an aristocratic American Garbo save that she hasn't got Garbo's warmth . . . whoever spotted her for the screen after her brief appearance on the stage in *The Warrior's Husband* knew the camera's power. Her personality is far more interesting and alluring on the screen than it ever was on the stage."

Kate's agent, Leland Hayward, thought the world of his star.

He ranked Kate "right up there with Garbo and Dietrich - definitely the best. God yes." He was eager to show everyone what he had already seen in her: "A certain look in her eyes, a style - an awareness of her effect on people - the way she holds herself, moves, a sense of her own mystery."

Hayward appreciated intelligent women. He had married, divorced, and then remarried Lola Gibbs, a beautiful Texas debutante and aviatrix who had taught Hayward to fly. His passion for planes brought him and Kate closer together during the filming of *Christopher Strong*, and Kate seemed to have reassessed her feelings for the man; she no longer loathed him. Then again, her supposed hatred of him may have disguised a hidden attraction. She may have concealed her true feelings for the same reason she stayed away from liquor - she always wanted to feel in control.

Hayward had been remarried to Gibbs for two years when he fell in love with Kate. He was good-looking and charming and looked nothing like most Hollywood agents, who were mostly Italians or Russian Jews. An affluent Princeton graduate, he waltzed through the executive offices of the major studios wearing white flannels and yachting sneakers. He was a brash and bold businessman who demanded outrageous salaries for his clients and often accomplished the impossible.

"The wives of the moguls were crazy about him . . . and kept talking about him," George Cukor said later, "because he was a very attractive, handsome, dashing man." Cukor added that if he were making a film about a successful agent and Hayward auditioned for the role, he would say, "You're out of your mind! This is not the way an agent looks."

But that was part of his success, the director noted. "Just charmed the birds off the trees, the money out of the coffers, and ladies into their beds."

Though Hayward and Kate were both married to other people, they spent a lot of time together. Kate and Harding had moved from their small Franklin Canyon cottage to a larger place in Coldwater Canyon with a swimming pool and a tennis court. Hayward spent hours there, lying on the couch and talking endlessly on the phone. Kate seemed to enjoy looking after him. "I could see very quickly that I suited Leland perfectly," Kate recalled later. "I liked to eat at home and go to bed early. He liked to eat out and go to bed late. So he had a drink when I had dinner and then off he'd go. Back at midnight. Perfect friendship."

Kate admired his qualities - he was strong, smart, successful, and decisive – and she also liked the fact that he appreciated her idiosyncrasies and independence and wanted to make her a huge star. Hayward negotiated a new contract for Kate at RKO that was an actor's dream, giving her an unprecedented percentage of the gross and allowing her to approve her co-stars and director. Her contract stipulated she make at least two films a year but also guaranteed time between films to appear on the stage.

Not long after finishing *Christopher Strong*, Kate was waiting for producer Pandro Berman to return to his office when she noticed a script on his desk. As she thumbed through it, she recalled, "I thought, 'Oh - my - God - that's the most wonderful part ever written for anyone.'" It was an unproduced stage play called *Morning Glory* that Berman planned to adapt into a film, written by Zoë Akins, whom Kate had clashed with while making *Christopher Strong*. She took it home to read it and when she returned it to Berman told him, "This is what I'd like to do."

The problem was that the role Kate wanted – a Broadway hopeful named Eva Lovelace – was written for Constance Bennett, one of the most popular and highly paid film stars of the time, who had yet to read it. Kate begged Berman, "Me, me, me!"

Akins had based the part on actress Tallulah Bankhead, but Kate considered her behavior too rude for the character of Eva. So she demanded that Howard J. Green, who was hired to adapt the play to film, make changes. The rewritten script had its limitations, but the role of Eva, the small-town girl who dreams of making it big on Broadway, suited Kate perfectly. She hounded Berman, insisting that it was the role she was *born* to play, until he finally relented, agreeing to pay her $2,500 per week.

Director Lowell Sherman defied convention and rehearsed and filmed simultaneously, shooting *Morning Glory* in an unheard-of eighteen days. Kate's co-stars in the film were Adolphe Menjou and Douglas Fairbanks Jr., who learned of her affair with Haywood when he took Kate out to dinner. Halfway through the date, Kate complained of a headache, so he drove her home, watched her go in the house and then run back out. "Another car I hadn't noticed was hidden further up the driveway under some trees," Fairbanks said later. "She hopped in, and I saw a man at the wheel [Hayward]. They drove right past me without noticing me. She was laughing happily, her hair blowing over her face."

Morning Glory premiered in August of 1933 at Radio City

Music Hall, and more than 130,000 people came to see it that first week. *Morning Glory* was a small film without any shocking plot twists, so most of the crowd likely showed up to watch Kate in an earnest and riveting performance.

One critic wrote: "Miss Hepburn shines as a stage-struck girl named Eva Lovelace, whose curious nature is a mixture of ingenuousness and cleverness, and persistence and pride. There are even moments when she does not appear quite rational, particularly when she declares that possibly when she reaches her zenith she will end her life. But let it be said here that she attains success and does not intend to be a morning glory, a flower that fades before the sun is very high."

With the success of the film and the validation of her acting abilities, Kate later recalled, "I can remember thinking, 'Oh, this is great! Oh, the camera! That's a friend. This is all very easy. Warm! Cozy!'"

Her newfound star status also invited criticism and a bit of ridicule. Her idiosyncratic mannerisms were easy to mimic and led to less-than-flattering parodies on the radio and in nightclubs. Frank S. Nugent of *The New York Times* wrote that Kate gave him the jitters. "The way she walks - those little scurrying steps . . . The way she talks - the breathless . . . so-soulfully brave, husky tones with the pipe of hysteria beneath them. The way she . . . flutters and is so fearfully feminine that almost any normal woman would seem a Tarzan in comparison."

Still, even her critics saw her as an original and audiences were fascinated by her. Cukor was slated to direct her next film, *Little Women*, and Kate was ecstatic; she considered him a genuine artist, who, like her father, treated her affectionately without letting her get away with too much.

Kate had long loved *Little Women*, but Cukor considered it simply a children's book. He was startled to discover that Louisa May Alcott's story was "very strong-minded . . . full of character, and a wonderful picture of New England family life." The character of Jo March also resembled Kate in her youth – a spirited tomboy who stages plays with her siblings before going to New York to pursue her dreams. The project would deepen the creative collaboration between Cukor and Kate, cement their friendship, and bind them professionally for years to come.

Throwing herself into the making of *Little Women* kept Kate from dwelling on the turmoil in her personal life. Harding had returned to the East Coast and their relationship had cooled. Kate was also trying to decide if her feelings for Leland were strong enough to warrant not one, but two divorces: Leland's from Lola and hers from Luddy.

The character of Jo March embodied many of Kate's best qualities: kindness, humor, loyalty, and willingness to play the fool when it was called for; she would later say it was the most autobiographical role she ever played. Kate modeled Jo after her mother's strong-willed mother, Caroline Garlinghouse Houghton; she even had wardrobe designer Walter Plunkett duplicate one her grandmother's dresses from a tintype she gave him.

Cukor said Kate cast "a spell of magic [over the film], a kind of power that dominated even those scenes she's not in." The script, by screenwriter Victor Heerman and his wife Sarah Y. Mason, stayed true to the novel, and the sets were plain and unpretentiousness. The Alcott house itself was replicated in great detail, and Walter Plunkett's costumes - which the four actresses borrowed from each other from time to time - were the epitome of New England frugality.

The production had its problems, however. Joan Bennett, who played Amy, was pregnant and hadn't informed the studio; she hoped to finish the film before her condition became noticeable. When she started to show, Plunkett had to rework Bennett's costumes, and Cukor had to shoot scenes so that Amy was seen only from the waist up.

Kate's role in *Little Women* called for her to draw on elements of her own personality. In one emotional scene, Cukor recalled, "Kate [who had not felt well] had to do take after take of a very emotional scene simply because the sound men kept messing it up. After the fifteenth take, or whatever, they got it - and Kate was so exhausted and agonized by all that weeping she threw up. But not until we'd got the take."

When it was released in November of 1933, *Little Women*, and especially Kate's performance, was a hit with the critics. And the studio launched an extensive marketing blitz that focused on Kate, with billboards that read: "Again she weaves her Magic Spell!" Full-page newspaper ads that included Kate's headshot dramatically announced, "The radiant Star of *Morning Glory* marches still deeper into your heart as the best loved heroine ever born in a book . . . See her . . . living . . . the immortal Jo."

Little Women was David Selznick's last picture at RKO before he left for Metro-Goldwyn-Mayer, but other executives quickly lined up potential projects for their new star:

an adaptation of Edith Wharton's *Age of Innocence;* a film based on the life of Sarah Bernhardt; Nell Gwyn's biography of Queen Elizabeth I, *The Tudor Wench;* and *Without Sin,* an original screenplay by Melville Baker and Jack Kirkland. She was also being considered for playwright Lula Vollmer's portrayal of a boyish, rough-hewn, faith healer in the Ozark Mountains.

But Kate was unimpressed with what Hollywood had to offer, professionally and socially. Her affair with Hayward – always provisional, even on their best days – was fizzling. Her relationship with Harding was devolving into a more conventional friendship, perhaps because Kate was spending so much time with a new friend, the popular actress Elissa Landi, who had appeared in Cecil B. De Mille's *The Sign of the Cross* with Claudette Colbert. Plus, Kate longed for Fenwick in Old Saybrook and New York City, where she could pursue her stage career. She decided to go home to Hartford.

Back on familiar territory, Kate became reacquainted with Jed Harris, who had playfully teased Kate on her last night of summer stock in Ossining, New York. The lean, handsome, Yale graduate was one of Broadway's top producers, having been featured on the cover of *Time* magazine. Intelligent, witty, and confrontational, Harris had a reputation as a womanizer; he was married and divorced three times and had two children, one out of wedlock with actress Ruth Gordon.

He also had a knack for making enemies with his abusive behavior. Laurence Olivier, whom Harris directed on Broadway in *The Green Bay Tree*, called him "the most loathsome man I'd ever met." The playwright and director George S. Kaufman once said, "When I die, I want to be cremated and have my ashes thrown in Jed Harris's face."

Still, even his worst critics admitted he had a tremendous talent for the theater. As for his powers of seduction, one of his contemporaries wrote that "he had the grin of a sorcerer . . . He purred when he spoke. His skinny jaw jutted. His eyes were dark and slightly upturned as if listening to some inner music." Women were attracted to "his athletic use of language, the fresh routes of his nimble mind," as well as his menacing demeanor.

When Kate arrived in Hartford, she was surprised to learn that Harris had called to offer her the lead in a play he was producing on Broadway called *The Lake*, by Dorothy Massingham and Murray MacDonald. When Kate asked him to send her the script, she casually mentioned that her parents were away and she had some time alone.

That seemed like an obvious invitation to Harris, who made a beeline for West Hartford with the playwright Edward Chodorov. For *The Lake* to succeed, Harris needed a star. He had produced a string of hits in the 1920s – including *The Front Page* and *Uncle Vanya* – but his most recent ventures had not gone well and he desperately needed a winner. In fact, Harris was financing *The Lake* himself and had sold his beloved 150-foot sailboat, the *Señorita*, to pull it off. Kate's box-office popularity would secure his investment, he believed, and under his expert direction, Kate could thrive in a difficult role.

Once in Hartford, Harris and Chodorov checked into a hotel, and Harris immediately called Kate. At her suggestion, he left Chodorov and drove to her house on Bloomfield Avenue. Stuck in a failing marriage, her affair with Hayward dying out, and her relationship with Harding increasingly distant, Kate was vulnerable to Harris's charm. She liked his energy and intelligence, which sparked her own. Beyond the dollar signs, Kate's appeal to Harris was that of the forbidden good girl: wealthy, beautiful, and raised in a society that typically excluded Jews like him.

Kate and Harris spent a lot of time together in the Hepburns' West Hartford home. Kate's mother especially enjoyed his company. Chodorov was surprised that Kate was taken with the abrasive and often scruffy producer, who didn't always bother to shave before going to the Hepburns' house. Kate agreed to take part in Harris's production of *The Lake*, but first, she had to return to Hollywood to make her next film, *Spitfire*.

Directed by stage and film actor John Cromwell and shot mostly in the San Jacinto Mountains of California, *Spitfire* was a vast departure from anything Kate had done so far – and an awkward follow-up to *Little Women*. Kate's character, a mountain girl with the power to heal, is feared, cursed, stoned, and almost lynched by her neighbors, not to mention deceived by a man she comes to love. Though Kate played the part with spirit, she wasn't suited for the role. A reviewer for *The New Yorke*r noted, "Her artistry does not extend to the interpretation of the primitive or the uncouth."

The filming of *Spitfire* was scheduled to be finished by five o'clock on November 15, so Kate could return to the East Coast to begin rehearsals on *The Lake* the next day. Rehearsals ran late, and Kate was forced to reschedule her flight for the next night. But she agreed to work only five hours and forty-five minutes, the time stipulated per her contract with the studio. When two scenes were still unfinished the next afternoon, Kate was exasperated. "You make other people live up to conditions you write into contracts," she told producer Pandro Berman, "It's time you learned to do so too."

"How much do you want to finish the scene?" Berman asked.

"Ten thousand dollars," Kate retorted. "I wanted to show them [RKO] that if I set a definite date," she later explained. "I meant to keep it . . . Time means a lot to me."

Even though her price for the entire four weeks of filming had been $50,000, Berman felt he had no choice but to agree to her demands.

The night of November 16, Kate boarded a plane for New York. When she learned that a mob of fans was waiting for her at Newark Airport, she landed at Cleveland and took a train to New York. It was a difficult trip because the stress of making four films in a little more than a year had taken its toll; she had lost weight, and her natural exuberance had dimmed.

But she looked forward to seeing Harris, especially now that Hayward was involved with a fresh flame – the Hollywood newcomer Margaret Sullavan, who seemed to be trying to out-Kate Kate by becoming the latest hot starlet. Only days after Kate left California to join the company of *The Lake*, the headline of the *Los Angeles Times* movie page announced: "BOW-GAYNOR-DIETRICH-GARBO-HEP-BURN - NOW IT'S MARGARET SULLAVAN."

Hayward had signed Sullavan - a petite, fun-loving twenty-four-year-old - six months earlier. The Virginia native, who fancied herself a femme fatale, was a relentless flirt with an adventurous streak that many men found irresistible – and Hayward's attraction to his new protégée bruised Kate's ego. Hayward had tried to prevent Kate from signing Harris's contract – and the fact that Harris, now her lover, was directing and producing *The Lake* made the whole arrangement a deeply satisfying form of revenge for Kate.

What she didn't know at the time was that Sullavan also had had an affair with Harris, a relationship that ended her marriage to actor Henry Fonda (who would later write about the affair in his book, *Fonda, My Life*). Kate was also unaware that Sullavan's affair with Harris hadn't actually ended. While Kate was on the West Coast filming *Spitfire*, Harris was seeing a lot of Sullavan in Virginia, where she was visiting her family. Harris spent so much time there, in fact, that New York newspaper columnists reported that he was working on a play by a Southern playwright.

Sullavan inspired that kind of devotion. Like Kate, she wore pants before they were fashionable and refused to make personal appearances - even on opening nights. Harris admired her talent as an actress – calling her a Southern Katharine Hepburn - and had initially considered her for the lead in *The Lake*. He wanted "a classy broad" to play the part, he said, and thought both actresses could fit the bill.

Unaware of Harris's duplicity – and believing that she was his first choice to star in *The Lake* – Kate dedicated herself whole-heartedly to the part. At age twenty-six, she had every reason to think her return to the Broadway stage would be as triumphant as her fledgling Hollywood career had been.

"When I returned to New York in 1933, I was a big hit," Kate recalled later. "As [Harris] became less successful, I became more so. Everything I did seemed to work. I apparently thought that I would renew Jed's luck if I did *The Lake* for him."

As it turned out, however, Harris – and Kate – would be sorely disappointed.

7

"THE GAMUT OF EMOTION FROM A TO B"

"My attitude toward the play was really cockeyed," Kate wrote in her memoir, describing her involvement with the Broadway production of *The Lake*. "I can't actually remember what I thought of it as a play - as an evening in the theater. I think I was anxious to be a help to Jed. I hardly dare write this. I actually thought that if I did the play, it would get him back on his feet. I thought that his position must be very embarrassing to him and now that I was `important,' I felt that as the little Mother of All the World, I could help him resume his proper status. How I could have been this dumb, I do not know."

The trouble started immediately. As rehearsals began in New York, Harris grew anxious about Kate's suitability for the role. She was playing Stella Surrege, a young socialite whose husband drowns in a lake on their first day of marriage; she becomes guilt-ridden because she has loved a married man instead. The play had been an unqualified success in London, where director Tyrone Guthrie had set a formal English drawing room tone with a cast of twenty-seven.

Harris had been warned that the story might not translate well to American audiences, who preferred strong-willed, rebellious heroines to meek and compliant characters like Stella. For the play to succeed, Kate would need to portray a supremely tragic creature.

In retrospect, she was horribly miscast. While Margaret Sullavan might be able to depict a doomed heroine whose plight could move an audience to tears, Kate's attempts at vulnerability seemed improbable because the audience knew her strength would overcome her weaknesses. Within forty-eight hours after arriving in New York, she and Harris were at a stalemate.

While Kate was confident of her ability to play the part, Harris could see that "she was hopeless. I fought with her - I begged her to stop posing, striking attitudes, leaning against doorways, putting a limp hand to her forehead, to stop being a big movie star and feel the lines, feel the character. I was trying the impossible, to make an artificial showcase of an artificial star, and she couldn't handle it."

Other members of the company disagreed. Some said Kate seemed unsure of herself and that Harris, rather than being supportive, was unnecessarily hard on her. One witness said, "If she turned her head to the left, he didn't like it. If she turned it to the right, he liked it still less."

Later, Kate realized that she still had a long way to go as a stage actress: "I was in my mid-twenties. Had exaggeratedly been referred to as the new Duse - Bernhardt. While I knew that all this adulation wasn't exactly deserved, still I did seem to have something. Just what it was I wasn't sure. And when it would happen I wasn't sure either. The acting, I mean. And this was indeed perilous. I could make them laugh. I could make them cry. But the atmosphere had to be perfect. O.K. in movies. Disaster on the stage."

In her films, when a scene was not working, Kate could always stop and do another take. No so on stage, where there is nowhere to hide. Plus, there is the relentless ticking of the clock as opening night approaches. On top of that pressure, Kate's infatuation with Harris, and his brutal treatment of her, had left her feeling vulnerable and confused; within a week, she was openly weeping in his presence. During one of these outbursts, Harris said, a crying Kate threw her arms around his neck and wailed, "I could have loved you so."

"I never thought of loving her or being loved by her," Harris said later. "I was intensely embarrassed. She clearly felt she could have been in love with me." In addition to rejecting her affections, Harris also stopped directing the play and gave the job to his stage manager, Worthington (Tony) Miner. Miner later recalled having to beg Kate to join the company in Washington, D.C., for the final week of rehearsals. They were preparing for public performances in Washington before officially opening on Broadway. "She was totally demoralized."

But Harris wasn't finished clashing with Kate. He vetoed her original costumes, leaving her only a week to find substitutions. When Harding, who was now coming to watch Kate's rehearsals, brought her more suitable clothes, Harris banned her from rehearsals. Then Harris took the drastic step of firing Tony Miner on the eve of the play's debut, deeply upsetting the cast and crew. Miner was replaced by Geoffrey Kerr, an actor and writer Kate had known from her summer stock theater days with the Berkshire Players three years earlier.

The Lake opened on December 17, 1933, at the National Theatre in Washington, D.C., to a packed house. It was a glittering premiere, with dozens of dinner parties hosted by prominent social luminaries prior to the show. The minute Kate stepped on stage wearing Harding's jodhpurs, the audience gave her a rousing ovation and her confidence returned in full force, lasting for the entire performance. When she spoke her last lines - "There are ghosts who are friendly ghosts. I shall be back" - the audience roared enthusiastically.

"I was terrified," she said later. "I really walked through the play in a daze. A few things hit. But mostly missed. I could actually feel the attention of the audience recede like the tide. I went through the motions but there was no heart in it - no joy . . . When it was over, the audience went mad . . . what the hell - she's young and all dressed up. Give her a hand."

The reviews were better than Kate had expected. A critic for *The Washington Post* said her timing was off, and her speech pattern was "staccato," but he also noted that "there was never an instant when she failed to command attention, hold the audience's undivided interest and win its unstinted acclaim."

Unfortunately, that was Kate's best performance of the entire week in Washington. But she got a break from her struggles when President Franklin Roosevelt invited her to tea at the White House. When they sat down – Kate terribly nervous and excited – the President said he had missed *The Lake* but had seen several of her movies. He hoped she might someday film an adaptation of a Kipling short story that was one of his favorites. "Franklin Delano Roosevelt was a man of great charm and he had the gift of laughter," she recalled. "And a great gift it is. Lightens the load."

When *The Lake*'s short Washington run ended, cast and crew headed to New York for the official Broadway opening. But Harris, without explanation, canceled all rehearsals before opening night and disappeared from the production. Years later, Kate remained mystified about why he did not allow the cast time to improve the show and why he dropped out of sight – though it may have been as simple as a captain abandoning a sinking ship.

"Now, it could be that Jed felt that he had over-directed me," Kate said. "And that he was letting me find my way back. But by this time back to where? He - Jed - was invisible. Never appeared at all, as far as I was concerned. And as for finding my way back. Not a chance. The trail had grown over. Alone there was no way back. I was lost."

The show opened on Broadway the day after Christmas. Kate's entire family, Harding, Frances Robinson-Duff, and Hayward were seated in front to show their support. Kate was petrified; celebrities in the audience included playwright George S. Kaufman, actress Kay Francis, writer Dorothy Parker, and aviation pioneer Amelia Earhart. Hayward came backstage to wish her well, which was both awkward and painful for Kate after his affair with Margaret Sullavan and her own failed romance with Harris.

Her performance was essentially a repeat of her first night in Washington. Her timing was off, and her pitch rose higher as she grew more frantic. As one New York critic put it, "Miss Hepburn began the first act in hysteria."

"It was perfectly awful," Kate recalled. "Like an automaton. My voice got higher and higher. I prayed. I prayed. I prayed. No use. I just went on and on and on. I hadn't died. I was there. Fully conscious of having given a totally nothing performance."

Playwright Noël Coward came backstage afterward and tried to reassure her. "Don't let it get your goat," he said.

"It happens to everyone." Her failure inspired one of Dorothy Parker's most famous quips, when she said of her performance, "She ran the gamut of emotion from A to B." Because of Parker's celebrity, her comment was printed in newspapers across the United States – and even in England – leaving a long-lasting mark on Kate's career. Later, Kate would admit, "Dorothy Parker was right."

The Lake was like a bad dream that would not end. Advance sales kept the show open through January and into February – tickets could not be returned – and Kate's contract required her to stay for the entire run. So she decided to make the best of it. "My main task now was to see whether I could learn to act under fire," she said later.

One night, a tall woman named Susan Steele appeared in Kate's dressing room, introduced herself as a singer, and said, "I think that I could help you." They went back to Kate's house and worked on her vocal technique. The two became close friends. Each night, Kate's performance improved a bit.

Spending time with Steele made Kate realize that she had committed the cardinal sin for a Hepburn: She had moaned and felt like a victim. Plus, she had lost the pure joy of acting. Slowly, her confidence returned. "It was thrilling," she recalled. "My dignity returned. I stopped making excuses. And I began to try to look at myself as the leader of a group. Not a poor little thing who was trying her best and had been mistreated . . . I was learning to act. I was learning to be a star."

Still, Kate was looking forward to wrapping up the show and getting on with her life. Then, about three weeks into the run, company manager Joe Glick told Kate the production would be going to Chicago. "What?" she cried. Despite the bad reviews, advance sales had kept the show afloat for a respectable fifty-five performances and *The Lake* actually turned a profit. That was enough to convince Harris that he could also make money on a Chicago tour.

After stewing about it for a week, Kate called Harris, whom she had not seen since the opening. "But, Jed, why?" she demanded. "I was roasted - but let's face it - so were you. Why send it out to –"

Harris cut her off. "My dear, the only interest I have in you is the money I can make out of you."

Angry and trapped by her contract, she asked Harris how much money it would take to convince him to close the show when the New York run ended.

"How much have you got?"

She reached for her bank account ledger, which she kept near the phone. "I have thirteen thousand, six hundred and seventy-five dollars and seventy-five cents in the Chase National Bank" – about $250,000 in today's currency.

"I'll take that."

The next morning, she sent him a check.

Years later, Harris went to Hollywood and asked Myron Selznick to help him get a job. "You've asked the wrong person," he said. "I'm Kate Hepburn's agent. She doesn't like you. You took all her money to close *The Lake*."

"Why, I didn't know that she was upset about that," Harris

said. "I'll send her a check."

Myron held out his hand. "I'll take it." When Kate got the check, she tore it up. "Sad money," she called it. Later, she called Harris "hands-down the most diabolical person I have ever met."

Not only was her professional life in ruins, but Kate's personal life was also a mess. Luddy was talking divorce, and Harding had been aloof and spending time with other friends.

When *The Lake* finally closed on February 10, 1934, Kate decided to take a vacation to Paris with Steele, her new voice coach and friend. Kate made reservations on the ocean liner S.S. *Paris* under the names K. Smith and S. Steele. The plan was to continue to Cannes, where she had won a Cannes Film Festival Award for *Little Women*, then spend a few weeks on the Riviera and touring France.

Just before departing, Kate got some stunning news that took some sting out of *The Lake* debacle: She had won the Academy Award for Best Actress for her performance in *Morning Glory*. It was the early days of the Oscars – only the fifth year since the awards ceremony began in 1929 – and she considered it just another glitzy industry event that she refused to attend, never dreaming she might win. But the award itself mean a great deal to her, boosting her confidence. "My first Academy Award," she said later. "I couldn't believe it!"

When word got out that the newly minted Oscar winner would be boarding the S.S. *Paris* on March 18, reporters and photographers scrambled over to the pier. Kate and

Steele refused to stop for questions or pictures; when they reached their cabin, they locked themselves in. When the press continued to hound them, Steele finally stepped out onto the pier and announced that she was "an old friend of Miss Hepburn's" and they would be "abroad for four or five weeks, visiting Paris and the Riviera."

Their six days at sea were difficult. To avoid attention, they ate meals in their cabin and took walks when most of the first-class passengers were dining. Kate and Steele soon started to bicker, and Steele began to drink heavily. By the time they reached Le Havre, they were barely speaking. Kate decided to return to the United States after only four days in Paris; Steele did not make the return trip.

Ernest Hemingway was also aboard the S.S. *Paris* and, when he heard Kate was a passenger, arranged to meet her. A great admirer of his books, she was thrilled to meet the famous author. During the trip, they took walks on the windy decks, dined together, and argued enthusiastically. When the ship docked in New York on April 4, 1934, they were sitting together as reporters rushed aboard.

"Don't be a mug!" Hemingway admonished Kate.

"I'm not a mug," she snapped, then flashed her best on-screen smile. "Really, I'm not disagreeable. How many reporters are there?"

Told that there were twelve, she asked the steward to bring them champagne.

"I never meant to cause you any inconvenience," she explained to the reporters. "The only reason I didn't see you when I went away was that I had nothing to say. I talk so little for publication because I'm so indiscreet."

With that, she opened herself up for questions, addressing every subject from her fondness for wearing pants to her eagerness to get back on a stage despite *The Lake's* poor reviews. She emphatically denied going to Paris to obtain a divorce. "I just needed a vacation and took it - that's good enough reason, isn't it?" she said. "And I came back because I got homesick."

"Obviously, Miss Hepburn needed a guide," Hemingway joked, before telling reporters he was heading back to Key West to do some intensive writing so he could earn enough to go back to Africa. Hemingway later said Kate had invited him to tea the next day at her house in Manhattan and told him that he need not wait to earn enough for another safari. She would provide the necessary money and accompany him and his wife Pauline on the trip. Hemingway considered Kate's offer but politely declined.

Despite her rocky trip to Paris, Kate soon boarded another ocean liner – this time to Mexico with Harding, with whom she had made up, to finally divorce Luddy. After five years of a marriage that wasn't much of a marriage, enough was enough.

Looking back later, she said the beginning of the end was when she went to Hollywood with Harding in the summer of 1932, leaving Luddy behind. Kate admitted she was thinking only of herself and her dream of becoming a movie star. In fact, the way she treated Luddy would remain one of the biggest regrets of her life.

". . . [H]ow can I describe to you my relationship with

Luddy?" she wrote in her memoir. "He really was close to me. He was like Mother and Dad. He was there. He was like breathing. My friend. I could ask him anything. He would do anything. You just don't find people like that in life. Unconditional love."

Without Luddy, she said, she would never have survived her move to New York in 1928. "I would have been frightened away from this big city and I would have shriveled up and died. And Luddy - all he wanted was me, and, of course, all I wanted was to be a great big hit star in the movies . . . Now as I write this, I am horrified at what an absolute pig I was. You can see that when I say about Luddy I spent his money, I broke his heart . . ."

Kate had even made Luddy legally change his name from Ludlow Ogden Smith to S. Ogden Ludlow to spare her the embarrassment of being confused with the singer Kate Smith or be burdened with the impossibly boring name of Mrs. Smith. "My aim was *me me me*" she said. "All the way - up - down - all about."

For a long time, Kate didn't care about divorcing Luddy, even when they were living apart, because she knew she would never marry again. But she wanted Luddy to have the freedom to take another wife – even though he was still in love with her and told one journalist he hoped she would come back to him. "I didn't want Luddy to be a deceived husband," she said.

Kate and Harding went to Miami to board a cruise ship, the *Morro Castle*, which stopped in Havana before sailing through the Panama Canal to Mexico. On April 24, 1934, Kate and Harding registered at the Hotel Itzá in Mérida, on

Mexico's Yucatán peninsula, and Kate met with a Mexican lawyer who filed the papers on her behalf, citing grounds of "deep disagreement as to life, incompatibility of character and separation for more than 300 days at a time."

At the hearing, Luddy was represented by an attorney who had been given instructions to be as helpful to Kate as possible. When the divorce became public two days later, the press emphasized the fact that the usual thirty-day restriction on remarriage had not been imposed. Because Luddy made it clear that he had no plans to remarry, the press speculated that Kate was the one looking to immediately wed again.

Harding, acting as Kate's official spokesman, set reporters straight: "Miss Hepburn has no plans to remarry." To avoid probing questions from the press when they returned to New York, they barricaded themselves in her Turtle Bay home while reporters camped outside.

Kate finally broke her silence when her new Persian kitten escaped through the kitchen door and she shouted to a reporter to stop it. When he scooped it up and brought it to her basement door, Kate thanked him and invited him in for an interview.

The reporter asked Kate to confirm reports that Leland Hayward had just divorced his wife and was flying to New York to marry her. "I will never have anything to say about Mr. Hayward or Mr. Smith," she said. "I won't discuss my personal affairs ever. They wouldn't be personal if I made them public."

Perhaps sensing that she needed to offer more, she became

reflective about her notoriety. "You pay a terrible price for fame," she said. "The most precious thing you have is your life and it's almost impossible to enjoy life after you have success in pictures. I suppose the newspapers hate me, but I'm not being rude in refusing to discuss my affairs. I always tried to be helpful to newspaper men but they go away dissatisfied and perhaps prejudiced. I fear this prejudice will affect my career and shorten it."

Responding to a question about her mother's activism, Kate said, "Mother has accomplished a great deal. I detest the newspaper references to her as Katharine Hepburn's mother. My mother is important. I am not."

Of her celebrity, she said, "I don't know how long I will last. Somehow, I wish I could paint pictures, play music or write books. Alas, I am not talented at all."

Becoming a movie star is what Kate wanted more than anything else. Now she wanted to run from fame, but it was too late. The die had been cast. Katharine Hepburn would become a Hollywood legend, no matter the cost.

8
"THERE WAS NO ESCAPING HER"

Early in her career, it was largely Kate's personality that charmed audiences; her success had little to do with her acting skills, which were still developing. It was her on-screen combination of charm and class – and her naturally photogenic look – that made her a star. But as she learned more about the art of filmmaking, the depth of her performances grew.

In 1934, however – despite having won the Academy Award for *Morning Glory* and being part of the ensemble cast that received an Oscar nomination for *Little Women* – she could not forget her failure on stage in *The Lake*, nor her disastrous miscasting as Trigger Hicks in the film *Spitfire*, which had been released in theaters during her Paris vacation in March.

Newly single, Kate decided that after her contract with RKO was up, she would return to the stage to prove that *The Lake* fiasco was an aberration. Meanwhile, RKO was considering her for two roles - the lead in *Joan of Arc*, a costume drama based on George Bernard Shaw's play, *Saint Joan*, and a biographical film based on the female French novelist George Sand. Kate turned them down. In early June, she went back to Fenwick to relax and think about her next move.

Feeling needy, she realized that she missed her Luddy. Ever accommodating, he joined her in Old Saybrook and stayed there in an upstairs room. Though the press had a field day with their unusual post-divorce friendship, buzzing about the prospect of a rekindled love affair, neither of them seriously considered getting back together.

In June of 1934, Kate agreed to play the heroine in George Brewer's tragedy, *Dark Victory*, at the Ivoryton Playhouse in

Connecticut. The company was excited about Kate joining the cast and hoped it might pave the way for the show being moved to New York. But, as usual, Kate clashed with cast and crew, especially her co-star, the British actor Stanley Ridges. Just as Kate was about to quit, Ridges used an illness in his family as an excuse to withdraw from the production, causing the theater to cancel the show.

Kate returned to Hollywood, where she and Harding rented a luxurious estate on Angelo Drive above Beverly Hills. The house, built in 1926 by silent-film director Fred Niblo, featured a pool and tennis courts and was later owned by Rupert Murdoch's family. It was so splendid that Greta Garbo asked to see it and even showed up for a visit one day with George Cukor.

Soon after they moved in, Theresa Helburn, a former casting agent and now co-producer for the Theatre Guild, mentioned to Kate that she was considering selling the rights to Eugene O'Neill's *Mourning Becomes Electra* to make a film featuring Kate and Garbo. Kate was ecstatic, but Louis B. Mayer at MGM, the studio that employed Garbo, wasn't interested in buying the play or borrowing Kate from RKO to make it happen. "Over my dead body," he told Kate. Helburn said it was a wonder Kate "didn't shoot him on the spot," but Kate and the legendary producer had great admiration for one another. "Mayer had the courage of his own convictions," she said later. "I liked that.

RKO brought Kate several scripts to read, but she turned them down, one after the other. She initially refused the role of Lady Babbie in *The Little Minister*, but changed her mind when she heard RKO was pursuing Margaret Sullavan for the part. Kate later confessed, "I really didn't want to play it until I heard another actress was desperate for the role. Then, of course, it became the most important thing in the world . . ."

As it turns out, her first instincts were right – *The Little Minister* wasn't a good fit for her. The James Barrie novel simply didn't translate well to the screen. Maude Adams, a talented stage actress, was responsible for the play's box-office success on Broadway, but her character was undefined, and the story was dated.

Kate believed she could overcome the deficiencies in the material, but both Harding and Hayward advised her not to take the part. As they predicted, even Kate's charm and acting skills were not enough to rescue the film when it came out in December of 1934. Audiences simply weren't interested.

Kate began seeing Hayward again, who by now had divorced Lola Gibbs for the second time. "Life with Leland had no problems," Kate recalled later. "There were solutions to everything. Joy was the constant mood. Everything was like a delightful surprise. He found life so easy. I don't remember any fights. We just enjoyed - enjoyed - enjoyed."

Hayward negotiated a six-picture deal for Kate at RKO for $50,000 per film, an astronomical sum during the Depression, when the annual income for a family of four averaged just $2,600. But he couldn't persuade Kate to be seen with him in public or to take his advice on which projects to tackle. They also had sharply different visions of their future together: Hayward wanted to get married, but Kate was adamantly against it.

"For an independent woman, the marriage problem is very great," Kate once told a journalist. "If she falls in love with a strong man, she loses him because she has to concentrate too much on her job," Kate said. "If she falls in love with a weakling . . . she can push around, she always falls out of love with him. A woman just has to have sense enough to handle a man well enough so he'll want to stay with her."

But Hayward was not a man to be handled. When Kate finished filming *The Little Minister*, she and Hayward flew to New York, where Kate casually mentioned to a reporter that she might marry Leland that month, triggering speculation that they might already be married. But after the couple visited her family in West Hartford the following week, Hayward flew back to Hollywood alone. What happened between them during that visit is not clear, but within weeks, Hayward was being photographed with other beautiful women on his arm.

Not long afterward, Kate was back in Hollywood as well, living with Harding and preparing to film a new movie. Hayward and Kate continued to date, but the relationship was rocky.

In early December 1934, life took a dizzying turn when Kate discovered Hayward was sick - prostate cancer was not ruled out - and she rushed him home to West Hartford so Dr. Hepburn could treat him. That triggered a media frenzy that resulted in Kate nearly walking into an airplane propeller while attempting to avoid the press at Idlewild Airport in New York (now JFK International). The paparazzi, still convinced that Kate and Hayward were married - or at least engaged - pursued the couple to Hartford Hospital, where they commandeered the lobby and waited to hear all the dramatic details about how the movie star's father saved her lover's life.

Coming and going through a basement entrance, Kate managed to avoid them for a few days, which sent some of the more persistent to keep vigil at the Hepburns' house. Hiding behind the garage, they ambushed Kate and her mother as they pulled up in their car. "I was in a blind, towering rage," Kate later said. On her way into the house, she grabbed a photographer's camera and threw it on the ground.

While Kit was trying to swat photographers away with a wire basket she had pulled from the garage, Kate yelled for her sister, asking, "Where's a shotgun?" Alarmed, the reporters finally left, but not before snapping a photo of Kit swinging at them in a rage. The picture was printed in publications around the country, but not in Hartford. Dr. Hepburn was not surprised by the omission. "I've operated on half the newspapermen in Hartford already," he said, "and I expect to operate on the other half."

After recuperating from his surgery, Hayward stayed for a short time at the Hepburn home before heading back to California. Kate returned later, unapologetic about her skirmish with reporters. When a friend asked if she was worried about the impact such incidents could have on her career, Kate responded, "What does it matter how much that quarrel cost me? . . . this invasion of people's private lives is rotten and wrong, and I've fought it in protest . . . I can live better with myself for doing it, and that's the most important thing in the world to me."

Kate's new project, *Break of Hearts*, was originally scheduled to co-star John Barrymore, but he turned it down and was replaced by the Austrian actor Francis Lederer, who was also replaced when the studio determined he and Kate had no on-screen chemistry. Sparks didn't fly with his replacement, Charles Boyer, either. The movie, originally titled *The Music Man*, told the story of a renowned musical conductor who falls for a promising composer, played by Kate, who gives up her aspirations to care for him as he descends into alcoholism.

Break of Hearts was indeed a heartbreaker when it was released in May of 1935: It did almost as poorly as *The Little Minister* at the box office. A critic at *Time* wrote, "Miss Hepburn makes it clear that unless her employers see fit to return her to roles in keeping with her mannerisms (*Little Women*), these will presently annoy cinema addicts into forgetting that she is really an actress of great promise and considerable style."

Kate's reputation was clearly faltering – a calamity for RKO, which had committed her to four more films at a cost of $200,000. They needed a box-office success just to break even. Pandro Berman, who had produced *Morning Glory*, hit upon a promising idea: Booth Tarkington's *Alice Adams*, a novel adapted to the screen by Jane Murfin. Kate's character would be a desperate social climber without the money or family connections to succeed – essentially competing in a race she couldn't possibly win.

In accordance with the contract Hayward had wrangled for her with RKO, Kate had final say in selecting the movie's director. George Cukor was busy filming *David Copperfield*, but she sought his advice in choosing between William

Wyler and George Stevens. Neither had well-established reputations at the time; producer Irving Thalberg had even nicknamed Wyler "Worthless Willy" for his uneven work ethic. Despite that, Cukor recommended Wyler, who had a bit more experience and whose two latest movies, *A House Divided* and *Counsellor at Law*, demonstrated his skill.

Berman disagreed. He wanted *Alice Adams* to be set in unremarkable, small-town America, sprinkled with bits of humor to lighten the tone. Humor, however, was not Wyler's strong suit – and his marriage to Margaret Sullavan didn't sit well with Kate, either. So she decided to go with Stevens, who had already done a number of comedies and seemed a better fit.

Doubts began to creep in, however, as soon as they began discussing the script. "Stevens was an odd duck," Kate recalled later. "Didn't talk much. Listened. Answered yes or no. Obviously, Pandro and I were doing all the talking. I must say that I felt we'd picked a rather peculiar director."

Kate and Stevens had their first argument about the very first shot; she was so infuriated that she stormed off to her dressing room and didn't return for hours. The tension on the set grew for the next three weeks. Though Kate would later admit that Stevens had a keen sense of how to evoke both pathos and humor, her frustration with him was palpable.

Their worst disagreement involved a scene in which Alice breaks down crying after losing a man she loves. Kate wanted to follow exactly what happened in the novel – she called it "my bible" – and throw herself onto her bed and bawl. But Stevens thought it would be more effective for Alice to look out the window first, then start to cry. For half of their twenty-first day of shooting, they were at a stalemate.

Kate finally had enough. "You dumb bastard, I'm going to cry on the bed!" she told him. Stevens replied that he'd go back to directing two-reelers before he'd let her win. "A quitter," Kate bellowed. "If I ever had any respect for you, it's gone now," she said. "You don't get your way, so you quit! You're yellow!"

Stevens grew quiet, and his voice was cold. "Miss Hepburn, just walk to the window, please, and stand there awhile. You needn't weep," he said. "I'll dub someone in, in a long shot and we can fake the sound track."

Angry, Kate took her mark, then proceeded to play the scene. Cameras rolled as she walked to the window and dissolved into tears, her face quivering. When the scene ended, she turned to Stevens and asked, "How was that, George?"

Despite their tempestuous start, Kate and Stevens would end up becoming good friends and make two more films together. And once *Alice Adams* was released in August of 1935, it helped put her professional life back on track: Kate was nominated for her second Academy Award for Best Actress (Bette Davis won for her role in *Dangerous*).

Her personal life, however, was in upheaval again. Her relationship with Hayward continued to swing from hot to cold, and – despite his other dalliances – he continued to resent her insistence that they keep a low profile off the set. Marriage was officially off the table.

Compounding Kate's feelings of rejection, Harding had moved back to the East Coast. Fan magazines had called her

"The Power Behind Katharine Hepburn," but, in truth, she was starting to feel inconsequential in Hollywood. "I had no interest in going into the industry," she said later, "I came from a totally different social milieu from either Hollywood or Kate. Our family was in railroads and the travel business [American Express], our friends were East Coast old money people, and I never even approved of Kate's bohemian ways. I adored her and still do, but in 1935 it had become obvious that I did not belong at the center of her life."

One bright spot was Kate's new friendship with Jane Loring, a film editor who had worked on both *Break of Hearts* and *Alice Adams*. Loring's film-cutting skills and her ability to showcase Kate's cinematic strengths quickly made her one of Kate's most trusted advisers and confidantes.

Kate appeared to be on a roll after the success of *Alice Adams*. But her next film, *Sylvia Scarlett*, released shortly after Hayward's operation, was a more dicey proposition. Kate played a female con artist who dresses as a man to evade the police at a time when gender-bending was not common on the big screen. The romantic comedy was her first pairing with Cary Grant, still two years away from stardom with his 1937 screwball hit, *Topper*. Grant was paid $15,000 for six weeks of filming for *Sylvia Scarlett*; Kate's pay was $50,000.

Grant later recalled what a force of nature Kate was: "She was this slip of a woman, skinny, and I never liked skinny women," he said. "But she had this thing, this air, you might call it, the most totally magnetic woman I'd ever seen, and probably have ever seen since. You had to look at her, you had to listen to her, there was no escaping her. But it wasn't just the beauty, it was the style. She's incredibly down to earth. She can see right through the nonsense in life. She cares, but about things that really matter."

George Cukor had had his eye on *Sylvia Scarlett* for several years and had given Kate the book it was adapted from, *The Early Life and Adventures of Sylvia Scarlett*, feeling she was right for the part. It took a lot of work to convince Berman to produce the unconventional film, but Cukor finally succeeded. Kate trusted Cukor completely and considered him one of her closest friends, going back to when he brought her to Hollywood for her very first film. She treasured her visits to his sumptuous estate, which was a magnet for prominent guests - Kate was once sandwiched on a sofa between Igor Stravinsky and Groucho Marx.

Whenever Cukor was involved in a project, Kate tried hard to be cooperative. For *Silvia Scarlet*, RKO implored her to play nicely with the press. She agreed, even inviting a reporter to her Manhattan home for a rare interview.

She told the reporter that her plans were not yet fixed, but she hoped to make a few films a year and at least one stage production. Her favorite screen actress, she said, was Greta Garbo. "Who can touch her?" Kate exclaimed. Her favorite director was George Cukor, "a grand fellow, understanding, imaginative."

Before the reporter could continue with his questions, Kate interjected, "Now, before you get around to it, I don't mind confessing . . . [that] I am crazy about Siamese cats, English bull terriers and English history. I am fond of golfing, horseback riding, skating, swimming and motoring. I'll tackle my bacon and eggs with any longshoreman, for I have a perfectly unladylike appetite."

As for her feelings about Hollywood, Kate said, "I like every damned thing about the place. Palms and brown hills and boulevards and geraniums six feet tall and flowers running riot everywhere and the grand roads and the golfing and the picture people and even the work, grinding as it is. I like it! Why in hell shouldn't I?"

In the resulting article, the interviewer concluded that Kate could "swear like the troops in Flanders" and that "head up, chin stuck out, [she is] a hundred and ten pounds or so of cold steel nerve . . . a lady of many angles, with a good deal of useful ego in her cosmos; but intellectually honest if ever there was such a creature. . . ."

That was as close to good press as RKO was going to get from Kate. She granted several more interviews, mustering as much grace as she could. Frankness was replacing the air of disdain that had made her seem aloof. In short, she was growing up, and it showed in the roles she wanted to play.

Playing a part in drag for *Sylvia Scarlett* would be unusual but not unprecedented. Marlene Dietrich had done that in 1930 in the film *Morocco*, and Mary Pickford in *Kiki* in 1931. Even the great Garbo had donned men's clothing in 1933's *Queen Christina*. What made *Sylvia Scarlett* different was its less humorous approach and its serious sexual undertones.

Cukor chose the British writer John Collier to write the script. Collier was known for his sophisticated and bizarre works of literature – particularly the satirical *His Monkey Wife*, about a man who marries a monkey – and Cukor later admitted that he knew hiring Collier would be risky. It was. His script portrayed Sylvia as a woman who not only dressed as a man, but who ultimately questions her true feelings about men – risqué stuff at the time.

To tone the script down, Cukor hired two additional screenwriters, Gladys Unger and Mortimer Offner, to make the character more feminine. They added a ten-minute prologue introducing Sylvia as a grieving daughter who just lost her mother, and a fifteen-minute ending showing the character as a gorgeous young woman. As a result, the plot was confusing and unbelievable. At the time, Kate said, "This picture makes no sense and I wonder whether George Cukor is aware of the fact, because I don't know what the hell I'm doing."

At the film's sneak preview in Pasadena, some audience members got up and walked out when actress Bunny Beatty, playing a maid who believes Sylvia is a boy, plants a kiss on Kate; they left in droves during a scene when Kate's character recites a long poem by Edna St. Vincent Millay. No one laughed at scenes the writers had thought were hilarious. Actress Natalie Paley, who had accompanied Kate to the screening, whispered, "Oh, Kate, why don't they laugh?" Kate responded that it simply wasn't funny. "It's a disaster," she said, slinking down in her seat.

When it was over, Berman was waiting for Kate and Cukor at Cukor's house. They told him to scrap the film and said they'd do another one for free. All Berman said was, "I never want to see either of you again!"

RKO executives tried to decide whether to shelve the movie or give it a complete overhaul; finally, they asked Jane Loring to eliminate the problematic scenes.

When *Sylvia Scarlett* was released two weeks before Christmas in 1935, the reviews called the film not only offensive but ineffectual in every way. When it came to Kate's performance, however, the comments were kinder: Richard Watts Jr., of the *New York Herald Tribune* wrote, "The dynamic Miss Hepburn is the handsomest boy of the season. I don't care for *Sylvia Scarlett* a bit, but I do think Miss Hepburn is much better in it than she was as the small-town wallflower in Alice Adams."

Time magazine wrote: "*Sylvia Scarlett* reveals the interesting fact that Katharine Hepburn is better looking as a boy than a woman . . . Miss Hepburn plays with her best intuition a scene in which a woman who has played a man so long that she has abdicated her sex tries to become a woman for the man she loves." Thornton Delehanty of the *New York Evening Post* wrote that Kate's talent was wasted on the part and that Cary Grant nearly stole the picture "with his bitingly humorous portrait of a Cockney ne'er-do-well."

Kate's talent notwithstanding, audiences were not ready for *Sylvia Scarlett*. In 1935, her thoughtful performance of a woman questioning her sexuality was unsettling, to say the least. It doesn't seem far-fetched to imagine that Cukor, whose homosexuality was an open secret, and Kate – who most likely had affairs with women, always wore pants, and as a child yearned to be a boy named Jimmy – were deliberately trying to challenge the status quo about gender roles.

In any case, making the film was a daring – perhaps even foolhardy – roll of the dice, one that undoubtedly damaged Kate's popularity and Cukor's career. And despite her best efforts, none of her next three movies - *Mary of Scotland, A*

Woman Rebels, and *Quality Street* – would be good enough to restore her reputation and pull her career out of the muck.

As her personal life became ever more turbulent, those films began generating whispers that would later grow into shouts: Kate Hepburn was becoming "box office poison."

9

"I'M LIKE THE GIRL WHO NEVER GREW UP, YOU SEE?"

Mary of Scotland had been a Broadway hit in 1934. Written by Maxwell Anderson, the play had starred Helen Hayes and Fredric March. Kate desperately wanted to play the sixteenth-century Scottish queen, Mary Stuart, in Dudley Nichols's film adaptation. She managed to beat out Ginger Rogers, who by then was already famous for her films with Fred Astaire. RKO executives felt Rogers would have been miscast as the wronged and martyred queen.

Kate wanted George Cukor to direct her, but after *Sylvia Scarlett*, producer Pandro Berman would have none of it. Instead, the producer gave the job to John Ford, whose reputation for storytelling was widely admired in Hollywood.

Unfortunately, the film failed to capture the essence of the title character and suffered at the box office. Later, Kate admitted that she never really got into the part. "I never cared for Mary," she said. "I thought she was a bit of an ass."

Still, the film's failure wasn't entirely Kate's fault; although she and Ford "fought, bickered, and fussed," throughout the production, she said, it was ultimately his heavy-handed machismo that reduced her character to mush. It probably didn't help that the script was written largely in blank verse.

Another contributing factor may have been Kate's infatuation with Ford. Nicknamed "Pappy," Ford was a big man - a "man's man" - and larger than life. A heavy-drinking Irish Catholic, twelve years older than Kate, he was talented, charming, successful, and authoritative - just Kate's type. Despite the fact that he was married with two children, rumors circulated among members of the cast and crew that he and Kate were having an affair.

Ford refused to tolerate Kate's being difficult; when he'd had enough, he'd stare her down and knock his pipe against a wall or into an ashtray - as a signal for her to stop. Then they would forget their quarrels and spend weekends at Kate's house or fishing and sailing on Ford's yacht, the *Araner*, where Kate would bait their hooks, rig the sails, and clean the decks.

Kate was proud of her physical abilities and loved to show them off; she never liked to use stunt doubles. In *Sylvia Scarlett*, she climbed a rainspout and fell from a dangerous height, saved by crew members who caught her. In *Mary of Scotland*, the script called for Kate to run down stone steps, leap onto the back of a horse, and ride away sidesaddle - all wearing high heels and a gown that weighed fifteen pounds. "Mary of Scotland supposedly did it, and I'm a damned good horsewoman," Kate said.

Ford tried to insist on a double for the scene, but Kate refused to surrender and did eleven successful takes in a row. The crew applauded, though her less athletic co-actors, who still needed stunt doubles, were not as enthusiastic. Ford, who did not enjoy having his authority challenged, wasn't thrilled either.

That didn't stop him from following her to Fenwick in the spring of 1936, where he and Kate sailed on the Long Island Sound and played golf. Kate's father did not approve of the director's philandering, but it wouldn't matter - their romance fizzled when summer ended. "I found him fascinating but impossible," Kate said later.

With Ford out of the picture, Kate began spending time with Hayward both at Fenwick and in West Hartford, but rumors were swirling that he was also – yet again – seeing Margaret Sullavan, whose marriage with William Wyler by then was kaput. When in Hollywood, Kate found companionship with her two cocker spaniels, Michael and Peter, a French poodle named Button, and a Siamese cat named Cocoa (her monkey had been donated to the Los Angeles Zoo years before) and was attended to by a cook, housekeeper, and chauffeur.

Kate's next film, *A Woman Rebels*, was based on the novel *Portrait of a Rebel* by Netta Syrett, which told the story of a magazine editor with an illegitimate child who struggles with the strict social conventions of Victorian England. RKO and Kate hoped to capitalize on the attributes that had made *Little Women* a success. But when *A Woman Rebels* was released in November of 1936, it had none of the innocent charm of Alcott's beloved book; instead, it was a controversial examination of whether a woman should marry for the sake of her child.

Director Mark Sandrich, whose forte was making musicals with Astaire and Rogers, was clearly out of his element; if not for Kate's deft handling of the material, the film could easily have turned into a soap opera. Sandrich was proficient with the more technical aspects of filming, such as lighting and costumes, but his lack of experience in working with more dramatic material showed. The film, which marked the film debut of future star Van Heflin, lost over $200,000 for RKO and was Kate's third box-office flop in a row.

With one film left on her six-film contract, RKO hoped it finally had a winner with her next project, *Quality Street*, which reunited Kate with director George Stevens. Jane Loring had edited *A Woman Rebels* but was not hired for the new film because Stevens hadn't liked Jane's work on *Alice Adams* and went so far as to ban her from the set. Stevens thought Kate's performance was adversely affected by the conflicting advice she got from Jane and other women friends, including her dresser-secretary, Emily Perkins, and her stand-in, Eve March, who substituted for Kate during lighting and camera setup.

"Kate was confused by them," Stevens said. "Their advice was so diverse, she didn't know what she was doing . . . she had a very good head on her shoulders, but she picked out lightweights to think with and that was a mistake. She doesn't need a lightweight . . . she needs someone who will question her judgments."

But Stevens also admitted he did not direct her well. "I don't think I did her any good," he said later. "She became precious, and preciousness was always her weakness." He added that *Quality Street* had been "a precious play . . . full of precious people" and confessed that he did not have "sufficient familiarity with the British background to save her."

As Kate was shooting the film, her personal life was unraveling yet again. Her friendship with Jane Loring hit a rough patch – perhaps owing to a lover's quarrel, since there has been much speculation that they were having an affair (though Kate, oddly, does not mention her in her memoir).

More devastating was the news that, in mid-November 1936, Hayward suddenly married Sullavan, who was pregnant. Though Kate sent the couple a congratulatory note, she was visibly distraught on the set of *Quality Street*, sometimes becoming nauseated, often sitting quietly on a stool, off by herself, arms on knees, smoking.

Hayward had gone back East when Sullavan appeared in the play *Stage Door*, written by another of his clients, Edna Ferber. The play was a hit, and so was Sullavan. "*Me*, far-away, became a sort of unreality," Kate recalled. "Years later he tried to explain it to me and he really couldn't - any more than I could explain my refusal to marry him."

When she got the news, Kate said, "I was thunderstruck. What is this! No - not nice - not fair! I called mother in Hartford. I was furious. Weeping. How could he? So wicked!"

"But you didn't want him, Kath," Kit reminded her. "Maybe he just wanted to get married. Poor man. You can't blame him. It's your fault. You must send them a wire. Don't be a poor sport. It's your fault."

George Cukor said the same thing: "Kate, what's wrong with you? You could have married him if you wanted him. You didn't."

"Oh, stop saying that!" she yelled. "What am I going to do?"

In her memoir, Kate does not mention the highly public tragedies that would later befall Hayward and Sullavan. The couple had three children, and Sullavan filed for divorce in 1947 after discovering that Hayward was having an affair with the socialite Slim Keith. Their oldest child, Brooke Hayward, wrote a 1977 memoir, *Haywire*, about their glamorous and dysfunctional family life, later made into a made-for-television movie. The sordid tale includes the mental illness and suicide of Brooke's younger sister,

Bridget, and Margaret Sullavan's death at age fifty from an overdose of barbiturates. In 2008, the youngest child, Bill, died of a self-inflicted gunshot wound.

After divorcing Sullavan, Hayward married Keith. In 1960, they divorced and he married another socialite, Pamela Churchfield, who later remarried and became well-known as the Democratic activist and diplomat Pamela Harriman. According to Kate, when Hayward was near the end of his life, in 1971, Pamela called her and said, "Leland is dying. He loved you more than he loved any of us. Will you go and see him?"

Kate paid Hayward a visit but does not report on what happened. "I think Pamela exaggerated his feeling for me," she said. "I think that as Leland looked back, he really was looking back at himself as a young man. We were both young and I had never married him, so he only had the experience of a thrilling love affair with me - no feeling of being locked in by a marriage . . . We met at a time when to each of us everything was joy and laughter and exciting and perfect. But we had such fun! Oh yes - Fun. I was lucky to know him."

In truth, Hayward was never locked in by any of his matrimonial arrangements, but after her relationship with Hayward ended, Kate nevertheless soon gravitated toward a man who shared her distaste for the institution of marriage. Howard Hughes, the tycoon and aviator, had been trying to get Kate's attention since the filming of *Sylvia Scarlett*: One day, while the cast and crew were enjoying a picnic lunch in Malibu, California, an airplane circled overhead and landed in the field next to them. "Who could that be?" Kate wondered. "Who the hell would - ?" Cary Grant piped up:

"That's my friend Howard Hughes."

Hughes joined the group at the picnic table but Kate – who had been tipped off that Hughes wanted to meet her – frowned at Grant and refused to even look at the party crasher. "What a nerve!" she thought.

But Hughes was persistent, his stunts becoming more audacious. Soon afterward, Kate was playing golf with the pro at the Bel Air Country Club. They were on the seventh hole of a nine-hole lesson when she once again heard the sound of an airplane and looked up to see Hughes landing right on the golf course! He calmly took his clubs out of the plane and finished the last three holes with them. "He had to have a truck come in and practically take the plane apart to remove it from the course," Kate recalled. "I must say it gave me pause. I thought that he had a hell of a nerve and was very pushy. The Club was furious."

Stranded at the golf course, Hughes accepted Kate's offer of a ride back to his hotel that day. But she was still resisting – if somewhat intrigued by – this rich and famous suitor, whom she later called "an oddball" even in his younger years.

When Kate wrapped up the filming of *Quality Street* – another flop for RKO when it was finally released in March of 1937, losing nearly $250,000 – she headed back to her sanctuary of West Hartford.

Reeling from Hayward's abandonment and her losing streak of films, Kate relied on her father to steady her, as she always did. Dr. Hepburn was still youthful at fifty-seven, with wide-set brown eyes dominating his strong face, and his red hair peppered with white.

Kate's trust in her father's judgment never faltered. Despite his nearly thirty-year-old daughter's wealth and independence, Dr. Hepburn took great care of her – and, unlike other men in her life, he had never let her down. "I'm like the girl who never grew up, you see?" Kate told writer Ralph Martin. "I just never really left home, so to speak. I always went back there [West Hartford and Fenwick] almost every weekend of my life when I wasn't filming. I kept my life there, my roots . . . And when I went back there I didn't go to *my* atmosphere: I went to *their* atmosphere - of which I was a part."

Returning to her father's house, she said, must seem odd. "That's very unusual, isn't it? Very, very unusual, that someone who's sort of made it in the big world could still want to go home to their father's house?"

None of her "beaux," as she called them, could match the closeness she had with her parents, which offered companionship and privacy at the same time. Kate was well aware, she said, that her personality grated on people's nerves. "I'm loud and talkative and I get onto subjects that irritate," she admitted. "If I feel these things causing a break, I know something has to give. I never think the man is going to give - or anyone else, for that matter - so I do. I just deliberately change. I just shut up - when every atom in me wants to speak up."

At Fenwick, to suppress her inner turmoil, she swam daily in the frigid waters of Long Island Sound and took brisk walks, some straight uphill, some through the woods and brush. She loved "getting up at 4:30 or five o'clock in the morning . . . the house absolutely quiet . . . a big roaring fire . . . and [eating] a great big breakfast [of] bacon, chicken livers, steaks and eggs . . . orange juice and a big pot of coffee . . . Then I watched the sun rise. Oh, golly, paradise!"

Soon, her glorious off-season vacation was interrupted by a telegram from the Theatre Guild offering her $1,000 a week to play the lead in *Jane Eyre*, first on tour and then in New York. She told the Guild she would take the part only if they increased her pay to $1,500; the extra $500, she explained, was for the humiliation of refusing to increase her salary from $30 to $35 a week during *A Month in the Country*, seven years earlier. The Guild agreed.

Jane Eyre, adapted for the stage by writer Helen Jerome from Charlotte Brontë's novel, got mixed reviews in London when it opened there in the fall of 1936. Actresses everywhere had clamored to play the part of Jane Eyre since the novel was published in 1847, but Kate worried it was too much like the period dramas that had caused her problems of late.

But it was the only stage role she had been offered, so she grabbed it, eager to get back to work. This time, remembering the debacle of *The Lake*, she vowed not to open on Broadway until the touring production, and her performance, were perfect.

Kate was happy to learn that Tony Miner, her director for *The Lake*, was slated to direct and that rehearsals would be held in New Haven, so she could make the forty-mile commute from West Hartford each day and be home for Christmas. Because she didn't want to make the drive herself after long days of rehearsing, she asked company manager

Herman Bernstein to rent her a car and hire a chauffeur. Bernstein hired the only available limousine in town, from Weller's Funeral Home, and owner Harry Weller was more than happy to act as chauffeur when he heard it was for the film star Katharine Hepburn.

A charming, old-fashioned Orthodox Jew, Weller would wear his best black undertaker's suit and wait outside the theater in New Haven until Kate appeared. They got along well, and she enjoyed his Yiddish stories. Once, after an ice storm doubled the length of their trip, she invited him in for something to eat. Weller hastily explained that he ate only kosher food and that his wife would kill him if he broke tradition. "But then on the other hand," he said, following Kate inside, "she'd kill me if I didn't go in and see your house."

Jane Eyre opened on December 26, 1936, in New Haven, with Dennis Hoey, an experienced English stage and film actor, playing the mysterious Mr. Rochester. Soon afterward, the show began touring – to Boston, Kansas City, Missouri, Cleveland, Chicago, Pittsburgh, Washington, D.C., and finally, Baltimore. Even though the tour grossed a record $340,000 before it ended on April 3, 1937, the Theatre Guild was afraid to bring it to New York. The third act of the play was fraught with problems, and even though it had been rewritten and the show had been well-attended on tour, the producers feared Kate's name would not work the same magic in New York as it had with less sophisticated audiences in smaller cities.

But the longer the show toured, the better the reviews of Kate's performance became. One Boston critic said she played "her not too exacting role with much simplicity and straight-forward intelligence." In Cleveland, a reviewer called her performance "thoroughly delightful . . . she essays the variety of moods her role calls for with the authority of a more seasoned stage player."

Theresa Helburn, co-producer of the Theatre Guild, said Kate's grasp of the role improved substantially as the tour progressed. "Kate . . . knew how to do the little pieces of the mosaic by which a film is built up, but she had no conception of building a character through three acts," she said. "It was wonderful to watch how she did it, groping her way from a stale performance that had a certain brilliance and charm, but no solid characterization, to the full realization of the woman whom she was portraying."

During the tour, Kate found herself terribly lonely. Though she enjoyed spending time with Tony Miner, they weren't especially close, and she never became friends with any of the other actors. But when the show was in Boston, she noticed in the newspaper that Hughes was in Boston. In fact, she learned that he had checked into the hotel at the Colonial Theater, where *Jane Eyre* was playing.

"I think that I must have been lonely, because Howard and I had supper with one another after the performance that first night," she recalled later. "Thus proving that persistence pays. We had supper the next night too - so . . ."

At first, Kate found him stiff and awkward. After seeing him a few times, she found him rather charming, but not everyone approved. "[I don't know] what she was doing with Howard Hughes," said friend Anita Loos, a screenwriter and author of the 1925 novel *Gentlemen Prefer Blonds*. "He had a whole stable of girls, and Kate simply wasn't the type to have anything to do with that kind of thing."

Kate, however, found the brilliant and mercurial Hughes to be a challenge she enjoyed. After inheriting his father's fortune as a teenager, Hughes had gone to Hollywood in the 1920s to produce films – one of which won an Oscar – and in 1932 formed the Hughes Aircraft Company and dedicated himself to setting flying speed records (in 1938, he set a record for flying around the world and was given a ticker-tape parade in New York). Clearly, Kate and Hughes each admired the other's adventurous spirits.

Hughes is best-known, of course, for becoming an eccentric recluse in his later years, which Kate said may have been caused by his deafness, which grew worse as he aged. "He had guts and he had a really fine mind, but he was deaf - quite seriously deaf - and he was apparently incapable of saying, `Please speak up. I'm deaf.'" she recalled. "Thus if he was with more than one person, he was apt to miss most of the conversation. This was tragic. But he was absolutely incapable of changing . . . I think that this weakness went a long way toward ruining Howard's life and making him into an oddball."

But in early 1937, Hughes was still a thirty-two-year-old bon vivant with his eye on Kate. When *Jane Eyre* arrived in Chicago, Hughes showed up unannounced, making national headlines and generating speculation that the two would be getting married. Kate did her best to keep a low profile, sneaking in and out of a theater to avoid being photographed.

When *Jane Eyre* wrapped up in April – without ever playing in New York – Kate moved into Hughes's home in Los

Angeles, located next to a golf course where they frequently played. Kate brought her own cook and maid to join Hughes's domestic staff. Hughes taught her to fly, and they flew around the country together. Once they landed a seaplane in the middle of Long Island Sound, dropped anchor, took off all their clothes, and dove off the wing.

Kate's family, however, did not get along well with Hughes. His hearing problems forced him to conduct most of his business by telephone, and his constant blabbing on the phone irritated Kate's relatives. Luddy was hanging around, too, always filming people with his movie camera, which annoyed Hughes. Once, when they were golfing, Dr. Hepburn said, "Howard, Luddy has been taking pictures of all of us for many years before you joined us and he will be taking them long after you've left. He is part of this family. Go ahead. Drive. You need a seven iron."

As her relationship with Hughes was heating up, Kate's film career was taking, in her words, "a real nosedive." After four consecutive flops – *Sylvia Scarlett, Mary of Scotland, A Woman Rebels,* and *Quality Street* – even the middling performances of her next few films could not keep the Independent Theatre Owners Association from ranking Katharine Hepburn Number One on its list of "box office poison."

It was some consolation to Kate that other independent, sometimes rebellious actresses who became screen legends – Joan Crawford, Marlene Dietrich, and Greta Garbo – also made the list, albeit a bit further down. According to the TOA, which based its rankings on box office sales, the most popular female stars of the time were Shirley Temple, Deanna Durbin, and Ginger Rogers, whose films did not rock

146

the boat. Facing the devastating effects of the Depression and ominous signs of unrest in Europe, people went to the movies to escape.

"The independent theater owners were trying to get rid of Marlene Dietrich, Joan Crawford, and me," Kate recalled later. "It seems that they were forced to take our pictures if they got certain ones which they *really* wanted. Actually, I felt sorry for [the theater owners]. I had made a string of very dull movies."

But Kate was ready to fight back – with or without the eccentric Howard Hughes by her side. "I did not want to marry Howard," she confessed later. "I liked him . . . but obviously I was obsessed by my own failure and I wondered whether I could put it right."

10

"WHAT'S WRONG WITH KATHARINE HEPBURN?"

After living with Howard Hughes for a while at his Los Angeles home in the spring of 1937, Kate decided to return to New York. Realizing how much she still loved the big city, she bought the four-story brownstone she had been renting on East Forty-Ninth Street for $33,000 – $560,000 in today's dollars (the place would sell for $21 million today).

Then Kate went to Fenwick for the summer to spend time with her family, Luddy, and Harding. Hughes visited her at Fenwick, and though their relationship was conflicted – he wanted to live on the West Coast while she preferred the East – he was still showing interest. And, as a significant player in Hollywood, his influence at RKO proved invaluable.

Despite Kate's floundering popularity – and her still-raw wounds over Hayward's marriage – Hayward remained her loyal agent and managed to negotiate a lucrative film deal for her at RKO, even better than the last one, an astonishing $75,000 per picture. At $1.3 million in today's dollars, more than twice what she paid for her home, that's a big paycheck for a few months of work, even by Hollywood standards.

Hughes was influential in the studio's decision, but similar deals were made with other stars. Like Kate, Joan Crawford had been on the "box office poison" list, but MGM still gave her a five-year contract to make three movies a year for $1.5 million, or $100,000 each. In one of those, *Mannequin*, Crawford was cast opposite Spencer Tracy, a new leading man who was quickly becoming an audience favorite.

A big pay raise, however, could not mask the fact that Kate's career was stalling. Her next film, *Stage Door*, had recently been a Broadway smash featuring – ironically enough

– Hayward's new wife, Margaret Sullavan. When Kate got back to Hollywood in September, it became apparent that RKO was well aware that box-office popularity polls ranked Kate seventieth while Ginger Rogers placed third. If the studio was going to pay Kate an astronomical salary, it would hedge its bet by also giving Rogers a major role.

Gregory La Cava, who had been nominated for an Academy Award for *My Man Godfrey*, signed on as director – which made Kate unhappy because he was hired without her approval. La Cava encouraged his actors to improvise, something Kate was not comfortable doing. He'd meet with the cast on the set, explain the scene, and have them interact as they would if they were not on stage. Rattled, Kate spent hours preparing, writing herself notes and memorizing parts – in fact, one of her scenes in *Stage Door* included lines she borrowed from *The Lake*, an inside joke for those following her turbulent career.

Kate, said La Cava, "is completely the intellectual actress. She has to understand the why of everything before she can feel. Then, when the meaning has soaked in, emotion comes, and superb work."

George Stevens agreed. When her emotions take hold, he said, Kate "isn't the kind of actress who counts six steps forward, then two to the left. She goes into a scene and lives it, and you have to steer her like an automaton through the mechanical part."

Making *Stage Door* would prove difficult for Kate, but she was delighted to make a new friend in Constance Collier, a British actress who played the drama coach in the film. Kate admired Collier, a well-known stage performer with extensive experience in Shakespearean productions, and frequently took her advice. Nearly thirty years older than Kate, she was warm and generous and shared Kate's love of intelligent conversation.

During filming, Kate and Rogers developed a heated rivalry, which La Cava was happy to exploit to enhance their performances. The director was notoriously manipulative. When Rogers needed to cry after Kate's character gave a speech, he lied and told Rogers that her house had burned down. He later said that was the only way he could elicit believable tears from her.

In the film version of *Stage Door*, Kate's character, Terry Randall, is a wealthy young woman who wants to be an actress. To help her, her father agrees to finance a production to ensure she'll get a starring role and the actress she replaces commits suicide. Terry, not surprisingly, is not popular with the other aspiring actresses and is especially loathed by Rogers's character, Jean Maitland. The suicide leads Kate's character to give a touching final speech that at last earns her the respect of Jean and their coworkers at The Footlights Club.

Though altogether different from the stage version, the movie came off smoothly, with well-honed comedy, even pacing, and an intelligent sense of style, earning La Cava another Academy Award nomination.

Stage Door, wrote a critic for *Life* magazine, marked career milestones for both Kate and Rogers. "Before this picture Katharine Hepburn, following a succession of costume pictures which stifled her talent, was in danger of losing her status as a star," the review said. "Ginger Rogers on the other hand had become No. 3 box-office attraction as one-half of a dancing team but still faced the problem of what she would do without Fred Astaire in a straight dramatic role. *Stage Door* answers both these problems. It proves that Miss Rogers is a talented comedienne and that Miss Hepburn really is, as her early pictures indicated, potentially, the screen's greatest actress."

Despite the good reviews, *Stage Door* was only a modest success at the box office, earning a profit of $81,000. Still, that was encouraging enough for RKO to team Kate up once again with Cary Grant in a new screwball comedy, *Bringing Up Baby.*

The script for *Bringing Up Baby* was specifically written to showcase Kate's personality. She plays an heiress who talks a handsome animal expert into taking care of her pet leopard, not realizing that he's a paleontologist rather than a zoologist. She soon falls for Grant's character and does everything she can to stop his upcoming marriage.

Kate worked well with the leopard. Throughout the filming, she wore a particular perfume that had a calming effect on the big cat. She also put resin on the soles of her shoes to avoid slipping, which could startle the animal. "If Miss Hepburn should ever decide to leave the screen she could make a very good animal trainer," said the film's animal trainer, Olga Celeste. "She has control of her nerves and, best of all, no fear of animals."

Shooting *Bringing Up Baby* was such a laugh riot for Kate and Grant that production had to be delayed several times when they couldn't stop laughing during takes. But movie-goers did not appreciate the film when it was released in

February of 1938. It wasn't until much later, in fact, that the film came to be regarded as the masterpiece of acclaimed director Howard Hawks's career. Film critic Andrew Sarris called it "the screwiest of the screwball comedies."

Kate appreciated Hawks's fast-paced directing style. He made an astounding twenty-two films in twelve years, including an eclectic mix of comedy - *Twentieth Century* (1934); adventure - *Ceiling Zero* (1936); and crime - *Scarface* (1932).

One element in *Bringing Up Baby* was particularly familiar to Hawks: men who had trouble communicating with women. In a few years' time, Hawks would marry the fashion icon Slim Keith, who would later have an affair with Kate's old beau Hayward. In the dizzying Hollywood game of marital musical chairs – or perhaps real-life screwball comedy – Keith later divorced Hawks and married Hayward, who by then had divorced Margaret Sullavan. Working in such a milieu, it's no wonder Kate never wanted to marry again.

Kate and Hawks shared a mutual respect. She appreciated his good sense and decisiveness; he admired her coordination. "She has an amazing body - like a boxer," Hawks said. "It's hard for her to make a wrong turn. She's always in perfect balance. She has that beautiful coordination that allows you to stop and make a turn and never fall off balance. This gives her an amazing sense of timing. I've never seen a girl that had that odd rhythm and control."

Bringing Up Baby gave audiences a chance to see Kate's light-hearted, comedic style. One critic wrote that Hepburn "proves she can be as amusingly skittery a comedienne as the best of them." Other critics called her performance "invigorating," "breezy," and touted her as "a comedienne of the highest order."

Nevertheless, RKO was disappointed by the film's performance at the box office – it did well in some cities but poorly in others – and that caused the studio to lose all faith in Kate. RKO had spent nearly $1 million on the film, and editing would cost another $100,000. In fact, before its release, executives were about to shelve it until Howard Hughes stepped in with a last-minute financial bail-out.

During its first run, *Bringing Up Baby* made $1.1 million in U.S. and foreign markets. RKO, still committed to Kate for two more films - at $75,000 a pop – was expecting bigger sales and did not think Kate was capable of making hit films. The studio wanted out of her contract.

Studio executives offered her the lead in a small-budget film, *Mother Carey's Chickens*, which the humiliated Kate refused. So RKO gave her two choices: Do the film or buy out her contract. After talking it over with her father, Kate decided to pay the studio $200,000, which freed her up to negotiate with other film companies.

Kate's next project came from her old friend George Cukor. He wanted her to star in a remake of the romantic comedy *Holiday* that he was directing for Columbia Pictures, with Cary Grant playing the lead. But first, he had to overcome resistance from Columbia president Harry Cohn, who wanted to pair Grant with Irene Dunne to capitalize on their success in *The Awful Truth* the previous year.

The forty-six year-old Cohn, striking and debonair, had a reputation for coming on to actresses and offering jobs to those who cooperated. He reportedly told Margaret Sullavan that the director Willie Wyler – to whom she was married for two years – told him, "You're great in the hay." Sullavan, incensed, stood and replied, "You didn't hear that from Willie. He is too much of a gentleman to discuss such things with you." On her way out, she added, "But I am."

Cohn tried something similar with Kate, saying he heard of her prowess from Hayward. Kate pretended she hadn't heard him. When he tried again, Kate continued to ignore him. Twice rebuffed, he never came on to her again – and, surprisingly, gave her the part.

Holiday was adapted from the 1928 Philip Barry play, which Kate knew well from her months as understudy for Hope Williams early in her career. It had all the makings of a great film. Kate and Grant had their usual chemistry and responded well to Cukor's direction; screenwriters Donald Ogden Stewart and Sidney Buchman had punched up Barry's original play by adding engaging dialogue. *New York Herald-Tribune* critic Howard Barnes praised Kate ("a vibrant, moving performance . . . first class screen acting"), but Frank S. Nugent of *The New York Times* was typically less kind: "Miss Hepburn - the 'New Hepburn' according to the publicity copy - is very mannish in this one, deep-voiced, grammatically precise, and is only a wee bit inclined to hysteria."

Even with decent reviews, the film didn't appeal to Depression-era audiences when it came out in June of 1938. They simply couldn't relate to Grant's character, who decides to quit a perfectly good-paying job and go on holiday, nor to the wealthy socialite (played by Kate) who encourages him.

With yet another box-office failure, Kate was not offered a second picture by Columbia. "Poor Harry," Kate said later, about Cohn. "He thought of taking out another 24-sheet [billboard] saying, 'What's wrong with Katharine Hepburn?' I advised him not to: 'Look out! They might tell you.'"

During this difficult period, Kate tried to shift her career into a higher gear by pursuing the coveted lead role in a highly anticipated picture, *Gone with the Wind*.

According to Kate's memoir, her first exposure to the story of Scarlett O'Hara came when the author Margaret Mitchell sent her the manuscript for her bestselling book, which she wanted to turn into a movie. "I read it and thought that it was fascinating," she said, and gave it to Berman, the head of RKO, who gave it to his assistant to read. "Joe Sistrom, the assistant, thought that it was a very unsympathetic part – bad for my career."

Berman himself wasn't keen about Kate doing another costume picture, and when RKO opted not to make the film, David Selznick – now at MGM – gave it a look. One day, Kate went to Selznick's house to pick up his brother, the agent Myron Selznick, to drive him to a social event. David came to the door with *Gone with the Wind* in his hands. "Don't read it, David," Kate said. "Just buy it."

Selznick bought the rights for $50,000 and hired Cukor to direct. But Selznick refused to even consider Kate for the part of Scarlett O'Hara, believing she lacked sex appeal. La Cava thought she had plenty, but only if paired with the right man. "To win her, to beat down that proud, impervious hauteur, is a challenge only the most virile and dominant male could afford to take up," the director said. "She's never had a leading man like that. They've always let her be the master."

Filming was delayed for two years as Selznick tried – successfully, ultimately – to secure Clark Gable for the role of Rhett Butler and interviewed a staggering 1,400 actresses for Scarlett. Kate continued to press her case, but Selznick was adamant: Why jeopardize the film's success by "having a girl who has the audience's dislike to beat down?" he argued.

Even Cukor – normally a strong advocate for Kate – was on the fence about whether she was right for the role. During one meeting with Kate, after an hour of discussion, Selznick finally offered to let her do a screen test. She refused. "You know what I look like on the screen," she told him. "You know I can act. And you know this part was practically written for me. I am Scarlett O'Hara. So what's the matter?"

"I just can't imagine Clark Gable chasing you for ten years," he said.

"I may not appeal to *you*, David," she shot back, "but there are men with different tastes!"

After calming down, Kate remained so desperate that she told Selznick if he were to make a mistake with an unknown actress - even two days before shooting - she would play the part for free, no questions asked.

In fact, Kate was under the impression that she might get the part by default. "By this time I felt that they were being forced to take me because they *had* to start the picture at a certain date or they would lose the property," Kate recalled. "I also felt that I would really be a disappointing choice [for Selznick]. And I knew that if I did a test they would sign me, but they would go on looking for an unknown and might find one and then just dump me."

Kate requested that press announcements not mention the possibility of her being cast because she dreaded the humiliation of losing the part to a nobody. But her name appeared on the list of contenders anyway. When Selznick fired Cukor three weeks into the filming and replaced him with Victor Fleming, Kate's chances to play Scarlett left with him. It was reported that Cukor and Clark Gable did not get along, but it's also possible that Cukor and Selznick simply had differing visions for the film.

In all, thirty-one women were screen-tested for the role of Scarlett O'Hara, from Tallulah Bankhead to Lana Turner to Paulette Goddard. Finally, it was a relative unknown, the British stage actress Vivian Leigh, who got the part. The rest, of course, is history: Leigh won the Academy Award for Best Actress and, despite criticism that it glorified slavery, *Gone with The Wind* became regarded as one of the greatest films of all time.

In early 1938, while Selznick was still trying to find his Scarlett, Kate reviewed her options. She had done excellent work on four strong films over the previous three years – *Alice Adams* and *Stage Door* (which received a combined six Academy Award nominations), *Bringing Up Baby,* and *Holiday* – but their uneven box-office performances had left her career foundering.

In fact, after *Holiday*, the only film role Kate was offered came from Paramount for just $10,000. She did not like the script and declined. "Howard was very upset with this," she said later. "He was really anxious for me to take that Paramount offer. I thought it would be a terrible mistake. He was very conscious of what he thought people were saying about him. He felt that I was embarrassed by my failure, but somehow I wasn't. Well, obviously it mattered but not enough to govern my actions."

At a dead end, Kate decided to move back east to the comfort of her family – and perhaps return to the stage, her first love. This created considerable tension with Hughes, who wanted her to stay with him in Los Angeles.

"Howard and I were indeed a strange pair," she recalled later. "He was sort of the top of the available men - and I of the women. We were a colorful pair. It seemed logical for us to be together, but it seems to me now that we were too similar. He came from the right street, so to speak. And so did I. We'd been brought up in ease. We each had a wild desire to be famous. I think that this was a dominant character failing. People who want to be famous are really loners. Or they should be.

"Certainly I felt that I was madly in love with him. And I think he felt the same way about me. But when it came right down to "What do we do now?" - I went East and he stayed West. We'd been together about three years. Ambition beat love, or was it *like?*"

In the spring of 1938, Kate and Harding took a train to the East coast, sharing the ride with actresses Marlene Dietrich and Gertrude Lawrence and playwright Noël Coward. The party of five spent a lot of time in Coward's cabin discussing the "box office poison" rankings, a list Dietrich made as well.

Kate got off in New York and stayed a few days, buying gifts for her family. Harding headed back to her New Jersey home. When Kate got back to West Hartford, her family was excited to hear her tales of Hollywood, and she delighted in listening to the latest exploits of her parents and siblings.

During her visit, Kate made it clear that she was through with Hollywood – at least for now. "I felt that I should get a breath of fresh air," she said later. "A real change of atmosphere." Back home in familiar surroundings, she relaxed immediately. Tapping into that indefatigable Hepburn optimism, she had a feeling that things were about to turn around.

11
"COME BACK, KATIE, ALL IS FORGIVEN"

As the weather warmed up in West Hartford in the spring of 1938, Kate passed her days playing golf at the country club, then returning home for lively conversation at the Hepburn table. Even Dr. Hepburn escaped his office on occasion and regaled Kate with the details of his latest cases. After lunch, Kate spent time with her mother, listening with pride to Kit's efforts to promote birth control. "Every time Kate looks at her mother," a family friend once said, "she recalls the meaning of service to others."

After one of Howard Hughes's visits, Kate's brother Dick, an aspiring playwright, began writing a new play about a handsome young millionaire who visits the family of an actress. Although a writer-director friend of Kate's said the script had potential, the family was far less enthusiastic and asked Dick to shelve it. Dick stubbornly refused and attempted to capture the interest of various producers, but no one wanted to risk a lawsuit from either Hughes or the Hepburns.

Despite the friction, the family eagerly cheered for Kate's sister Marion when she became engaged to Ellsworth Grant on Valentine's Day 1938; the couple married the following June, with Kate as maid of honor. Pleased that at least one of his daughters was finally wed, Dr. Hepburn told Kate, "All you New England girls look at a man like a bull about to charge. You're very forthright and truthful, but you do sort of put a man off."

But Kate, at age thirty-one, was not about to change now. She still liked to behave exactly as she pleased, and spent her summer at Fenwick, swimming and walking on the beach. "It was June and the weather was heavenly and the golf-tennis-swimming-sailing were ever available," she recalled later.

"The family were all there, and it was fun. Lots of talk. Lots of exercise. The people there were not really aware of my peculiar [career] predicament so it was never discussed."

One day, the telephone rang. It was playwright Philip Barry, who long ago had fired Kate and endured her screaming tirade in response. By now, seven years later, all had been forgiven. "I have an idea," Barry said. "I want to talk to you."

Kate invited him to Fenwick, where they sat on a pier as Barry explained that he was working on two plays. One was about a father and daughter; the second was called *The Philadelphia Story*. Kate said she liked the second idea best and, a few weeks later, received a draft of the first act in the mail.

He read the play script and loved it. It was a romantic comedy about a prominent society family that shunned the spotlight, and an equally famous and well-to-do ex. But the similarities to the Hepburns ended there. The main character was not an actress, her father was not a doctor, and her mother was not an activist. Still, there was little doubt that Barry had written the part of Tracy Lord in *The Philadelphia Story* with Kate in mind.

Excited, she called Hughes to tell him about the play she would soon be starring in. "Buy the film rights before you open," he advised her. So she did, with Hughes's money. It was a shrewd move, giving her complete control over hiring the director, screenwriter, and cast when it came time for the movie version.

Hughes also readily agreed to help finance the stage production. Because the Theatre Guild couldn't afford to fund it alone, Kate and Hughes put up half the money and the

Guild the rest. As a result, Kate owned a quarter of the play and was entitled to a share of profits. In lieu of a salary, she opted to take 10 percent of the gross from the Broadway run, and 12.5 percent of profits on the road tour. For the first time in her life, Katharine Hepburn was an entrepreneur, fully in charge of her own destiny.

Performing in a new play on Broadway was just what Kate needed. She was looking radiant and feeling good. Hughes arrived often in his private plane and showered her with lavish gifts, which Dr. Hepburn thought a ridiculous waste of money. Not much of an athlete, Hughes would go boating with Kate or take her flying in his plane; sometimes he'd let her take the controls, and they'd soar to Maine to meet with Barry about the play.

As she prepared for her role as Tracy Lord, tragedy struck. One of the most destructive hurricanes ever to hit New England whipped through the region in late September of 1938. Connecticut had no hurricane warning system at the time, so all the Hepburns knew was that a big storm was brewing somewhere out in the Atlantic.

By the time the storm made landfall, the summer season was over and most residents of the coastal town of Old Saybrook had already returned to Hartford, including Dr. Hepburn. But Kate was still at Fenwick with a friend named Jack "Red" Hammond, her mother, brother Dick, and their cook Fanny. Kate and Hammond played golf that day and went for a swim, noticing that the wind was so strong that Kate could lean against it, and it held her up.

Then the hurricane unleashed its full fury. When a repairman came over to fix the porch screen, the family was shocked to see the man's car suddenly lifted into the air and sent flying into a nearby lagoon. "An ordinary-sized car - just lifted up by the wind," she recalled later. "What goes on!"

Soon afterward, the Hepburns' big laundry wing was ripped off the house and the tide began creeping across their lawn. The big house shook like a leaf. "Windows were being blown out or sucked in," Kate said.

As the storm raged, the family decided to escape by dropping a rope out the dining-room window, climbing out, and crossing a field. When they reached higher ground, they turned and watched in horror as their beloved house, built on brick piles three-and-a-half-feet high, slowly turned and floated away on a brook that fed the lagoon.

"It just sailed away - easy as pie - and soon there was nothing at all left on the spot where the house had stood for over sixty years," she recalled. "Our house - ours for twenty-five years - all our possessions - just gone, look - we live there! Hey - what is happening!"

They pushed on through the storm, arriving at an empty nearby inn called the Riversea, and forced open the door to escape the wind. "Slowly the storm calmed, the tide went down, the water receded, the wind calmed," Kate recalled. "Darkness fell. We all slept at the Riversea."

When they went back to their property the next day, all that was left was a bathtub and a toilet. Later, they learned the grim statistics: Fenwick was one of more than 57,000 homes destroyed by the hurricane of 1938, which killed more than 600 people and caused $306 million in property damage -

more than $4 billion today.

Kate lost 95 percent of her belongings in the storm, she said, including her 1932 Academy Award, which was later recovered. Photographs taken of her after the hurricane showed her clad in a thick sweater and muddy pants as she combed the beach for family mementos; miraculously, she managed to find some of her mother's silver and tea set. While she could endure the loss of her possessions, Kate could not do without Fenwick. So she spearheaded ambitious plans for the waterfront home to be rebuilt, scheduling the work to begin in the spring of 1939.

After the hurricane, it became clear to Kate that her love affair with Howard Hughes was over, though they would remain friends and business partners for many years. "Howard had a pilot fly in with bottled water - and I knew that Howard and I had become friends and not lovers," she said later. "Love had turned to water. Pure water. But water."

As with many of Kate's affairs, the absence of commitment was the fatal flaw. "I look back at our relationship and I think that we were both cool customers," she reflected later. "He could do anything he wanted. And when I decided to move East, I think he thought, Well, I don't want to move East. I'll find someone who will stay West. I always thought it was lucky that we never married - two people who are used to having their own way should stay separate."

As the Hepburns recovered from their devastating loss, Kate got news in November that she was still in the running for Scarlett O'Hara in *Gone with The Wind*, even after her squabble with David Selznick. On November 21, Selznick asked his assistant to notify the final candidates – among them Kate, Jean Arthur, Joan Bennett, Loretta Young, Paulette Goddard, and Doris Jordan.

On December 10, Selznick met with Vivien Leigh, even as the scenes of Atlanta burning were being filmed. In a note to his wife, Irene Selznick – who would later become a close friend of Kate's – he wrote, "Not for anybody's ears but your own: It's narrowed down to Paulette, Jean Arthur, Joan Bennett, and Vivien Leigh." In early January, Kate found out she had been removed from the list – and Leigh signed - by way of a press release.

It was a big disappointment for Kate, but – after such a long search – she could not say she was surprised. Fortunately, she had *The Philadelphia Story* to keep her busy. The third act of the play needed to be rewritten, Kate and director Robert Sinclair agreed; to lighten the drama, they had Barry edit out some of the characters' more awkward confrontations and sprinkle in some clever dialogue.

Even before the revision of act three was completed, the play opened in New Haven in early 1939 and then moved to Philadelphia, where it was well-received by show-goers and critics alike. When the show opened in Washington, D.C., with the new third act, the cast played to a full house every night.

Because Kate had a hand in choosing her co-stars, all the actors in the production had great rapport, which contributed to a family-like atmosphere on the set. Van Heflin played Mike, a young journalist and writer who falls for Tracy Lord, and Joseph Cotten was Tracy's dapper ex-husband, C. K. Dexter Haven. The chemistry between Van Heflin and Kate was so convincing that rumors swirled that they were having an affair.

When the play finally closed in Washington in the spring, the major players - Kate, Barry, Sinclair, and The Theatre Guild's Lawrence Langner and Theresa Helburn – had to decide what to do next: Take the show on the road or head for New York?

Clearly, Kate was not ready for New York. "For God's sake, don't throw away your money," she said. "Let's be practical about this. We've got a fortune if we stay out of New York."

Helburn, fearing "the bloom would be off" if they went on another tour before New York, wanted to head for Broadway immediately; Barry, while acknowledging the risks of going straight to New York, was willing to try. In the end, Kate was the only one who wanted to delay the play's opening on Broadway. Ever since she had been roasted for her performance in *The Lake*, the city had been hostile territory.

With opening night scheduled for March 28, 1939, instead of returning to her Turtle Bay home, Kate checked into the Waldorf-Astoria Hotel with her friend and secretary Em Perkins, drew the shades, avoided calls, and paced the room repeating to herself, "This is Indianapolis, this is Indianapolis." She was attempting to convince herself that New York was no different than any other city.

As it turned out, her fears were completely unfounded. On March 29, the day after *The Philadelphia Story* opened in New York, critic John Mason Brown wrote, "The radiant Miss Hepburn brings a loveliness to our stage such as has not been seen hereabouts in years. Her fine chiseled face is a volatile mask. If it is difficult to take one's eyes off of her, it is because she is also blessed with an extraordinary personality. Slim and lovely as she is, Miss Hepburn likewise possesses a voice which in her emotional scenes can be sheer velvet."

Kate, said *New York Times* film critic Brooks Atkinson, had finally found her voice. "A strange, tense little lady with austere beauty and metallic voice, she has consistently found it difficult to project a part in the theater," Atkinson wrote. "But now she has surrendered to the central part in Mr. Barry's play and she acts it like a woman who has at last found the joy she has always been seeking in the theater."

The *New York Herald Tribune*'s Richard Watts Jr. applauded her bravery. "Few actresses have been so relentlessly assailed by critics' wit, columnists, magazine editors and other professional assailers over so long a period of time," he wrote, "and, even if you confess that some of the abuse had a certain justice to it, you must admit she faced it gamely and unflinchingly and fought back with courage and gallantry."

Finally, Kate felt vindicated as a stage actress, the deep scars left by the trauma of *The Lake* beginning to heal. The role of Tracy Lord perfectly matched Kate's strengths as an actress, and she relished her opening-night success, particularly because her parents were there to see it. She had longed for their respect; for the first time, she felt they were actually proud of her career. "I still grin to myself when I think of the party Kate gave [on opening night]," Helburn later said, explaining how she treated her frugal New England family differently than her glittering show-business crowd. "As long as her family was there she served beer; when they had gone she brought out the champagne."

The Philadelphia Story ran for 415 performances in New York, closing nearly a year later, in March of 1940. It grossed $961,310 and garnered Kate $96,131 in salary plus 25 percent of the net; the show's 254 performances on the road grossed an additional $753,538. Counting the film version released in December of 1940, Kate - once labeled "box-office poison" - would eventually make more than $500,000 from *The Philadelphia Story*. She had taken charge of her career in a way few women dared at the time.

The show's success had a tremendous impact on Kate; she was finally able to relax. Now that her romance with Howard Hughes was over, Van Heflin was seen frequently at her Turtle Bay home when they were not at the theater. As always, Harding and Luddy were her dearest friends.

To fill her days during the New York run, Kate played two hours of tennis daily, took an hour-long nap in the afternoon, and ate a healthy dinner before arriving at the Shubert Theatre an hour before curtain. She spent her weekends supervising Fenwick's reconstruction and visiting the Harding estate in New Jersey.

"I'd find Kate out picking little flowers that nobody else would have picked," Harding said. "She loves nature and she loves streams and she loves rain. She's really very Scotch in her love of mist. I used to find her . . . having breakfast under a tree that I'd never sat under . . . She's friends with all of it and sees things and makes something of it that nobody else would."

Kate's friends and neighbors noticed her new composure. Though still a tomboy, with age she had acquired a degree of grace in her movements, and her voice had mellowed, except when she got riled up and spewed unladylike profanity. She had grown surer of herself and dressed less like a refugee, though she still avoided jewelry and makeup, with the exception of lipstick.

When it came time to negotiate the details of producing the film version of *The Philadelphia Story*, Kate put on her businesswoman hat, which she wore well. Soon after the play opened in New York, the legendary producer Louis B. Mayer of MGM discovered that she owned the film rights and requested a meeting. "You know, Mr. Mayer, you are charming me," she said after they had chatted for a while. "I know that you are deliberately charming me, and still I am charmed. That's a real artist."

Mayer then got right to the point, asking how much money she wanted. Kate replied that she was not looking to make a profit. "What interests me is who I play with, because people say that I am poison at the box office. I want it cast."

"Who do you want?"

"Give me Tracy and Gable," she said. "I presumed that they probably wouldn't, but ask them."

Mayer asked. Both said no. Clark Gable had other commitments and Spencer Tracy had starred in four successful films over the previous six months and needed a break. His problems with alcohol had begun to interfere with his work and many days he simply wasn't fit to face the cameras.

"I can give you Jimmy Stewart because we have control over him," Mayer said, adding, "I'll give you a hundred and fifty thousand dollars to get anyone else you want or can get. You get them. You can name the director."

Kate readily agreed – it was a dream situation. She liked Mayer, calling him "a shrewd man with enormous understanding of an artist. He was not stupid, not crude. He was a very sensible fellow - and honest. In all my dealings with Mayer, I can say that he was the most honest person I ever dealt with in my life."

Gone, however, were any illusions about the business of film-making. "You're selling yourself," she said later, "and if everybody begins to say, 'Oh boy, we've had enough of that' . . . then it becomes a little embarrassing. Then it's up to you to say to them: 'Just a minute, fellows. Here's something you haven't seen yet.'"

Empowered by her MGM deal, Kate chose George Cukor to direct and approached Cary Grant, who wanted to play her character's ex-husband, C. K. Dexter Haven. Getting Grant signed, however, was a complicated matter. He was under contract with both RKO and Columbia, who would need to "loan" him to MGM. He asked for, and got, $137,500 in salary, which, after paying loan-out fees to the studios, he donated to the British War Relief Fund.

To complicate matters further, both Grant and his studios wanted him to get top billing above Kate, to ensure they would reap the benefits of the film's success; an actor's name appearing above that of the other stars not only suggested greater star-power but gave studios a reason to charge more when loaning out their actors. Kate resisted this demand for a while but decided it wasn't worth the fight. She finally agreed to share lesser billing with James Stewart, who would play the young journalist Macaulay "Mike" Connor, Van Heflin's part on the stage.

Producer Joseph L. Mankiewicz asked screenwriter Donald Ogden Stewart to make some changes to the screenplay, including rolling two parts – Tracy Lord's ex-husband and brother – into one, and adding a prologue, which briefly but humorously depicts the end of Tracy's marriage to Grant's character.

During the filming in Los Angeles, Kate lived in John Barrymore's former house near the top of Tower Grove, enjoying both privacy and a grand view of Beverly Hills. Harding visited, as did Kate's old boyfriend, the artist Bob McKnight, who painted a nude portrait of her. When Garson Kanin came for dinner that night and commented that Kate appeared to be in pain, she said, "I got too much sun today - sat out in the garden with no clothes on like a fool." Kate explained that her old friend was in town and "wanted to do a little figure of me and so there we were . . ." Kanin thought she was kidding until he saw the evidence in her living room a few weeks later.

The filming of *The Philadelphia Story* went swimmingly. It took eight weeks, required no retakes, and was Kate's first taste of control over her films, a euphoric experience for her. She was so energetic that she started pulling pranks on the crew, including putting a dead opossum in a snazzy box and giving it to script clerk Jack Greenwood, who didn't find it nearly as amusing as she did. "We had great fun doing it, as we always did on one of George's pictures," Kate said later.

Even before filming began, Kate made a shrewd calculation. "I don't want to make a grand entrance in this picture," she said. "Moviegoers . . . think I'm too la-di-da or something. A lot of people want to see me fall flat on my face." So the film begins with Grant knocking her flat on her backside. As Hepburn biographer A. Scott Berg put it, her character was carefully crafted to have audiences "laugh at her enough that they would ultimately sympathize with her," which Kate felt was critical to restoring her public image.

It worked. The film was an enormous success, both financially and critically, when it was released the day after Christmas in 1940, earning Academy Awards for Stewart (Best Actor) and Smith (Best Screenplay). Kate was nominated for Best Actress, but the award went to Ginger Rogers for playing the title character in *Kitty Foyle*. *The Philadelphia Story* also was nominated for Best Picture, Best Director, and Best Supporting Actress (Ruth Hussey).

Kate did, however, win the New York Film Critics' Award, and her performance as Tracy Lord earned glowing reviews, all praising her and agreeing that the story perfectly suited her personality, physicality, and distinctive voice. "And when Katharine Hepburn sets out to play Katharine Hepburn," one critic wrote, "she is a sight to behold. Nobody is . . . her equal."

Once filming was finished, Kate headed east and took the stage production of *The Philadelphia Story* back out on the road in October of 1940. The tour wrapped in February 1941, with its final performance in Philadelphia. After the last scene, the curtain was left up, allowing time for a lengthy applause as the performers remained motionless in their final positions.

After a few minutes, Kate walked to the front of the stage, motioned for silence, thanked the audience and then the entire crew, calling them on stage to applaud their efforts.

"When I started this play, these people knew I was on the spot," she said. "They could have treated me as a climber and a phony. Instead, they treated me as an actress and a friend."

She then pointed to two props on the stage, a fire screen and a green vase, and said, "See those? I've had my eye on them for two years, and now I'm going to get them." She tried to pick them up, but they were fastened firmly to the set, giving the audience a good laugh. After a couple of tries, she waved goodbye and left the stage.

For Kate, it was a triumphant comeback on both stage and screen. *Time* magazine's review of the film version of *The Philadelphia Story* perfectly summed up the prevailing sentiment of critics and audiences alike as she pondered her next move: "Come on back, Katie, all is forgiven."

12

"I DISCOVERED WHAT 'I LOVE YOU' REALLY MEANS"

What Kate learned from *The Philadelphia Story* was that she was more likely to succeed when she was firmly in control of her career. Owning the rights to a story written for her, with a cast of box-office favorites chosen by her, had worked spectacularly well.

Now, thanks to writer-director Garson Kanin, another custom-made opportunity was about to present itself.

In the spring of 1941, Kanin approached Kate about playing the lead in a story inspired by the renowned journalist Dorothy Thompson, whose poignant political columns had made her one of the most influential women in America, second only to Eleanor Roosevelt. His fictional film version centered on Sam Craig, a high profile sports reporter, and an international affairs correspondent named Tess Harding, who struggle to balance the demands of their careers with the demands of their relationship.

Kanin, a twenty-eight-year-old former actor who had already directed five films, turned the project over to his brother, Michael Kanin, and Ring Lardner Jr. to develop further.

Garson Kanin was confident that his brother, who had co-written the screenplay *They Made Her a Spy*, and Lardner, whose journalism background could give the story realism, would adhere to his vision for the film. While neither had much screenwriting experience, and Lardner had a reputation as a troublemaker for participating in the Screenwriters Guild's labor disputes, the two wrote a stellar script. Within three weeks, they had transformed Garson Kanin's idea into a 30,000-word gem and, with Garson's approval, sent it to Kate in West Hartford. It would be called

Woman of the Year.

Kate loved the script and began to formulate a plan to sell it to MGM and play the female lead herself. Although the names of the writers would have to be kept secret – MGM's chief story editor, William Fadiman, had said publicly that the studio would never hire Lardner - Kate went ahead and pitched the story to Joseph Mankiewicz, who had produced *The Philadelphia Story.*

When Kate let Mankiewicz know that she would soon be sending him a script for a new film she wanted to make, Mankiewicz asked who wrote it. "I can't tell you. It's a secret," she said, then hung up before he could press her for more information. She got in her car and headed for New York and by the time she arrived three hours later, Mankiewicz had already read the script. Guessing that it had been written by the acclaimed Ben Hecht and Charles MacArthur, Mankiewicz asked how much they wanted for it. Kate reiterated that the author would remain a secret for the present.

"Look, Kate," MacKenna said. "I can't send up a story [to the front office] unless I know the author's name and the price he expects."

"I'm not going to tell you his name, and as for the price, all I'll tell you is that it's going to be high," she replied. "I own the story, and I'm not going to sell it anyway, unless [Spencer] Tracy will play it."

Getting Tracy was originally Garson Kanin's idea. Later, he recalled Kate's initial reaction: "Oh - I don't know. I wonder whether we would be good together. We're so different."

Then he suggested it to Tracy, who said, "Oh, really - do you think that we would be good together? We're - so sort - of different."

Tracy also reportedly said, "How can I do a picture with a woman who has dirt under her fingernails and who is of ambiguous sexuality and always wears pants?" Kate, addressing part of her memoir to Tracy, wrote, "I think that you imagined that I was a lesbian. But not for long."

Mankiewicz, unwilling to let the project slip out of his hands, sent the script to Tracy in Florida, where he was shooting a film. Though Tracy obviously knew who Kate was, he had never seen any of her films and had to request a screening of *The Philadelphia Story*. After seeing it, he called Kate, "a damn fine actress," told Mankiewicz that he thought the script would suit the two of them well, and flew to California to meet Kate and the producers.

A successful Broadway stage actor in the 1920s, Tracy had a well-received Hollywood debut with *Up the River* in 1930 – appearing with another promising rookie named Humphrey Bogart – and then made a series of forgettable films before winning consecutive Academy Awards in 1937 and 1938 for *Captains Courageous* and *Boys Town*.

By the time he flew to California to meet Kate in the spring of 1941, Tracy was a major box-office star – and also a raging alcoholic whom the studios had to handle with care. His contract with MGM, the director Fritz Lang said, included a clause that specified "if he had so much as a glass of beer they could throw him out."

Though he never showed up drunk on the set, Tracy would

sometimes miss days of shooting and once stayed with Mankiewicz for a week in an effort to remain sober. Still, his talent was undeniable; after watching him crack nuts for hours to prepare for a scene, Mankiewicz said, "Christ, he used up five pounds of nuts and then he pretended on the set it had just occurred to him."

Tracy's knack for "under-acting" and his seemingly effortless performances made him a favorite of other actors, who appreciated his innate abilities. "The thing about his acting is there's no bullshit in it," Bogart once said. "He doesn't go in for those hammy disguises some clowns think is acting . . . Feels it. Says it. Talks. Listens. He means what he says when he says it, and if you think that's easy, try it."

Clark Gable, a close friend of Tracy's who used to call him "The King," said his only complaint about the actor was his feigned humility. "Don't you believe it," Gable said. "He knows how good he is. And that's as good as anyone has gotten up to here and now in this business. Any actor or actress who's ever played a scene with Spencer will tell you - there's nothing like it. He mesmerizes you. Those eyes of his - and what goes on behind them. Nobody's better than when they act with him."

Even Laurence Olivier, who would later be considered one of the best actors in the world, said, "I've learned more about acting from watching Tracy than in any other way. He has a great truth in everything he does."

Captivated by his natural on-screen style, Kate watched his films again and again. She'd heard about his alcoholism but felt reassured by the fact that he never brought it to the set with him; if he wasn't sober, he simply wouldn't come to work.

As negotiations for *Woman of the Year* progressed, Kate met with Joe Mankiewicz and MGM executive Benjamin Thau in Louis B. Mayer's office in Hollywood. Afraid that Mayer would charm her into a bad deal, she put on a pair of platform shoes that she had had made specifically for the occasion - adding four inches to her five-foot-eight frame to give her additional leverage.

Mayer got right to the point: "How much do you want for it?"

"Two hundred and fifty thousand dollars" Kate replied, explaining that half would go to her, and half to the screenwriters. When Mayer argued that he could not agree to that after only seeing a first draft, Kate agreed to deliver sixty pages on Monday. When Mayer left the room to take a call, Kate grabbed her head and said, "This is absolutely terrible! I don't know what I am doing!"

When Mayer came back, Kate announced she had to leave. Mankiewicz left with her, and, once they were outside, kissed her forehead and said, "I've just kissed the Blarney Stone."

Crossing the lot to the studio commissary for a cup of tea, they arrived just as Tracy was leaving. In what turned out to be a historic occasion, Mankiewicz introduced them. Still shaky from her meeting with Mayer and towering above the five-foot-ten Tracy in her four-inch platforms, Kate said, "I'm afraid I'm a little tall for you, Mr. Tracy." Smiling, Tracy replied, "Don't worry, Miss Hepburn. I'll cut you down to my size."

Later, when Mankiewicz told Tracy he predicted the two

would have great chemistry together, Tracy told him, "Not me, boy, I don't want to get mixed up with anything like that."

For the rest of the week, Kate, Michael Kanin, and Lardner worked hard revising the script, with Garson Kanin contributing some last-minute touches. At 7:00 a.m. Sunday morning, Kate surprised George Stevens at home and asked if he'd direct the film.

It was hard for Kate to bypass her great friend, the director George Cukor, with whom she had made so many memorable films, but she felt that Cukor was not the best fit. "I had to explain to Cukor that this script had to be directed by a very macho director from the man's point of view and not the woman's," she said later. "I'm sure that George was very disappointed."

Stevens had another advantage over Cukor: He had been dating Kate in recent months, despite their previous conflicts, though the affair proved to be short-lived. In any case, Stevens agreed to direct and offered some suggestions about the script. Kate took his ideas back to the writers at her bungalow, where they worked through the night with the help of two typists whose fingers got so tired they could barely hold a cigarette.

On Monday, she delivered 106 pages to MGM, far more than the sixty she had promised. On Tuesday, she got a call from studio executive Sam Katz, who offered her $175,000 for everything. "You don't seem to understand," Kate told him. "I really want 250,000."

"Well, you know we're going to give it to you," Katz told her.

" . . . So now you can tell us. Who wrote it?"

She told him. For a moment, he didn't respond. Finally, he said, "Mike Kanin and Ring Lardner have never made more than $3,000 for a script before, and we're paying them $62,500 each? This picture should be called *Agent of the Year.*"

In May of 1941, Kate sold the screenplay to MGM, and the studio spent the next six weeks making revisions. Tracy read the revised script, which centered primarily on Kate's Tess Harding character, but he offered no complaints. He was impressed with Kate's tenacity and admired the courage it took for her to stand up to a powerful Hollywood studio.

When it came time to shoot, the electricity between Kate and Tracy was palpable. They were the quintessential example of opposites attracting: the strong, gruff, hard-drinking Irishman and the independent, outspoken, Yankee WASP. Everyone involved with the film felt their chemistry immediately, especially Stevens, who quickly eased out of his relationship with Kate – no doubt to keep peace on the set.

Kate and Tracy were evenly matched: Both intensely private, they shared a range of interests, from food to sports to politics, and enjoyed the banter of a good debate. Each had a unique sense of humor and hated pretension as much as they loved their work. Despite their sizable egos, they both treated everyone on the set - from producer to crew - with the utmost respect.

Their first scene was shot on a set replicating a bar frequented by the staff of the *New York Herald Tribune*. "I accidentally knocked over a glass," Kate recalled. "Spencer handed me a handkerchief, and I took . . . [it] and I thought, 'Oh you old so-and-so, you're going to make me mop it up right in the middle of a scene.'" That she did, even crawling underneath the table to mop up the floor as well. Tracy just watched as the camera rolled. "Spencer just smiled," Kate said. "He wasn't thrown at all."

The first few days on the set, Tracy called Kate "Shorty" and "That Woman." Suddenly, however, as if they had called a truce, he began calling her Kate or sometimes even Kath. Everyone relaxed.

Stevens commented that early in Kate's relationship with Tracy - both on film and off – "Spence's reaction to her was a total, pleasant, but glacial put-down of her extreme effusiveness. He just didn't get disturbed about doing things immediately; she wanted to do a hundred and one things at once; he was never in a hurry. She 'worried the bone'; he just took it and padded off with it. Slowly."

While Kate loved to rehearse at length and shoot scenes repeatedly, Tracy felt too much preparation could make a performance stilted and stale. He preferred to trust his instincts, and they were usually right: His first takes were often his best. Eventually, Kate was forced to adapt to his method, which ultimately seemed to improve her own acting.

Once the camera started rolling, Tracy disappeared into his character. Actress Jean Simmons described him as "a sort of sorcerer" who became so immersed in his role that he pulled everyone deeper into theirs.

As their characters fell for one another in *Woman of the*

Year, so did Tracy and Kate. "Someone asked me when I fell for Spencer," Kate said later. "I can't remember. It was right away. We started our first picture together and I knew right away that I found him irresistible. Just exactly that, irresistible."

As Kate was learning, however, Tracy had an extremely complicated personal life. He was married, albeit in name only, to his wife of eighteen years, the former stock theater actress Louise Treadwell Tracy. But they had been living separate lives for many years, and Tracy had already had many affairs, including co-stars Loretta Young (*Man's Castle*), Joan Crawford (*Mannequin*), and Ingrid Bergman (*Dr. Jekyll and Mr. Hyde*). But as a Catholic, he did not believe in divorce. So when he was filming, he would stay at the Beverly Wilshire Hotel and spend his evenings in Hollywood nightclubs, occasionally returning home on the weekends to visit his family.

A major source of Tracy's despair was his relationship with his son John, deaf since birth. Rather than committing him to an institution, Louise dedicated herself to learning how to communicate with the boy and eventually – miraculously – taught him to speak. While she devoted her days to his care, her husband - feeling as if he'd failed his family - drank.

"I wanted to help with the boy, but I was no damn good at it," Tracy later said. "I would come in after Louise had been working with him for hours and start undoing the good she had done. Maybe she had been working with him all day on a word like 'shoe,' showing it to him and saying the word over and over, trying to get him to read her lips. So I would pick up the damn shoe and throw it across the room and scare the poor kid half to death. I had no patience, and it's amazing how much she had - and has."

Louise – who in 1942 created the John Tracy Clinic in Los Angeles to help other deaf children and their families – understood her husband's guilt and frustration. Aware of his infidelities and alcoholism, she had always welcomed her husband back home. And Tracy reciprocated by never abandoning her. When Louise accepted her husband's 1938 Best Actor Academy Award for his role as a Portuguese fisherman in *Captains Courageous* – he was apparently hospitalized to help him sober up – Ed Sullivan wrote, "Mrs. Tracy stole the show. She is just the sort of person you expect Spencer Tracy's wife to be. Simple and unaffected."

Though Stevens cautioned Kate that Tracy would never divorce his wife, she was undeterred; she actually preferred a secret relationship. As for Tracy's drinking, she brewed a lot of strong tea to serve on the set.

As filming progressed, both Kate and her character softened and became more vulnerable; though Kate never gave up her pants, she began wearing new ones that complemented her figure. When describing her character to a reporter, Kate said, "I'm alive, alert, enthusiastic - and also egotistical. I love Spencer, but I won't give up too much of myself to him . . . I try to dominate him, put things over on him. I almost lose him."

Watching Kate fall in love with Tracy, friends reminded her she'd never be anything but the other woman; Louise was and would always be Mrs. Spencer Tracy. Even the letterhead of the new John Tracy Clinic shouted, "MRS. SPENCER TRACY, PRESIDENT." Metro's publicity department used her spotless reputation to its advantage; to avoid humiliating her, Tracy would not be seen on the town with other women.

That was fine with Kate. At last, she could have the privacy she always demanded in her relationships without causing problems; meanwhile, the press would oblige her out of their respect and admiration for Mrs. Tracy. Without question, Kate had fallen hard for Tracy, who, in turn, was beginning to see her as someone who could help him shoulder some of his burdens. He even curbed his drinking temporarily. A legendary love affair had begun.

Obviously, theirs wasn't the first secret relationship in Hollywood. Vivien Leigh and Laurence Olivier were a couple long before they divorced their respective spouses. Louis B. Mayer had quietly paid Clark Gable's wife, Rhea Gable, $100,000 to divorce him so he could marry Carole Lombard. As for Kate and Spencer Tracy's affair, Mayer made sure it never became public knowledge.

Those in Hollywood knew, of course, and loved to speculate about whether Kate would leave him or whether they might marry. None of it bothered Kate, who had always enjoyed keeping people guessing and was good at keeping secrets; she also liked the fact that her relationship with Tracy kept other men away from her. Kate felt that she'd finally found the perfect man - smart, outspoken, quick with a joke, deliberate, and ridiculously talented. She trusted him implicitly and likened his dedication to his religious beliefs to her father's commitment to medicine.

Tracy was forty-one years old when they met – seven years older than Kate – and was already suffering serious health problems from his dependence on alcohol. He went on periodic binges and suffered deep depressions – and Kate was often the target of his short fuse and cruel sarcasm. Halfway through the filming of *Woman of the Year*, he disappeared; Kate went from bar to bar until she found him, brought him home, and sobered him up. Taking care of Tracy and keeping him away from booze would become her new mission in life. Somehow, his vulnerability was as irresistible to her as his strength.

Garson Kanin later explained that Kate and Tracy supported each other in many ways. While she helped him cope with his drinking, he kept her grounded. "Spencer kept his partner-friend down to earth," Kanin wrote. "She can be flighty, whimsical, impractical, wildly over-imaginative, and often unrealistic. Spencer kept his sharp eye on her and used the tender weapon of humor to reveal her to herself; to show her a better way."

By the time *Woman of the Year* was finished, Kate and Tracy were spending as much time together as possible. It's no exaggeration to say that Kate had been utterly transformed by love. "It seems to me I discovered what 'I love you' really means," she wrote in her memoir. "It means I put you and your interests and your comfort ahead of my own interests and my own comfort because I love you . . . This was not easy for me because I was definitely a *me me me* person."

After seeing a sneak preview of the film, Mankiewicz and Stevens insisted that the ending be rewritten; the original showed Tess Harding embracing baseball, her husband's passion, and coming to love it even more than he did – an outcome Mankiewicz and Stevens felt most American women would find unrealistic. They believed Tess needed some flaws to humble her and wanted the last scene to reveal them.

Stevens decided to reenact a kitchen routine he had done once in a silent film, where a wife, attempting to prove her domestic abilities by making breakfast, fails miserably. Lardner and Mike Kanin strongly objected when they found out that writer John Lee Mahin was assigned to revise the ending – and Kate was appalled, calling it "the worst bunch of shit I've ever read." But while she, Lardner, and Mike Kanin thought the script had been vulgarized, women at the next preview cheered, Mankiewicz, said, "not only with admiration, but relief. Now they could turn to their schmuck husbands and say, 'She may know Batista, but she can't even make a cup of coffee you silly bastard.'"

Filmgoers loved it and *Woman of the Year* went on to become even more successful than *The Philadelphia Story*. Critics agreed that Tracy and Hepburn were a match made in movie heaven. "The title part is played by Miss Hepburn, who has never looked more beautiful," the *New York World-Telegram* wrote. "It is played with such humor, resourcefulness and contagious spirit that I think it is even better than her performance in *The Philadelphia Story*, and that was just as fine as anything could be. No less satisfactory is Mr. Tracy. There isn't a false note in his characterization of the sportswriter. And the things he can do with a gesture, with a smile, are nobody's business . . . what an actor!"

Donald Kirkley of *The Baltimore Sun* wrote that "each complements the other . . . Gone for good are [Miss Hepburn's] mannerisms, the tricks, the superficiality which marred much of her previous work. Her performance in *Woman of the Year* shows even more subtlety and depth."

Kate would be nominated for another Academy Award for best actress for the film, though the award would go to Greer Garson for *Mrs. Miniver*. Despite the fact that the film's title focused on Kate's character, Tracy got top billing, as he would in all nine of the movies they ended up making together. When Garson Kanin once asked Tracy why he did this, he responded, "Why not?"

"Well," Kanin said, "she's the lady. You're the man. Ladies first?"

"This is a movie, chowderhead," Tracy replied, "not a life-boat."

In the years of taking care of Tracy that followed, there were moments when Kate must have felt like she needed a life-boat. But conflict and upheaval were not confined to their personal lives. Just days after the sneak preview of *Woman of the Year*, the Japanese bombed Pearl Harbor. Tough times lay ahead, even for those living in the Hollywood bubble.

13

"HE COULD BE A MEAN BASTARD IF HE GOT TOO DRUNK"

Most in Hollywood considered Kate an intellectual; Humphrey Bogart once said she could speak as intelligently about St. Thomas Aquinas's Summa Theologica as she could about spreading manure. Tracy could, too, which was one of the things that knit them together. He also shared Kate's love of the water, and both enjoyed painting scenes of the places they went together, sometimes from rooftops or through hotel windows. Kate relished Tracy's colorful stories and could listen for hours to his blarney. She loved his masculinity and called his size seventeen neck a "man's neck."

Their social circle was limited to Kate's closest friends – George Cukor, Laura Harding, Garson Kanin and his wife Ruth Gordon, and producer-director Chester Erskine - and Tracy's drinking buddies, director Victor Fleming and actors Lynne Overman, Pat O'Brien, and James Cagney. They had to handle Tracy with care. Said one friend, "He could be a mean bastard if he got too drunk."

Tracy would occasionally drink with reporters, too. "Kate and I never go any place where you bastards will see us," he told them. "It's as simple as that."

Another of Tracy's drinking mates was Clark Gable, who had known Tracy since they made the hit film *San Francisco* together in 1936. Both had played Killer Mears in stage productions of *The Last Mile*, and both had had serious affairs with Loretta Young. After making the films *Test Pilot* and *Boom Town* together, they became close friends and often broke studio rules by having drinks in each other's dressing rooms.

Gable could hold his booze better than Tracy, however, and

did his best to cut his friend off when things got ugly. Before Gable married Carole Lombard in 1939, the two would go on wild drinking sprees; once, when MGM boss Louis B. Mayer called them in Tucson, Arizona, an incoherent Tracy told Mayer that Gable couldn't talk right then because he was playing a wild game of jacks for big gambling stakes and was "on his threesies." Then he hung up.

But the party ended – at least for awhile - when the United States entered World War II. Gable's wife Carole Lombard – the highest-paid Hollywood star of the late 1930s – died in a plane crash on January 16, 1942, on her way to Los Angeles from a war bond rally in her home state of Indiana. Devastated, Gable enlisted in the Air Force, something Lombard had urged him to do, and joined a B-17 combat group in England, where he flew in five missions.

Other stars joined the war effort, too. Jimmy Stewart signed up for the Air Force and Cukor enlisted in the Signal Corps. Inspired by their courage, Kate and Tracy felt compelled to contribute, too. Tracy wanted to fight, but was not allowed to enlist because of his poor health. So he narrated Kanin's Army recruiting film, *Ring of Steel,* instead.

Kate also narrated a government propaganda movie - *Women in Defense,* directed by John Ford - that outlined the various ways women could help their country (urging them, among other things, to raise children, "which has always been the first line of defense"). She also entertained servicemen at the Stage Door Canteen, a recreation center in Manhattan for servicemen on leave.

All this pro-war activity was a marked shift for Hollywood, which during the depression had trafficked mostly in escapist fare and feared offending the prevailing isolationist sentiment of the time, even as dictators like Mussolini and Hitler rose to power in Europe. The situation began changing with 1939's *Confession of a Nazi Spy* starring Edward G. Robinson, and 1940's *The Great Dictator*, which was hugely popular and today is considered a classic.

Once the United States entered the war, the American government insisted that Hollywood enthusiastically support the cause. The Office of War Information made sure that filmmakers portrayed the war positively and censored images of American casualties under a ban that lasted until 1943.

After Lombard died and Gable joined the Air Force, Tracy sank into a deep depression. When the Theatre Guild offered Kate the lead role in a new Philip Barry stage comedy, *Without Love,* she asked if Tracy could co-star. But the producers, concerned about his drinking, said no. Unwilling to leave him alone in California, Kate persuaded him to come along on the tour.

Without Love, a witty tale about a widow and a scientist-investor who marry for convenience and eventually fall in love, was scheduled to open in New Haven on February 26, 1942, then go to Boston and Washington, D.C., before opening in New York in late March.

But there were big problems from the start. Kate and co-star Elliott Nugent didn't mesh well, on or off the stage, and Lawrence Langner of the Theatre Guild blamed her for the play's failures. "And as a result of Kate's feeling about Nugent not 'working' with her, she overplayed extremely, trying to make up for his deficiency, his inadequacy, and her whole performance failed to soar," he said. "We all knew it was a blunder. It was very hard on poor Elliott."

Langner, however, didn't realize the pressure Kate was under. Between Nugent and Tracy, she had two heavy drinkers on her hands and was worried about keeping both sober while trying to conceal the fact that Tracy was with her on tour. What she had hoped would be a romantic adventure was anything but that. Because the show had not been well received, the key players decided to keep touring rather than take the show to Broadway. Kate suggested going to Hartford; when everyone agreed, they booked the play for the end of April at the Bushnell Memorial Auditorium, where her family filled the sixth row on opening night.

By now, Kate's stress level was soaring. Tracy had gone back to Hollywood alone to film *Tortilla Flat*, and Kate was gravely concerned about his drinking. She also was losing patience with Nugent and his lackluster performances. Touchy, irritable, and unapproachable, she refused an interview with a student from Hartford High School and a request for a photograph from a fifteen-year-old aspiring actress. She also called the police on a group of fans standing outside the Hepburn house.

After Hartford, Kate and the Theatre Guild agreed that *Without Love* would end its tour; they told the press that it would not debut on Broadway until Kate's next movie with Spencer Tracy was completed in the fall.

Meanwhile, Donald Ogden Stewart, who had won an Oscar for his screenplay for *The Philadelphia Story*, had written a new script called *Keeper of the Flame*, adapted from an unpublished novel by I. A. R. Wylie, and George Cukor agreed to direct. Cautious MGM executives were unsure if it was the best follow-up to *Woman of the Year* for Kate. But, fascinated by her character, Kate was determined to make it work. She was intrigued by the possibilities of her role as Christine, the widow of a famous and beloved civic leader who suddenly dies in a mysterious accident.

Later, Kate said that Christine was the first mature woman she had ever played. All the others, she said, were "girls, all sorts of girls, shy, whimsical, sensitive, flamboyant, tempestuous, but never a woman . . . I looked upon Christine as a new acting experience, the one I had been preparing years to play."

Tracy was again her co-star, playing a reporter who discovers that Christine's late husband had betrayed his country. Kate was happy to be back in Hollywood where she could keep an eye on him because when he was lonely, he drank more and ran with the wrong crowd. While making *Tortilla Flat*, he had rented a suite at the Beverly Hills Hotel while Kate rented a house in exclusive Malibu Beach.

Kate's life with Tracy was a busy one. She was not only his companion, but his secretary, nurse, and driver, taking him to and from the studio, then back to her house, where she fed him and stroked his ego before carting him back to his suite. She did her best to keep him occupied; on weekends, they walked together, painted together, and spent time with her friends rather than his drinking buddies. When he went on a bender, she escorted him out of bars and nursed his hangovers, even putting up with his abusive behavior when he mocked her mannerisms and called her his "bag of bones." There were only four subjects Tracy would not joke about: his religion, Franklin Delano Roosevelt, Louise, and his children. Everything else was fair game.

Through it all, Kate, like Louise, stood staunchly by his side. She would later say Tracy represented "the simple and pure things in life . . . He was like water, air, earth. He wasn't easily fooled . . . He was onto the human race - but with humor and understanding. Yet he was enormously complicated and tortured. He looked out from a terribly tangled maze, like a web. Yet from the center of this tangle would come the simple statement, the total clarity of his work."

She loved Tracy and admired his work so much that she tailored her own career to suit his needs. Hollywood writers called these the Tracy-Hepburn years: Between 1942 and 1950, she made ten films, six of them with Tracy. Though her movies without him were not terribly successful, the opposite was true for him: All but one of the eight he made without her during that time were box-office hits.

Kate was constantly on the lookout for scripts suitable for her and Tracy, which was not easy considering their distinct personalities. Kate often had a smaller role than Tracy, as in *Keeper of the Flame* and later in the film version of *Without Love*; it was not until *Adam's Rib* in 1949 that she had the chance to play a strong female lead again.

Keeper of the Flame may have disappointed audiences when it was released in March of 1943 because it lacked the romance of other Tracy and Hepburn films. Fans who showed up to see them sizzle instead saw a chilling, gloomy, mystery movie. The film also enraged MGM head Louis B. Mayer and Republican members of Congress because it had a clear leftist slant that seemed to equate wealth with fascism.

Keeper of the Flame marked the beginning of another slowdown in Kate's career. Since the outbreak of World War II, films had to depend solely on revenues from within the United States, since foreign markets now presented a risk. Movie deals were easy to come by for pin-up girls like Betty Grable and Rita Hayworth, but Kate appealed to a narrower audience - mostly middle-aged, educated, upper-middle-class men and women who wanted a diversion from the realities of war. Kate had demonstrated her charm and talents in comedy and romance, but now, during these volatile times, she had to tread carefully.

In September 1942, Kate got a surprise when Luddy suddenly filed for divorce in Hartford on grounds of desertion, explaining to the court that he doubted the validity of the divorce granted in Mexico in 1934. Kate did not attend the hearing, but to establish Connecticut as her legal residence, Dr. Hepburn testified on Kate's behalf. A week after the proceedings, Luddy, at age forty-three, was finally able to move on with his life, marrying Elizabeth Albers, a twenty-four-year-old Boston socialite, with whom he would have two children.

Now officially divorced for the second time, Kate returned to New York for the stage production of *Without Love* – which she decided to do only because Tracy promised to spend most of his time in New York with her. Although the original director, Robert Sinclair, had been replaced by Kate's old friend Arthur Hopkins, Nugent was still the male lead, resulting in a stilted and stiff performances from Kate.

In New York, Tracy stayed in the Waldorf Towers, just a few blocks from Kate's Turtle Bay apartment. Once he arrived, both Kate's mood and her performances improved. But she was still met with a chilly reception from critics when the show opened in November of 1942 at the St. James Theatre: "Even at her best, Miss Hepburn is not a virtuoso actress," wrote Brooks Atkinson of *The New York Times*. "As a wealthy Washington widow with a New England heritage, she has several stunning visual moments to contribute to *Without Love*. But it is hard for her to sustain a scene in a trifling play that is generally uneventful."

Still, Kate's star power kept the show running for its scheduled fourteen weeks, playing to mostly full houses, and ending in February 1943.

In May, Tracy was back in Hollywood shooting *A Guy Named Joe* – it would become his highest-grossing film to date – and Kate went to West Hartford to visit "her father's house," as she continued to call it. During this visit, she later recalled, she spent a lot of time on her "wonderful English racing bike [doing] 90 million miles an hour" through the suburbs of West Hartford, wearing frayed, white shorts and an oversized sweater "like an old bum."

"I get my hands way down on the bars, and my bottom way up on the seat and I go like mad," she said. "People see my bottom in white shorts and my long legs pedaling madly and from the back I guess it really looked like I had absolutely nothing on. It was enough to make them say, 'What the hell is that?' Then they'd see it was me and try to be nice."

Kate played tennis and golf, weeded her father's garden, and spent time with Marion's four-year-old son, Jackie. It was a happy time until she learned in mid-June that Tracy's film was being postponed. Uncomfortable with the thought of Tracy being left to his own devices, she renewed her search for a script that would suit them both and give her work to do back in Hollywood.

For a while, she hoped to convince MGM to make a film adaptation of Eugene O'Neill's play *Mourning Becomes Electra.* Though Greta Garbo had been in seclusion for a year, Kate thought she could persuade her to suspend her retirement to co-star with her. Kate approached Mayer, who agreed to a meeting to consider the mammoth project, which in its original form consisted of three plays, with four or five acts in each, based on a Greek classic, *The Oresteia* trilogy by Aeschylus.

"He listened to the whole thing," Kate recalled later. "He heard it told by Mrs. Frank, his storyteller. It was customary for the heads of the companies at that time to have someone tell them the stories which were sent to the studios for possible pictures. I thought this was idiotic until I heard Mrs. Frank do it. I used to laugh at the idea of her telling the stories. I was wrong. She was brilliant. I was absolutely riveted and fascinated when she told *Mourning Becomes Electra.*"

Mayer concluded that the project was too risqué, and Kate offered a passionate rebuttal to the press. "Really deep consideration of the issue of sex, the problems that may arise because of it, has no chance to be translated onto the screen under the present system of censorship," she said. "It makes no sense at all when at the same time in musicals and other lighter entertainment you find sex exploited in an intriguing and vaguely peeking sort of way that is more meretriciously alluring than artists' dramatic studies and impressions. It all seems so terribly false and unintelligent and even harmful if you want to believe harm arises from such things."

The press was surprised by its new relationship with Kate. No longer the reticent glamor girl, she could now be depended on to voice her opinions regarding social issues intelligently and succinctly. Tracy encouraged her to speak out in the same way her father had encouraged her mother, drawing her even closer to him.

She fought hard for *Mourning Becomes Electra*, carefully articulating her arguments in the media. The *Los Angeles Times* quoted her as saying, "I will fight to have this picture produced and others I believe would benefit the screen - there is need to think of the post war world when we will again be appealing to the European public as well as our own. We simply cannot confine ourselves to typical musicals and light comedies and expect in all ways to satisfy the people in foreign countries."

She continued: "I'm afraid I agree with George Bernard Shaw who said that censors are like decayed teeth - not good for the purpose for which they were intended and the cause of much painfulness besides."

Despite her extensive lobbying, Mayer held firm and in retrospect seems to have been right. *Mourning Becomes Electra* was finally produced by RKO in 1947. While the film, which starred Rosalind Russell and Kirk Douglas, was nominated for two Academy Awards, it had to be re-released after being cut from nearly three hours to 105 minutes and lost $2.3 million, making it one of the biggest flops in the studio's history.

Meanwhile, MGM had other projects in mind for Kate. Pandro Berman had moved to MGM from RKO three years earlier and had let bygones be bygones after Kate and Cukor's debacle with *Sylvia Scarlett*. Now he wanted to cast her as a Chinese woman in *Dragon Seed*, adapted from the Pearl S. Buck novel of the same name. Mayer approved the project because of its critique of Japanese imperialism and the studio's previous success with another Buck novel adaptation, *The Good Earth*.

Dragon Seed would cost $2.8 million to make - by far the most expensive film Kate had ever worked on – and its ambitions meant extra responsibility for her. It was filmed mostly in the San Fernando Valley, and Kate was expected to arrive at 6:00 each morning to give the makeup artist time to transform her into an Asian woman. The set itself was an entire Chinese peasant village, constructed for the movie on 120 acres. The filming was a grueling experience for Kate, but her newly restored friendship with Berman and the presence of her old friend, film editor Jane Loring, now at MGM, helped her through.

Berman was also producing *The Seventh Cross* with Tracy, who was playing a German liberal who escaped from a concentration camp. During the filming, Tracy replaced alcohol with coffee, which he drank all day long, leading to chronic insomnia.

Although *Dragon Seed* was successful at the box-office when it opened in July of 1944, grossing $4.6 million worldwide – Kate's performance was harshly criticized: Reviewers mocked everything from her clothing to her Chinese accent. Cast mates Walter Huston and Aline MacMahon created compelling characters – in fact, MacMahon was nominated for a Best Supporting Actress Oscar – and wartime audiences were enticed by the exotic background and enthralling story. But the film never drew as many movie-goers as *The Good Earth* and, partly because of its high production costs, lost $281,000 overall.

After that difficult experience, what Kate really wanted was a light-hearted comedy for her and Tracy. After much persuasion, she was able to convince Mayer to buy the rights to *Without Love* and hire Donald Ogden Stewart to adapt the play for the screen. While her widowed character had taken the spotlight on stage, now that Tracy was on board as her scientist love interest, the male lead part was given more substance, and Kate's performance was more subdued. This made the film less exciting than the original, but it was good for the Tracy-and-Hepburn team, which for Kate now took priority over her ego.

To ensure the film's success, Kate took a new interest in the production process, and when she was unhappy, she clearly let her displeasure be known. Set director Ed Willis remarked, "People always said to me, 'She's trying to do everything.' And my reply was, 'The thing I'm afraid of and you should be afraid of, is that she can do everything.' Producer, director, cameraman! That's what she was! Her idea of everything was always better than you could ever have envisioned."

When it opened in March of 1945, *Without Love* received mostly favorable reviews. It was called "witty and engaging" by *The New Yorker*'s Wolcott Gibbs, who said Hepburn and Tracy "succeed brilliantly" in the lead roles. The film also did well at the box office, earning a profit of $619,000 on a gross of $2.7 million.

With Tracy still on the wagon, Kate was optimistic about his chances of recovery from alcoholism and had richly enjoyed their time together on the set. But life was never simple for Katharine Hepburn; even she must have sensed that such bliss wouldn't last.

14

"I LIKE TO CHECK IN AND CHECK OUT"

In the spring of 1945, just months before the end of the war, Kate finally brought Tracy to Fenwick to meet her family, an experience Tracy described as overwhelming. "The Hepburns all love to talk," he once said. "Even when they look like they're listening, they're really only sitting there thinking what they're going to say next."

To Tracy, the Hepburns were egotistical, self-righteous, and hypocritical. "They won't let charity letters go through New England's mails unless [Dr. Hepburn's] name's on the letterheads. And her mother helps Margaret Sanger with young girls that got knocked up . . ." Later, Kate would overhear Tracy describe her family to director Frank Capra as "ultra-liberal New England aristocrats that work their ass off for the poor, poor folk, but never see one."

While staying with the Hepburns in Fenwick, Tracy - outside looking for some peace and quiet - saw a man with a fishing rod sneak past the Hepburns' barbed wire fence en route to the Sound. Tracy joked that the good doctor should invite the fisherman in for lunch. Instead, Dr. Hepburn grabbed a shotgun and a megaphone he kept handy and screamed at the man that he shouldn't be trespassing.

"The poor old fisherman dove through that barbed wire and runs for his life up the beach trailing barbed wire from his legs," Tracy recalled. "Papa Hepburn hangs up the megaphone and says to me, 'Getting so a man can't enjoy any privacy anymore. At least twice a week some nervy interloper tries crawling through that fence!' And he goes right inside and joins the hot family discussion about the rights of the poor."

In her memoir, Kate was far more circumspect – one might

even say evasive – about the frosty relationship between the people she loved most, which must have pained her tremendously. "He went to Hartford several times and to Fenwick," she recalled. "But they were never close. I think that they liked him - but Spence felt a bit uncomfortable with them. After all, he was a married man. I don't think that Dad and Mother were bothered too much by this. But there it was as far as Spence went - and he felt uncomfortable - unrelaxed. So we seldom were together when I went home."

Despite that family tension, Kate was delighted with Tracy's progress - he had been sober several months, and it showed. On April 1, he received a letter from President Franklin Roosevelt asking him to go overseas and tour U.S. military bases to boost morale; he eagerly accepted. But before Tracy could make the trip, on April 12, 1945, the president suffered a stroke and died. The tour was canceled.

When the war officially ended, old friends George Cukor and Clark Gable returned to Hollywood. Cukor's home was still Kate's favorite refuge; she despised going out or eating in restaurants, where people stared at her while she chewed and eavesdropped on her conversations.

She became close friends with Garson Kanin's wife, Ruth Gordon, a fellow New Englander who knew a lot of Kate's former stage friends. At forty-nine, Gordon was eleven years older than Kate – and sixteen years older than her husband – and had already had a successful Broadway and film career. Later, she would win an Academy Award for Best Supporting Actress in 1969's *Rosemary's Baby.* She is still venerated for her role in the 1971 cult classic *Harold and Maude.*

Like Kate, Gordon had survived an entanglement with that notorious lothario Jed Harris. Gordon and Harris never married, but they had a son in 1929 and lived together in an attempt to provide him with a normal upbringing. By the time the child was four, however, Harris was having affairs with both Kate and Margaret Sullavan.

Gordon had appeared on Broadway in leading roles in two plays she had written herself, and her success as both an actress and writer rivaled her husband Garson's acclaim as a writer and a producer. Garson and Ruth and Kate and Tracy shared similar interests and were well matched. Like Kate and Tracy, the photographer and set designer Cecil Beaton wrote, Gordon and Kanin knew how to "dispense with all unnecessary impediments, driving right to the point, sticking to it, and brooking no interruptions."

Beaton likened Gordon and Kanin to "a couple of athletes; their training is rigorous . . . It is typical of [Ruth] and her husband that they both have much work in hand while there is much already ready for production. Garson with a couple of film scripts and a play, Ruth with three plays."

Gordon and Kanin quickly became Kate and Tracy's closest friends and even bought a home next to Kate's on East Forty-Ninth Street in Manhattan. Kate liked the fact that that they did not drink and hoped their abstinence would rub off on Tracy.

Though she no longer needed their constant companionship, Kate maintained her friendships with Harding and Luddy, but these were mostly long-distance relationships now that she was with Tracy. Always fiercely loyal, she clung to them tightly, even though their busy lives rarely intersected.

Meanwhile, Kate was thrilled with her relationship with Tracy, who had managed to stay sober for so long that Kanin asked him to star in his latest stage directorial effort, *The Rugged Path* by Robert E. Sherwood. Tracy was happy to get the work but understandably apprehensive - he hadn't been on the stage for fifteen years. "I'm coming back to Broadway to see if I can still act," he told a journalist in April.

"Most of all there hung over him the fear of losing so much as a single round in his continuing battle against alcohol," Kanin later said. "A few days lost in the production of a film was no great matter. The discipline of the theater was far more stringent."

Tracy leveled with Sherwood. "I could be good in this thing all right," he said. "But then, who knows? I could fall off [the wagon] and maybe not show up."

Kate encouraged Tracy to do the play, and with MGM's permission, he began rehearsals in the summer of 1945. After the show opened in Providence in the fall, however – to a sold-out crowd and tepid reviews - Tracy came down with what he called "history's worst case of the flu." With Kate's help, he took the stage anyway, fearful that if he missed a performance, the press would conclude he was drinking. By the time the show reached Boston, however, he was almost too ill to go on.

On top of his health problems, Tracy was also surprised to realize that, after such a long hiatus, he hated stage acting. As he later explained to a friend, "I couldn't say those goddamn lines over and over and over again every night . . . At least every day is a new day for me in films . . . But this thing

- every day, every day, over and over again."

Later, Kanin wrote, "In the ten days prior to the New York opening all the important relationships had deteriorated. Spencer was tense and unbending, could not, or would not, take direction." They both knew, he added, that "the circumstances had sullied our fine friendship."

The morning the play was set to open on Broadway, Kanin was unable to find Tracy, who finally arrived just in time for the show. He did his job, but the play itself was fundamentally flawed. Critic George Jean Nathan said his performance "injected at least a superficial belief into the unbelievable materials provided him."

Tracy speculated publicly about leaving the show even before it opened on Broadway, and he lasted there just six weeks before announcing he would be leaving in January of 1946, forcing the show to close after eighty-one performances. The producers and cast and crew were furious at Tracy for publicly disparaging the play and jumping ship even when ticket sales were brisk, throwing 250 people out of work.

Sherwood, who continued to rewrite the play until it reached Broadway, blasted Tracy for having "the morals and scruples and integrity and human decency of a louse." Tracy had also gone back to drinking and, according to some accounts, was in a stupor for the final ten performances.

Both Kate and Tracy were relieved to return to the far more hospitable and lucrative environment of Hollywood – and Kate was anxious to get her career back on track after a long absence spent tending to Tracy. They agreed to co-star in

MGM's *The Sea of Grass*, based on Conrad Richter's novel about a tyrannical cattleman (Tracy) who forces homesteaders off government-owned property. Kate played his wife, who, unable to get him to change his ways, has an affair and bears an illegitimate child.

Elia Kazan, who at the time had directed only one other film, *A Tree Grows in Brooklyn*, had a difficult time working with Kate and Tracy. Kate was cool to him, and Tracy wouldn't buy into his ideas about acting. Kazan's belief in the "Method" approach – in which actors use their own experiences and emotional states to create their characters – did not sit well with Tracy, who appeared to use acting as a way to escape from his private demons rather than confront them.

Because MGM had an ample supply of background footage in its library, all outdoor scenes were shot on a sound stage with a rear projection screen, saving the studio money. This disappointed Kazan, who had eagerly looked forward to filming on location out on the Great Plains. When *The Sea of Grass* was finished, Louis B. Mayer was unsure of what to do with it and decided to shelve it for the time being.

Kate, meanwhile, was trying to get MGM to back a film adaptation of Anita Loos's play *Happy Birthday*, but Eric Johnston, president of the Motion Picture Association of America (MPAA), would not allow it. Johnston argued that the story – Kate would play a teetotaler who gets drunk and ardently pursues the man of her dreams - promoted alcohol abuse.

At the same time, Kate was still taking care of a suffering Tracy, who – with *The Sea of Grass* under wraps - had gone almost a year without making a film. They continued to live separately, Kate in her Coldwater Canyon home near Beverly Hills, and Tracy in a modest guest cottage on George Cukor's estate. This would be Tracy's home for the rest of his life. Kate would later consider it her home, too, and lived there alone for over a decade after his death.

Though both had lived in California for more than fifteen years, neither felt settled in; Tracy, in particular, eschewed possessions, believing that "everything you own . . . gets to be a burden . . . I like to check in and check out." Though he visited Louise and the kids at the ranch every Friday, he didn't feel at home there either.

Even though she was approaching forty, Kate still called Fenwick and West Hartford her home and continued to send her money home to daddy, who had a secretary pay her bills and provide her an allowance. In Hollywood and Turtle Bay, her personal belongings could fit into a few pieces of luggage.

With a small staff, Kate managed both her household and Tracy's with no interference from her beau, who considered anything connected to domestic life to be woman's work. Since he was still technically married, he appreciated Kate's willingness to live alone. But whatever she did, she did with Tracy in mind, subjugating her own needs to his.

Kate finally got back to work with Edward Chodorov's film, *Undercurrent*, her first attempt at the suspense genre. Upon meeting director Vincente Minelli, she told him, "I'm sure we'll get along," which sounded to him like both an order and a thinly-veiled threat. "Never had I met anyone with such self-assurance," he said. "She made me nervous."

Kate was nervous, too: Her character was continually terrified and "getting the right horrified reaction" was a challenge. Though she and Minelli clashed at the beginning, Kate eventually warmed up to him and also befriended his wife, Judy Garland, and their young daughter, Liza Minelli.

The plot of *Undercurrent* centers on Kate's character, Ann Hamilton, a naive woman who marries Alan Garroway, a charming, successful businessman, played by Robert Taylor. Alan tells his wife that his brother Michael - played by Robert Mitchum - is psychotic and has committed murder. When Michael shows up, however, he's kind and articulate. Kate's character falls in love with Michael as she gradually realizes that the psychotic murderer is actually her husband.

Kate thought someone like Ingrid Bergman would be better suited to the role but nevertheless enjoyed making the film and her new friendship with the Minellis - and Garland in particular. Aware of Garland's fragile emotional state, she did her best to be cooperative with Garland's husband on the set.

She was not, however, fond of Mitchum. When she passed by his dressing room one day and saw his stand-in, Boyd Coheen, drawing, she told him, "You know young man, you have obvious talent. You really should do something with it instead of working for some cheap flash actor like Mr. Mitchum."

Coheen, loyal to Mitchum, replied, "Thanks for the advice, Miss Hepburn. Now, may I make a request?"

"Yes, of course," she said.

"Should I survive you, would you bequeath me that lovely

collection of bones?" he said, then shut the door in her face.

Turning around to find Mitchum standing behind her, she said, "You can't be all bad with friends like that."

Kate's performance in *Undercurrent* was not her best, but the film was a commercial success when it was released in November of 1946, earning a profit of $1 million at the box office. It also gave her something to focus on while she took care of Tracy without draining too much of her energy.

In April of 1947, *The Sea of Grass* was finally released and fared better than predicted, with some critics oblivious to the studio's use of rear projection. One even gushed that the "vast, flat New Mexico desert with the 'sea of grass' high on a table-rock mesa, waving now lazily, now stormily, ended like a sea as far as the camera eye can reach." Despite Mayer's reservations – and Kazan admonishing his friends not to see it – the film did remarkably well at the box office, earning a profit of $742,000.

Toward the end of 1947, Tracy starred in MGM's *Cass Timberlane* while Kate made *Song of Love*, the story of nineteenth-century German musicians Clara and Robert Schumann. To authenticate her portrayal of Clara, Kate took daily piano lessons and eventually mastered some of Schumann's more difficult compositions. *Time* magazine wrote that Kate played Clara "with skill and feeling . . . She is fascinating to watch at the piano, using the claw-like nineteenth century style."

The story, directed by Clarence Brown and co-starring Paul Henreid as Robert Schumann, closely paralleled Kate's own life: a strong, successful woman who had dedicated herself to a remarkable but tormented man. Though the film would ultimately lose more than $1 million for the studio, it was one of Kate's most skillful performances.

Around this time, with a presidential campaign heating up, Kate's art began imitating her life in other ways. Her roller-coaster career was about to take a sharp political turn to the left, both on and off the set.

Both Kate and Tracy had supported President Franklin Roosevelt but pursued separate political paths when the president died and Vice President Harry Truman suddenly became commander-in-chief. Tracy remained faithful to the Democratic Party, but Kate could not condone Truman's decision to drop the atomic bomb on Hiroshima and Nagasaki or his increasing antagonism toward Russia. In the 1948 election, she backed the Progressive Party candidate Henry A. Wallace, who had been Roosevelt's vice president before Truman.

Because Wallace was endorsed by both the Communist Party and the American Labor party of New York State, his supporters were seen as pro-Communism and labeled "pinkos," a derogatory term for anyone with leftist leanings. A vocal Hollywood contingent also supported Wallace, which resulted in congressional investigations into the movie industry and some of its brightest stars.

In 1947, the House Un-American Activities Committee, a Congressional committee formed to root out Nazi sympathizers during the war years, sent its Chairman, J. Parnell Thomas, to investigate possible subversive activities and un-American influences in motion pictures. Those who refused to cooperate with the committee often lost their jobs and were blacklisted by the film industry, effectively prevented from working; some even served prison terms after being cited for contempt of Congress.

When Wallace was denied permission to lease the Hollywood Bowl for a political speech, Kate and other members of the Hollywood elite spoke at a massive rally on his behalf at Los Angeles's Gilmore Stadium in May of 1947. In an embarrassing faux pas, she accidentally wore pink. "At first I was going to wear white, and then I decided they'd think I was the dove of peace so I wore pink," she said. "Pink! How could I have been so dumb!"

At the rally, a number of passionate speakers denounced the House committee's witch hunt, but Kate stole the show. "J. Parnell Thomas is engaged in a personally conducted smear campaign of the motion picture industry," she said. "He is aided and abetted in his efforts by a group of super patriots who call themselves the Motion Picture Alliance for the Preservation of American Ideals. For myself, I want no part of their ideals or those of Mr. Thomas. The artist since the beginning of time has always expressed the aspirations and dreams of his people. Silence the artist and you have silenced the most articulate voice the people have."

Judy Garland chimed in as well. "Before every free conscience in America is subpoenaed, please speak up! Say your piece. Write your Congressman a letter! Let the Congress know what you think of its 'Un-American Committee,'" she said. "Tell them how much you resent Mr. Thomas's kicking the living daylights out of the Bill of Rights!"

Later, Kate explained why she took part in the rally. "[The actor] Edward G. Robinson was supposed to make that speech, and I thought, Well, here I am. He's Jewish and very left of center, so he would certainly be suspect by that committee. My ancestors were `on the *Mayflower.*' There's nothing that they can tack onto me. I've never been a member of any organization of any kind in my whole life. I'll make the speech."

But she was shocked by the reaction: "The headlines against me and the articles against me were vicious, absolutely vicious," she recalled.

Kate had yet to make her next movie with Tracy – the political comedy *State of the Union* – but she was already deeply embroiled in her own political controversies that threatened to derail her career.

15
"THERE ARE ACTRESSES – THEN THERE IS HEPBURN"

The negative press caused by Kate's defiant speech against censorship in May of 1947 was creating big problems for her studio, MGM. The studio had one Hepburn film playing in theaters – *The Sea of Grass* – and another – *Song of Love* – scheduled for release in the fall.

MGM Chief Louis B. Mayer – a staunch Republican – sent for her. When she sat down with him, he asked, "Katharine, why did you make that speech?"

"I think the situation is idiotic and out of hand," she told him. "People are being crucified who can't afford it, and I can afford it."

On the other hand, said, she understood his difficult position. "Mr. Mayer, I do not blame you at all for being upset. You have got to sell the picture with me in it, and you are going to run into trouble. I agree with you; as I am under contract to you, I put you in an enormously embarrassing situation by making the speech. Had I asked you if I could make the speech, you would have said no.

"Now let's face it," she continued. "I would have done it anyway. That would have put me in a very embarrassing situation. Anyway, I made it. On the other hand, I think you have a perfect right not to pay me a weekly salary from here on in, because I don't know how you can cast me in anything."

"That's not what we're discussing," he said.

"Mr. Mayer, maybe we should be discussing that, because I have done something which an employee of a large institution has no right to do. If you presume to take a weekly salary from someone, maybe you haven't got a right to go out and walk naked down the street."

"We are not discussing that," he repeated.

Finally, Kate left the office, and Mayer did not take any action against her. "He never tried to use force or say, `I'll take your money away,'" She said. "[MGM] did not force their people. It was a paternalistic organization in the best and worst sense of the word. I have to say that Mayer never forced me to do anything that I didn't want to do."

Kate had made it clear that if subpoenaed by the HUAC, she would not name names. But she still had to watch her friends' careers suffer under its heavy-handed treatment, including screenwriters Donald Ogden Stewart and Ring Lardner, Jr.

For his part, Tracy also loathed J. Parnell Thomas and his committee but did not believe actors had any business dabbling in politics. When asked about those who did, he often said, "Remember who shot Lincoln."

In her on-screen political life, Kate was not Frank Capra's first choice for the female lead in *State of the Union*; the director had initially hired Claudette Colbert, but she backed out of production three days before filming began, reportedly because of disagreements with Capra. In desperate need of a replacement, he called Tracy and asked if Kate would consider taking the role of Mary Mathews, the estranged wife of Grant Mathews, played by Tracy, a dark horse Republican presidential candidate.

"I don't know," Tracy said. "But the bag of bones has been helping me rehearse. Kinda stops you, Frank, by the way she reads the woman's part. She's a real theater nut, you know.

She might do it for the hell of it." Capra was delighted when Kate called and accepted the job, appearing on the set Monday, even before her contract was negotiated. Waiting for her costume to be sewn, she played the first scenes in her pajamas and bathrobe.

"There are women and there are women - and then there is Kate," Capra said. "There are actresses and actresses - then there is Hepburn. A rare professional-amateur, acting is her hobby, her living, her love . . . If Katharine Hepburn made up her mind to become a runner, she'd be the first woman to break the four-minute mile."

On the set, there was predictable tension between Kate and Adolphe Menjou, who played the Republican political strategist Jim Conover. Menjou was an outspoken far-right conservative who had testified before the HUAC and named every liberal he knew in the industry as pro-Communist. "Scratch a do-gooder, like Hepburn, and they'll yell, 'Pravda,'" he said, referring to the official newspaper of the Communist Party in the Soviet Union. Tracy, infuriated by the remark, told Capra, "You scratch some members of the Hepburn clan and you're liable to get an ass full of buckshot."

On the set, Kate talked to Menjou only when she had to; in the film, Kate's character disliked his, making their antagonistic real-life relationship well-suited to their scenes together. Kate's strong feelings also enhanced her on-screen chemistry with Angela Lansbury's venomous character, the Republican newspaper magnate Kaye Thorndyke – who "sinks a fine fang," said the noted critic James Agee in *Time* – who attempts to get her lover, Tracy's character, into the

White House.

Unlike the stage version of *State of the Union*, in which writers incorporated current events to give the dialogue authenticity, the film version released in April of 1948 lacked a sense of immediacy and relevance – and abandoned some of the play's more controversial themes. Still, *State of the Union*'s spectacular cast and famous director generated a slick political film that, unlike the real world, had more charm than controversy (it even had some real-world impact, as some advisors to President Harry Truman believe the film helped convince him to run for re-election that year). And while Lansbury's performance received more acclaim - she was nominated for an Academy Award - the movie further solidified the glamorous Hollywood pairing of Hepburn and Tracy.

Toward the end of 1948, George Cukor asked Tracy to join him in England to play an obsessive father in the melodrama *Edward, My Son*, and he happily accepted. With Kate's old friend Edwin Knopf producing and Donald Ogden Stewart writing the screenplay, it was a perfect opportunity for Kate to tag along with her old pals and spend quality time with Tracy away from the prying eyes of the American press. Though Kate was considered for the female lead, the part went to Deborah Kerr, who was better suited for it.

When Tracy was filming, and Kate was exploring the shops and museums of London, Garson Kanin was working with Ruth Gordon on a screenplay that would be ready for them when they got back to the States. Sure enough, when Kate returned home in February 1949, she was handed the script for *Adam's Rib*.

Gordon and Kanin had been inspired by the real-life case of William and Dorothy Whitney, married lawyers who ended up divorcing and marrying their respective clients. The husband-and-wife filmmaking team, who knew a few things about a married couple in the same business, changed the story to create a battle-of-the-sexes comedy featuring married lawyers who find themselves on opposite sides in the trial of a wife accused of attempting to murder her philandering husband. The characters in *Adam's Rib* were flawed and temperamental, and the script's satirical quality and over-the-top comedy made a perfect vehicle for the Tracy-Hepburn team.

As always, Kate was closely involved in the development of the script. She and Cukor attended script conferences and visited courtrooms in Los Angeles on the lookout for details to make the film more authentic. Cukor decided to shoot in New York City, allowing Kate to remain at her Turtle Bay home while Tracy stayed at the nearby Waldorf Towers, close enough that they could walk to work.

Shooting in New York also allowed the director to give the film a nearly documentary feel in certain scenes. As the film opens, the cameras follow Doris Attinger through the subway and other actual locations as she tracks her cheating husband, giving the movie the atmosphere of what film critics in the 1960s would call *cinéma vérité*.

Behind the scenes, *Adam's Rib* also showed that Kate had matured into a more generous soul eager to help others rather than focusing exclusively on herself. As they were casting the film, she was eager for Judy Holliday to play Doris, the jealous wife who stands trial. Not only did they think Holliday would do a splendid job, but it might help her land a role in another film that she desperately wanted. Holliday had been a big hit in Kanin's Broadway play *Born Yesterday*, but the head of Columbia Pictures, Harry Cohn, wanted an established movie star for the film version.

"Judy was friendly with Spence, George Cukor, me, and of course the Kanins," Kate recalled later. "We all felt Judy must play the part [in *Born Yesterday*]. We, or actually Garson and I, went East to try to get Judy to play a tiny part in our movie [*Adam's Rib*], which would show Harry Cohn what she could do and how she could look."

Holliday was grateful but resisted; *Adam's Rib* was really a Hepburn-Tracy vehicle, and she worried that the relatively small part could set her career back. "We finally convinced her - makeup, clothes - a tiny scene but a great scene," Kate said. "And with my back always to the camera, her face always in view - big close-up."

Kate sent the scene to Cohn, who loved it and soon signed Holliday to star in *Born Yesterday*, also directed by Cukor. It proved to be a very wise move: Holliday won both an Academy Award and Golden Globe for Best Actress for her portrayal of Emma "Billie" Dawn, an uneducated young woman married to an older, wealthy mobster. The comedy/drama was a top box-office hit in 1950 and today is considered a classic.

Adam's Rib was also a resounding success when it came out in November of 1949 – not only for Kate and Tracy, but for the studio, too. The film made a sizable profit for MGM and earned Gordon and Kanin an Academy Award nomination for Best Screenplay.

Today, it is clear that *Adam's Rib*, with its story of married attorneys fighting over sexual double standards, was far ahead of its time. "A boy sows a wild oat or two, the whole world winks," Kate's character says about the charges against her female client. "A girl does the same – scandal!" Critic and historian Robin Wood called it "perhaps the most explicitly feminist of all Hepburn movies."

In fact, *Adam's Rib* was the logical extension of the battles over sexual stereotyping seen in some of Kate's earlier films, such as *Woman of the Year.* And it had a lasting impact by inspiring many similar films: a short-lived 1973 ABC television series starring Blythe Danner and Ken Howard; Joel and Ethan Coen's comedy *Intolerable Cruelty* in 2003 with George Clooney and Catherine Zeta-Jones; and 2004's *Laws of Attraction* with Pierce Brosnan and Julianne Moore.

With nothing on the horizon for the Tracy/Hepburn duo after *Adam's Rib*, Tracy agreed to play a former prisoner of Alcatraz in another Knopf-produced film, *Malaya* - the type of tough guy role that had made him famous. He looked the part. At forty-nine, Tracy appeared to be an older man; his hair was gray and his face deeply creased from a lifetime of cigarettes and booze. But since his career did not depend on playing romantic leads, casting directors didn't seem to care.

Kate, now forty-two, was still lean and healthy, although years of heavy smoking had deepened the tenor of her voice. She had learned a lot from Tracy, and it showed: Her technical skills had improved, and her knowledge of film-making had expanded, permitting her to take almost any role and make it her own. Like Tracy, she was no longer interested in glamorous or romantic roles, just good ones.

Despite all they had been through together and meant to each other, the relationship between Kate and Tracy had grown fragile. Tracy didn't take as kindly to Kate's interfering with his drinking and resented others who tried to help. By the time he finished *Malaya*, the two had separated.

Meanwhile, the HUAC was still trying to purge the film industry of "un-Americans," and included Kate on a list, released in June 1949, that named hundreds of actors, writers, and directors that the committee believed "followed or appeased some of the Communist party line program over a long period of time." Frank Sinatra called the list "the product of liars, and liars to me make very un-American leaders . . . and I'm Right not Left."

Many on the list attempted to defend themselves in the press, but Kate "refused to dignify [the] un-American accusation with a reply."

During this time, Kate missed the theater and was planning a return to the stage when Lawrence Langner of the Theatre Guild asked her to play the part of Rosalind in Shakespeare's *As You Like It*. She was hesitant to accept: It would be her first attempt at Shakespeare, and she would have to dress like a boy again, which had left the public cold in *Sylvia Scarlett*.

Langner persisted, however, and Kate finally consented. His co-producer, Theresa Helburn, was in London when she received a cable from Kate and Langner, saying, "Kate definitely wants to do *As You Like It* . . . both feel that there can be some good casting done in England . . . Kate says 'Don't be cheap - we only live once' and [I] say 'Don't be extravagant either.'"

To direct the play, Helburn suggested the British Shakespearean director Michael Benthall and persuaded him to fly to Hollywood so Kate could meet him. Appreciating his sensitivity and good sense of humor, Kate approved, and asked Constance Collier, the Shakespearean actress she had befriended during *Stage Door*, to help hone her performance. A few days later, Kate flew to New York with Collier and her secretary, Phyllis Wilbourn, a young British woman who would later spend decades as Kate's trusted assistant.

As You Like It wasn't one of Shakespeare's more popular works in contemporary theater - its longest run in America had lasted only sixty performances in New York in 1902. Still, the part of Rosalind was a substantial one, and some of the greatest stage actresses of the day were drawn to the role - Sarah Siddons, Madame Modjeska, Lily Langtry, and Julia Marlowe - but they had played it on tour or in repertory. Kate liked the character's optimism and hope, which reminded her of early days in New York. "I was so happy and so wild with excitement that my feet never touched the pavement. I was always five feet above the sidewalk," she later recalled. "We all like to see life in terms of fairy tales," she said, and *As You Like It* was a "pure, idealized, fabulous romance."

Kate worked with Collier three hours a day for six months to synchronize the rhythm of the dialogue and learn to speak Shakespearean English naturally. She worked hard to soften Rosalind and avoid the mannishness of her *Sylvia Scarlett* performance, ultimately creating a character who was restrained and ladylike.

Tracy, having undergone a change of heart, was calling her

at all hours of the day. Kate finally agreed to meet him when the play opened in Cleveland. At their clandestine meeting, he promised to stop drinking, and she agreed to see him in New York when the show hit Broadway.

Like most of her theater tours, *As You Like It* was well attended and financially successful, and the press even complimented her on her legs. New York critics were still churlish, however; when the show opened on Broadway at the Cort Theatre in January of 1950, Brooks Atkinson of *The New York Times* wrote, "There is too much Yankee in Miss Hepburn for Shakespeare's glades and lyric fancies." He admired James Bailey's costume designs, but said Kate was too "honest and straightforward" to play a "helpless, bewitched, moon-struck maiden swooning through a magic forest . . . Miss Hepburn has too sharply defined a personality for such romantic make-believe."

Later, Kate dug up those old reviews. "Looking back on my notices, which I had not read at the time, I have the impression that I was irritating to the critics," she said. "They liked me in *The Philadelphia Story,* but in Shakespeare - well - it was sort of `she has a nerve to be doing this.' Well I don't know. I did study and work hard and Constance was a great help and it was exciting. At least I enjoyed it."

Kate endured the criticism with aplomb and continued working with Collier, improving as the show went on. Audiences loved it. Even today, her version of *As You Like It* remains the longest-running Broadway production of the play, at 145 performances.

Tracy couldn't keep his promise to stay sober, and after endless shouting matches, Kate once again expelled him from her Turtle Bay home. He returned to Hollywood before her Broadway show ended.

After its New York run, *As You Like It* headed to the Midwest for another tour. Without Tracy, Kate was lonely and miserable as she waited for the scenery to be set up in one obscure theater after another. Other than performing, she did little more than sleep, eat, and curl her hair.

By the time the tour reached Tulsa, Oklahoma, she was an irritable mess. When her driver was stopped for going eighty miles an hour, Kate was summoned to court, where she paced the floor and hissed at the officer, "We would have been glad to slow down if you had just warned us. You don't have enough sense to be an officer." Then she leaned against an electric heater and burned her mink coat.

"It probably did not hurt that one thousand dollar coat too much, Miss Hepburn," the judge told her.

"One thousand? This coat cost five thousand," she responded.

The fine was $10, the exasperated judge told her, "but you better leave this courtroom now before I change my mind."

When Kate went back to California for the Christmas holidays, she and Tracy called another truce for a few weeks and spent their time together strolling around Cukor's estate, playing chess, and talking. MGM kept Tracy busy with *Father of the Bride* and *Father's Little Dividend*, keeping him in Hollywood for the early months of 1951.

As the tour of *As You Like It* wound down, Kate was ready to make a new film, but at forty-four, she had a harder time finding good roles. The increasing popularity of television was forcing Hollywood to give audiences something they couldn't find on the small screen, and studios were struggling with antitrust laws requiring them to divest themselves of their theaters. The economics of filmmaking were changing as new and independent producers began offering stars better fees and percentages.

It was during this precarious time in Kate's career that producer Sam Spiegel (then going by the name S. P. Eagle) began to explore the idea of a film adaptation of an adventure novel, set in Africa in the early 1900s, that could match Kate with another famous leading man, Humphrey Bogart.

16

"HOW I WENT TO AFRICA WITH BOGART, BACALL, AND HUSTON AND ALMOST LOST MY MIND"

While Kate was in Los Angeles on tour with *As You Like It,* Spiegel sent her the novel *African Queen* by British writer C. S. Forester. "I read it," Kate recalled later. "What a story! I was thrilled."

Published in 1935, the tale of a prim spinster and the drunken boat captain who takes her down a river in Africa had made the rounds in Hollywood for years. RKO considered making it with Charles Laughton and his wife, the actress Elsa Lanchester, but concluded that it would never work.

"It is dated, incredible, quite outside acceptable dramatic screen material," read the notes of one RKO script reader. "Its two characters are neither appealing nor sympathetic enough to sustain interest for an entire picture . . . Both are physically unattractive and their love scenes are distasteful and not a little disgusting. It's no bargain at any price. No amount of rewriting can possibly salvage this dated yarn."

Warner Brothers bought the rights in 1946 and considered making it with Bette Davis in the female lead, but within a year had abandoned the idea and was looking to unload the property. The director John Huston, who always loved the book, asked Spiegel, his producing partner, to secure the rights for their independent film company, Horizon Pictures. By then, Huston was already becoming a screen legend for the classic films he made with Humphrey Bogart: *The Maltese Falcon* (1941), *The Treasure of the Sierra Madre* (1948), and *Key Largo* (1948).

When pitching the idea to Kate, Spiegel told her, falsely, that Bogart had already agreed to co-star and Huston would direct. Kate agreed to do the film for $65,000 in cash, an equal amount in deferred payments, and 10 percent of the film's profits. Spiegel then told similar lies to Bogart and Huston, both of whom, unaware that he had yet to secure the rights to the property, also agreed.

Now Spiegel had two big stars and a famous director but not the $50,000 Warner Brothers wanted for the rights to the story. So he went to Sound Services Inc., a company that supplied studios with sound equipment, to propose that it finance the project. Sound Services didn't usually do this kind of thing – it wasn't a bank or a film-production company – but Spiegel not only promised to pay back the loan promptly but offered to give the company credit in its titles in exchange for using its equipment on location in Africa. It was an unusual arrangement, but the company agreed.

In January 1951, as Kate was wrapping up *As You Like It*, she got word from Spiegel that shooting would begin in Africa in April. That left Kate six weeks to prepare before she had to leave for London for wardrobe fittings.

The story of *The African Queen* is centered on Kate's character, Rose Sayer. With her missionary brother, she ministers to the natives of German East Africa during World War I. After her brother dies, Charlie Allnut, a scruffy riverboat captain played by Bogart, persuades her to escape the war-torn area in his small steamboat, *The African Queen*.

As she was preparing for her role, Kate learned of a fashion historian named Doris Langley Moore, who grew up in Africa and had an enormous collection of period clothes. "She said that the materials we used must be able to stand *sweaty* heat - and not muss too easily and not show dirt and not show whether they were wet or dry," Kate recalled. "So our first meeting [was] with her and Huston and me. He was fascinated by the underwear. I tried on every variety of split-pants, of chemise - and I was terrified that he was going to have me wear nothing but an envelope chemise [a loose-fitting, shirt-like undergarment] in the picture."

But Kate still hadn't seen a script. From the beginning, Huston had insisted that his friend James Agee help him write the screenplay. Agee was a poet, novelist, journalist, and film critic known today mostly for *Let Us Now Praise Famous Men*, his 1941 study of Alabama sharecroppers. The two holed up in a resort hotel outside of Santa Barbara to work on the screenplay but Agee – a heavy drinker and smoker – had a heart attack that put him out of commission before the script was completed.

"I kept asking for a script - but none appeared," Kate recalled. "I felt foreboding but Bogie, who had worked with John Huston before, said, `Don't worry. This is the way he does it . . . You'll see - it's worth it.' So I went along with Bogie."

In March, exhausted from the *As You Like It* tour and intense preparations for *The African Queen*, Kate went home to West Hartford. By this time, all her siblings had married and moved away, but her father, at seventy-five, was still going to the office daily, and her mother was still campaigning for accessible birth control and women's rights. With fourteen grandchildren, their Sunday dinners were as boisterous as ever, and their daily afternoon tea was served promptly at 4:00 p.m. in the dining room.

On St. Patrick's Day, Kate and her father went to Fenwick, leaving her mother in Hartford to take her afternoon nap.

Later, they returned for tea. "When we got home, we walked into the living room," she recalled later. "No fire in the fireplace. Mother's chair was empty. No fire? We rushed upstairs and opened the bedroom door. Mother was there in bed - dead."

"Oh no - no," her father said. "I can't - she can't –"

"Go down, Daddy," Kate said. "Go down - don't look –"

Her father went downstairs, and Kate tried to figure out what had happened. "She was getting dressed for tea. She must have felt something queer. She went from her dressing room into the bedroom, got into bed and with her left hand was pulling the covers up - and bingo - dead.

"I stood - my mother - dead - my darling mother - the only mother I'll ever have - gone.

"I took her hand - still warm - unclasped her fingers from the sheet she had pulled up - and I kissed her and went down to Dad. No goodbyes. Just gone."

Ever stoic, her father did not cry. But, Kate said, it was the only time she ever saw him "what shall I say? - thrown for a loop."

Kit was seventy-three years old. "She had had her share of serious problems," Kate said. "Her father's suicide. Her mother's death at thirty-four of cancer. She had been sixteen at the time. The responsibility of her two sisters as children twelve and fourteen."

Following the example of her parents – who, she recalled, never talked about their son Tom after he hanged himself at age fifteen – Kate's response to her mother's death was simple and clear: Be tough and move on with life. "The thing about life is that you must survive," she said later. "Life is going to be difficult and dreadful things will happen. What you do is to move along, get on with it and be tough. Not in the sense of being mean to others, but tough with yourself and making a deadly effort not to be defeated."

On April 13, just weeks after her mother's death, Kate got "on with it" by packing her bags for Africa, and, with Constance Collier, boarded a freighter-passenger ship to Liverpool, England. From there, Spiegel hired a Rolls-Royce to take them to Claridge's in London, where he had reserved a luxurious suite that Kate doubted he could afford. At a welcoming party in one of the ballrooms, she announced, with typical dramatic flair and exaggeration: "I'm tall, skinny (117 pounds) with a lot of freckles, and I can't stop growing. I'm five feet eight inches now, and I've put on an inch in the last year. You could call me an antelope; swift, lean, graceful (I hope) and freckled."

The *Sunday Express* wrote that Kate "wore her favorite attention getting costume - slacks and a severely cut jacket, which made her look like a male impersonator." Bogart's wife, the film star Lauren Bacall, who had accompanied her husband on the trip, exclaimed, "There was a press conference at Claridge's for which I got myself all done up in a Balenciaga suit, and Katharine Hepburn stole the show in her pants."

Kate, Bogart, and Bacall flew to Rome, where they waited for Spiegel to arrive with the completed script – the novelist and screenwriter Peter Viertel having taken over after Agee's heart attack - before boarding a plane for the Belgian Congo. Kate hid in the airplane bathroom to avoid the media, causing a temporary scare that she had been lost somehow. Bacall found her in the ladies room, "laughing uproariously at having outwitted the press."

At the time, it was highly unusual to film a Hollywood movie in a remote location like Africa, but Huston insisted. "I wanted these characters to sweat when the script called for it," he explained in an interview. "On a sound stage you fake it, but in Africa you don't have to imagine that it's hot, that it's so hot, that it's so humid and wet that cigarettes turn green with mold; it really is hot and clothes do mildew overnight - and when people sweat it isn't with the help of a make-up man. Africa was the only place to get what I was after."

After arriving in Léopoldville, the capital of the Belgian Congo, they traveled by boat to Stanleyville, where Spiegel and Viertel threw them a welcoming party featuring local dancers in full costume. The next day, their party boarded a small train to take them deeper into the Congo, where people living in grass huts stared at them as they rolled past.

Switching to cars and jeeps in Ponthierville, they drove to the Ruiki River and loaded their vehicles onto a raft and crossed to the opposite bank. After another hour's drive, they finally arrived at their camp and met Huston, who talked late into the night sharing stories about Africa: the terrain, the locals and their superstitions, the bugs, and the hunting he'd done on the trip.

When the sun came up the next morning, Kate got a closer look at her new living arrangements: a hut made of bamboo and palm leaves, with dirt floors covered by grass mats; a basin with a bottle of water sitting next to it; and an outdoor toilet and makeshift shower - essentially a platform with a bucket hanging above it. When the user pulled a string, cold water poured out through holes in the bottom of the bucket.

Living in the jungle with no close companions, Kate nervously chatted with Huston and the Bogarts - who would eventually become good friends - as they waited for the rain to stop: two days of downpours, followed by swarms of mosquitoes. Ever prepared, Kate had brought salve and passed it around to ease everyone's discomfort.

The boat used for the film, the *African Queen*, was a fully functional riverboat. To shoot the sequences as the boat steamed down the river, the crew devised a caravan made from four rafts powered by the *African Queen* herself.

One of the rafts carried a replica of the *Queen*, used for mock-up shots; another carried the lights and props, and a third one hauled a generator for power. The fourth raft - designed specifically for Kate by Huston – had a bathroom, full-length mirror, and a dressing room, but wound up being left behind after a few days because it was too cumbersome to haul.

In 1987, Kate wrote a book called, *The Making of the African Queen; or How I Went to Africa with Bogart, Bacall and Huston and Almost Lost My Mind.* In it, she tells of some priceless direction Huston gave her about how to improve her portrayal of Rose Sayer, which he felt she was playing too seriously.

"And I wondered - well – let me put it this way," Huston said one morning during breakfast in Kate's hut. "Have you by any chance seen any movies of - you know – newsreels - of Mrs. [Eleanor] Roosevelt – those newsreels where she visited the soldiers in the hospitals?"

"Yes, John – yes - I saw one," Kate replied. "Yes."

"Do you remember, Katie dear, that lovely smile?"

"Yes, John - yes - I do."

"Well, I was wondering. You know, thinking ahead of our story. And thinking of your skinny little face – a lovely little face, dear. But skinny. And those famous hollow cheeks. And that turned-down mouth. You know – when you look serious – you do look rather – well, serious."

A solution, he said, could be to "put on" a smile. "Like Mrs. Roosevelt - she felt she was ugly - she thought she looked better smiling – so she - chin up. The best is yet to come – onward ever onward - The society smile."

A long pause. Kate certainly knew all about putting on that "society smile" in the face of adversity.

"You mean – yes - I see," she said. "When I pour out the gin I - yes – yes - when I –"

"Well," he said, getting up to go. "Think it over . . . Perhaps it might be a useful –"

"He was gone," she said later. "I sat there. That is the goddamndest best piece of direction I have ever heard . . . I was his from there on in."

In her memoir, she said of Huston, "He was an amazing character. He had flashes. And those flashes were brilliant."

The cast and crew filmed seven days a week from 6:30 a.m. until the sun went down. The obstacles they encountered were numerous. At one point, the raft carrying the generator got stuck in a thicket on the riverbank, causing a boiler to topple over, nearly burning Kate, Bogart, and assistant director Guy Hamilton. Another day, black wasps attacked, leaving everyone badly stung. Poisonous black mamba snakes invaded the company's portable bathrooms. A few nights after the boiler incident, the *African Queen* sank. Huston radioed Spiegel to tell him, and the producer laughed, saying, "I thought you said the *African Queen* sank."

"That's right," Huston told him.

"Oy!" Spiegel said.

It took fifty-five Africans and thirty British crew members to lift the boat out of the muck and weeds.

After the steamer had been cleaned and fixed and the crew sailed back to their camp, they found their lodgings crawling with ants - inches deep on their floors and infesting their clothing and toiletries. To ward them off, they dug ditches lit with kerosene fires and swatted ants relentlessly, fighting them to the death. Huston called Kate "the Jeanne d' Arc [Joan of Arc] of Ruiki."

Despite the hardships, Kate fell in love with Africa and wrote of her adventures in long letters to Tracy.

Bogart, however, did not like Africa. The son of a successful portrait painter and a cardiopulmonary surgeon, he was accustomed to urban living. Despite his rough and rugged persona, Bogart was a well-bred man with a natural gentility and a keen intellect. The British television personality Alistair Cooke once observed, "Upon meeting Bogart, [I found I was] dealing here with two characters, one fictional, the other private . . . There was the movie Bogart, a character at once repellent and fascinating; and the complex private man . . . a product of upper middle-class respectability."

Spiegel was delighted with the chemistry between Bogart's Charlie Allnut, the disillusioned, hard-drinking riverboat captain, and Kate's Rose Sayer, a stout-hearted, yet brittle spinster; he was confident the film would be a hit. Everyone else on the production crew just wanted to make it out of Africa with their health intact. Some got malaria, others suffered with dysentery.

"The big joke was on me because I was rather self-righteous and I thought, 'Well, I'm traveling with two drunks [Huston and Bogart] I'd better not drink anything' - so I drank lots and lots of the water," Kate later said. "John [Huston] never got sick, Bogie never got sick - and I nearly died of the dysentery because the water was poisoned. Shows how sensible they were."

Nearly half the location shooting was done at Ruiki, and when it was finished, local dancers in full regalia performed for the company as part of a musical farewell organized by their chief. Bacall called it an "old fashioned jam session." The cast and crew were certain the worst was over as they moved on to a site near Butiaba to film the beginning of the story, which takes place in a German East African mission run by Rose's brother, Reverend Samuel (Robert Morley).

In the film, after their settlement is attacked and burned, her brother dies and Rose is forced to rely on Charlie and his riverboat. The crew constructed a village they could burn down, and with permission from their chief, Huston recruited locals to play the villagers. But the day they were supposed to arrive, none of them showed up. Huston later learned they had feared it was a trap and that they would be cannibalized - a ritual still practiced in the Congo at the time.

Crew members stayed on a steamboat while filming in Butiaba, living in small but comfortable cabins and enjoyed similar accommodations when they moved to Murchison Falls two weeks later.

Meanwhile, Huston frequently hunted in the mornings or late afternoons, a pastime that baffled Kate. "You seem to be such a sensitive person," she told him. "How can you shoot anything as beautiful as these creatures? Are you a murderer at heart?"

To understand, he told her, she would have to go with him. So she did - more than once. While she never shot anything, she carried his rifle and reveled in the beauty and the excitement of the jungle. One day, Huston hired a professional hunter to search for elephants, and after an hour, the three realized they were surrounded by a herd.

"The thing to do in such a situation is to retrace your steps as quietly as possible, getting clear of the herd," Huston said. "We started to do this, but the elephants picked up our scent [and], panicked and trumpeting, began to crash through the jungle all around us like big locomotives."

Suddenly, the herd dispersed, leaving them safely alone. On the return trip, Kate, wielding her eight-millimeter movie camera, approached a wild boar to capture it on film; luckily, it ignored her and trotted after its family instead of charging her down.

Bogart never joined them on a hunt, preferring to stay in camp drinking, telling stories, or reading books he'd brought along. He didn't care much for his character Charlie - Huston had talked him into the role - but when the cameras rolled, Bogart transformed himself into the gritty steamboat captain. Before he did, he'd turn to Huston and ask for help to stay in character: "John, don't let me lose it. Watch me. Don't let me lose it."

In Murchison Falls, the river water was found to be contaminated with tiny worms carrying a disease called bilharzia, as was the bottled water from Nairobi. Spiegel, who arrived at Murchison Falls for the last segment of the shooting, was horrified. "The worms penetrate the skin and stay with the victim for up to thirty years," Spiegel said. "The disease affects the liver and weakens you, and can eventually kill you. It's said to be the most agonizing way to die. At one time or another, practically everyone fell into the water. We would quickly fish them out, dry them down, spray them with a disinfectant and pray."

When a tarantula bit Spiegel on the back of his neck, Bacall gave him massive doses of penicillin she had brought along, possibly saving his life.

"The country is like a great sponge – it finally absorbs you," Kate wrote in her book about the making of *The African Queen*. "Eventually you will get malaria or you will get dysentery and whatever you do, if you don't keep doing it, the jungle will grow over you. Black or white, you've got to fight it every minute of the day."

On July 17, 1951, only two days later than scheduled, the company finished filming in Africa. Tracy was waiting for Kate in London when her flight landed, though they didn't get to spend as much time together as she wanted. She had to spend six weeks with Bogart filming at either Shepperton Studios or Worton Hall, where they shot scenes that required being in the water. Scenes with Rose's brother Reverend Samuel (Robert Morley) were filmed there, too, as was footage of them navigating the rapids.

All of the danger, discomfort, and diligent attention to detail, underscored by tremendous performances by Kate and Bogart, paid off. When the film - shot in Technicolor - opened in theaters just before Christmas, the audience not only saw Kate's flashing red hair and clear, gray eyes, they witnessed a more mature side of her – a woman whose dogged determination bears her through horrific hardships.

For her dazzling performance, Kate earned her fifth Academy Award nomination for Best Actress, although she would lose to Vivien Leigh, who won for *A Streetcar Named Desire*. The film received three other Oscar nominations: Huston for Best Director; Huston and Agee for Best Screenplay; and Bogart for Best Actor, which he won.

Throughout it all, Kate was still in love with Tracy. Huston said, "Many nights I sat with Katie on the top deck of the paddle boat [at Murchison Falls] and watched the eyes of the hippos in the water all around us; every eye seemed to be staring in our direction. And we talked. We talked about anything and everything. But there was never an idea of romance - Spencer Tracy was the only man in Kate's life."

Tracy was not nearly as devoted to her, however. While waiting for Kate to return from the Congo, he was in England with actress Joan Fontaine, first to make *Ivanhoe* and then *Decameron Nights*. After meeting mutual friends for dinner one night, Tracy called Fontaine at her hotel and asked her out. Out of respect for Kate, Fontaine turned him down and laughed when Tracy said that he and Kate were just good friends. Calling Fontaine in Sweden a few days later, he asked if she would reconsider going out with him when she got back to London.

"I'm afraid not," she said. "Not only is there Kate to consider, but you are a married man."

"I can get a divorce whenever I want to," Tracy responded. "But my wife and Kate like things just as they are."

While Kate was in Africa, Dr. Hepburn married a nurse who had worked in his office for many years, Madelaine Santa Croce, whom everyone called Santa. "I had always felt that Dad married Santa because he didn't want any of his children to feel that they were responsible for him," Kate said later. "It worked. Santa had always been in love with him, and she was thrilled with the idea. He gave her a wonderful life - full of adventure and study."

Kate eventually got used to the idea – "They had fascinating trips to Greece and Egypt. I went with them twice." But it was hard for her to accept her father's decision so soon after her mother's death.

Kate returned to the States in the summer of 1951. Three weeks after landing in New York, she boarded a train to Hollywood. With her mother gone, her dad remarried, and

Tracy as undependable as ever, the emotional foundations of her life were shaky at best. But Kate fell back on what she always did when times were tough – she kept on moving. In her mid-forties, an age when many actresses begin to fade away, Katharine Hepburn was just getting started.

17
"I WAS SWIMMING - AGAINST THE TIDE, BUT SWIMMING"

Accompanying Kate on the train to Los Angeles in the summer of 1951 were Ruth Gordon and Garson Kanin. They had written a new script, a romantic comedy called *Pat and Mike*, specifically to showcase Kate's athletic abilities. "As I watched Kate playing tennis one day," Kanin said later, "it occurred to me that her audience was missing a treat." Their screwball tale of Pat Pemberton, a female gym teacher and amateur athlete, and a sports promoter named Mike Conovan was a perfect vehicle for the Hepburn-Tracy team.

When she arrived in Hollywood, Kate moved into the house of Irene Mayer Selznick, a socialite and theater producer whose father was MGM head Louis B. Mayer. Irene had vacated the house after her divorce from David Selznick and was living happily in New York. Since 1947, she had allowed Kate to live at the house whenever she was in Hollywood. With Tracy still living in Cukor's guest house, Kate resumed her double housekeeping duties and focused again on his sobriety, which he once again vowed to maintain.

When she wasn't there, Tracy – now somewhat of a recluse off the set – read, listened to music, and smoked, and when he felt overwhelmed, he drank. To help him create new habits, Kate started brewing his coffee again and enforced cold showers and daily swims. He had put on some weight but wore it well and still had no problems getting the roles he wanted. He seemed pleased to have Kate back and was eager to make another movie with her.

Shooting for *Pat and Mike*, with George Cukor directing, began in January of 1952. Kate's character is a brilliant athlete who loses her confidence whenever her fiancé is around. She enlists the help of Tracy's shady sports promoter and together they face mobsters, a jealous boxer, and a growing mutual attraction. Famous athletes of the day appear in cameo roles or play themselves, including golfer Babe Didrikson and tennis champion Don Budge.

Kate worked hard to get in shape for the part, and it showed. When the film was released in June of 1952, *New York Times* film critic Bosley Crowther wrote, "She can swing a golf club or tennis racquet as adroitly as she can an epigram." Kate also swam, cycled, boxed, and played basketball in the film, looking youthful and fabulous. Her on-screen magic with Tracy earned Gordon and Kanin another Academy Award nomination, won approval from the critics, and made a splash at the box office. Later, Kate said that of the nine films she made with Tracy, *Pat and Mike* was her personal favorite.

It was a familiar, comfortable experience for Kate to be back in her old skin, making witty quips on a studio set. But for her, the era of playing in charming comedies had ended; *The African Queen* had ushered in a new phase of her life, and she yearned for more challenging roles. *Pat and Mike* also marked the end of her contract with MGM, and she decided not to renew to give herself more freedom to choose her projects. Looking to make a change, she moved back to New York while Tracy made his next film, *The Plymouth Adventure*.

Tracy also was frustrated with MGM but wasn't nearly as interested as Kate in traveling or living out of a suitcase while making independent productions. He wanted her to come back to California but she refused, instead accepting an offer in England that would pose one of her greatest challenges: the lead role in George Bernard Shaw's play *The Millionairess*.

Kate had turned the part down twice before, but this time felt good about taking it on. Shaw had written the play in 1936 specifically for the British actress Edith Evans, who rejected the lead role of Epifania, a spoiled heiress in search of a suitor, calling it "too icy."

Epifania, a sledgehammer of a woman who wields her millions like a weapon, was a role well suited to Kate's personality and acting style; Shaw had said the actress who played the part would have to be watched carefully, "for she'll have to play a scene where she applies jujitsu to her leading man, and she'll kill him if she isn't careful."

On March 15, 1952, Kate sailed for London with her friend and acting coach, Constance Collier, and Collier's secretary Phyllis Wilbourn; the three women stayed in a suite at Claridge's for the run of the play. Directed by Michael Benthall – who had directed Kate in *As You Like It* – the play was produced by Hugh "Binkie" Beaumont of the theatrical production company H. M. Tennent, which invested thousands of dollars in it. Beaumont funded pricey designer costumes for Kate and co-stars Robert Helpmann, who played Epifania's love interest, and Cyril Ritchard, her previous love interest who takes a beating from her jujitsu.

After six weeks of rehearsals, the show began a tour of English provinces, performing to enthusiastic full houses. By the time they wrapped in Brighton, their last stop, they knew they had a hit on their hands.

The play opened in London's New Theatre on June 26, 1952 - the hottest day of the year. The nearly 1,000 patrons who attended the show, however, did not seem to mind, nor did Kate; she played Epifania "with such a furious, raw-boned, strident vitality that it sweeps away likes and dislikes and presents the creature as a force of nature," wrote the *London Times*. Its critic, A. V. Cookman, described her portrayal as "so vivid in her vicious arrogance that she brings us quite as close as we want to come to feeling the same horrid fascination that Shaw felt in the middle thirties for unprincipled men and women who are born to boss the world by sheer force of personality."

The New York Times wrote that Kate "hit London with such a crack that she might have been a thunderbolt generating the sweltering weather." Even her harshest reviewers praised this performance: Britain's *News Chronicle* said Kate demonstrated "enormous range"; *The Times* noted her "rhythmic beauty"; and the *Daily Express* called her "a human hurricane." *The Sunday Times* wrote, "One feels as excited as the man who went over Niagara in a barrel."

Still, some critics were unimpressed. "This millionairess," *The Times* wrote, "the born-boss, who simply cannot help dominating people, and equally cannot help spreading devastation in her successful tracks, is not a live character. Shaw could not make a woman of her and Miss Hepburn does not try. What she has seen in this part is that it makes a superb vehicle for violence and it is on her ability to be violent in about twenty-five different ways that her triumph depends. Every now and then she is quiet for a space and the effect is that of a sudden shutting off of power in a boiler-factory. This is magnificent in its way, but it is still not acting."

Kate was no stranger to this kind of criticism. For decades, critics had damned her with faint praise, calling her performances a projection of her own personality rather than actual acting. But there was no denying that Epifania's personality was vastly different from Kate's own, just as Rose Sayer's had been. Though her distinctive voice, athletic form, and grace remained the same, Kate had grown as an actress, and her performance in *The Millionairess* was powerful proof.

But trouble lay ahead. Following her triumphant opening night, Kate came down with a bad case of laryngitis that she could not shake. "I pitched [my lines] louder and wilder than I could sustain and I began to have trouble," she recalled later. "After about six weeks or so I began to get hoarse, then worse and worse."

Beaumont was panicked - he knew that the success of the play rested on Kate's virtuoso performance. To combat the problem, Kate stopped talking completely when she was not on stage. For three months, she scribbled notes to anyone she needed to converse with, even when buying antique furniture to take back to the United States. "At the end, I never talked at all offstage," she said. Her restraint saved her – at least for the time being. Once she was on stage, only a keen ear could detect the slight scratchiness in her voice.

After the final performance of *The Millionairess* - number ninety-six - Kate's fans stormed the stage door, making it impossible for her to reach her car. The stage-doorkeeper came to her rescue, but once she was inside the car, her admirers blocked the driveway and refused to move. No longer needing to conserve her voice, Kate shouted, "Drive on. We'll sweep up the blood later!" As the car began to roll, fans finally dispersed as Kate waved goodbye from the window.

A few days later, Collier and Wilbourn took a cruise vacation on the luxury liner *Nieuw Amsterdam* while Irene Selznick joined Kate on a flight to Jamaica, where they met Noël Coward and his secretary Cole Lesley. Irene and Kate got extravagant, cruising around Jamaica in a sports car convertible they had had shipped to the island, something few Jamaicans had ever seen.

After this relaxing interlude, Kate flew to New York to star in the Broadway production of *The Millionairess*. Deciding to bring the show to New York was a difficult decision for Kate: She worried about spending more time away from Tracy, who was still in Hollywood, and how New York critics would react to her portrayal of Epifania. But the Theatre Guild was keen to produce *The Millionairess* stateside, so Benthall brought the play to New York with the original London company.

Advance buzz was strong, and the producers nearly sold out the entire ten-week run before opening night. But after just two dress rehearsals in the fall, disaster struck. Kate's voice gave out – again.

"We'll postpone the opening," said Lawrence Langner of the Theatre Guild.

"Oh bunk," Kate rasped in despair. "What's the point? I'll either die or I won't die. I've had a whole summer off. What's the point of kidding ourselves? Keep a-going, going. The question is, when comes 'gone'?"

The play opened at the Shubert Theatre on October 17, 1952 – and, as Kate had feared, her performance was panned by the critics. Brooks Atkinson of *The New York Times* wrote that while Kate had "doubtless more endurance than any actress alive . . . she takes every line in about the same key and tempo. What wit there may be lurking in the lines gets short shrift in this treatment . . . As a piece of theater literature *The Millionairess* is not worth all the energy she is squandering on it."

What the critics didn't seem to realize was how much Kate was suffering from vocal problems. "I struggled through that opening - half-strangled," she recalled. "Naturally, with such a limited range vocally, my performance hadn't the thrill and abandon required. No ring. So the play suffered and I certainly suffered. No zing. And it was a story about a woman of great zing.

She went to a doctor. "Well, Miss Hepburn, you're all wound up, aren't you?" he said. "Why don't you just take a little drink and relax . . ."

"My God . . . take a drink! I can't take a drink . . . my God! My mind would go. Don't you know anyone - any teacher - someone - some help - I've got a whole company . . . I've got to keep going. There must be something . . . someone . . ."

"Well, there's a man named Alfred Dixon. Why don't you . . ."

By this time, she was spending her weekends at Columbia Presbyterian hospital, "contemplating jumping out the window." Bobby Helpmann, her co-star in the play who had become a good friend, went to fetch Alfred Dixon. "Bobby came in the door of my hospital room," she recalled. "With him came a man - not tall, not short - inclined to be hefty. Fat, really. Big head - eyes far apart - big face. Sitting in bed, in despair, I thought, Well, he's not going to save my life . . .

"I'm Alfred Dixon . . ."

"Yes - so - what do you teach in a case like this?" she demanded. "What can you do?"

Dixon explained his theory about why she was so hoarse and explained his method of voice projection. "Something about dogs and panting," Kate recalled. "Good grief. Desperate, that's what I am - I'm desperate and you're talking about panting dogs. I want to die. I want to dive out that window and die. He's a big, pompous ass and I just wish he'd leave me to suffer."

Finally, the men left. "I sat there staring at space. Tomorrow another week would begin . . . agony." Kate went back home. "I was really low. Down – down . . . What to do? . . . Then I began to think. Don't be a hysterical ass. Try it."

She called Dixon and arranged to meet him at his studio on Thirty-Sixth Street that afternoon. He asked her to do a group of exercises. "The central idea of the whole thing was to get off the vagus nerve, which - when one is excited, scared, as actors are most of the time - makes one tighten up one's neck and throat and stop the natural flow of air from the diaphragm through a relaxed passage. My tendency had apparently always been to grab with my throat."

Kate understood immediately what he was talking about. These were the same ideas her first acting coach, Frances

Robinson-Duff, had tried to explain to her back in 1928, when she first arrived in New York as a naïve, ambitious twenty-one-year-old – "but at that point in life I didn't get the message," she recalled. "I suppose I was too occupied with my own adorable self. Now, just about to drown, I could feel that somehow it made sense."

After spending an hour with Dixon, Kate felt better. "I wasn't actually any better as far as my enraged vocal cords were concerned," she said. "But my mental attitude had changed. Instead of cowering, waiting for disaster, I was trying to find a path - a hole - a ray - a way out. I was going forward, not floating. I was swimming. Against the tide, but swimming."

Kate went to see Dixon every day. "And although I did not get better, I did not get worse. And I began to realize that if I could do it this way, I would not get worse. I could control it. Not it - me. And I maintained my status quo - just. I had a positive attitude. I kept afloat."

Kate got through the ten-week run that ended in December of 1952, and *The Millionairess* was considered a success. Pleased, Kate wanted to obtain the rights, adapt it to film, and star in it. After wrangling with Gabriel Pascal, who owned the rights to Shaw's plays, they finally agreed on a price Kate deemed reasonable.

Kate then hired Preston Sturges, one of Hollywood's most clever satirists, to adapt the play to the screen, and together, the two devised a script Garson Kanin called "beautifully conceived, hilariously written." Kate now owned the rights, had a well-written script and Sturges as director. But while

Kate's star was still high in Hollywood, Sturges's was not.

In an astonishing five-year period from 1939 to 1943, Sturges had turned out seven films, four of which – *The Lady Eve*, *Sullivan's Travels*, *The Palm Beach Story*, and *The Miracle of Morgan's Creek* – have been ranked among the American Film Institute's 100 funniest films of all time. But after that, he endured a string of failures, had gained a reputation as a temperamental headache, and was resented by studio chiefs for the unusual power he wielded as a rare hybrid writer-producer-director. When it came time to shop *The Millionairess*, not a single major studio or independent film-maker – in the United States or Europe – wanted to make the movie with him.

Meanwhile, Kate was concerned by some suspicious lesions on her skin, which turned out to be skin cancer, likely caused by sun exposure, possibly during the filming of *The African Queen*. On August 6, 1953, Kate underwent surgery at Hartford Hospital to have the lesions removed, and after her recuperation at Fenwick, went back to work trying to get a buyer for *The Millionairess* film package.

In January 1954, she approached John and James Woolf of the British production company Romulus Films, who had helped finance *The African Queen* and went on to work with director John Huston on *Moulin Rouge* (1952) and *Beat The Devil* (1953). When they declined the deal, she flew to London, and from her hotel room at Claridge's, made a series of desperate phone calls to the Woolf brothers, offering to work for nothing so she could pay Sturges. While the Woolfs appreciated Sturges's clever script and agreed that Kate was perfect for the role, they were concerned that the story and its characters would not transition well to the big screen.

What finally doomed the Hepburn-Sturges version of *The Millionairess* – which she later called the biggest disappointment of her career – remains a matter of speculation, especially since Kate does not mention the episode at all in her memoir. Some thought Kate, in her mid-forties, was becoming too old to be credible in the role and that producers preferred a younger actress. When 20th Century Fox finally produced a version of *The Millionairess* in 1960 – using a new script by Wolf Mankowitz only loosely based on the Shaw play – the leading role went to the sexy new star, Sophia Loren, twenty-seven years her junior. Co-starring Peter Sellers, the film was a huge success internationally, especially in England.

Kate felt like a failure. In addition to her frustration over her career – it had been two years since she made her last film, *Pat and Mike* – her relationship with Tracy had deteriorated, and he had started spending more time with his wife and children. With Louise, he was drinking less and was more subdued, but, as always, hardly seemed happy.

The rejection hurt Kate deeply. She was used to getting her way. According to accounts published much later, one of her staff members (who remained anonymous) said she sank into a depression and became "sullen, peevish, and argumentative. She behaved badly, was rude, cutting." When the offended staffer threatened to quit, Kate called her a deserter "leaving the sinking ship." In the end, however, "she asked me to stay (which I did), although she never was able to bring herself to apologize."

It was at this low point in her life that English director David Lean sent her the script for a new film he was making called *Summertime*. Lean was already highly successful, especially for his adaptations of novels by Charles Dickens (*Great Expectations* and *Oliver Twist*) but had yet to produce the big-screen epics that he would be best known for (*The Bridge on the River Kwai*, *Lawrence of Arabia*, and *Doctor Zhivago*). Lean had collaborated with the English writer H.E. Bate to write the *Summertime* screenplay as an adaptation of *The Time of the Cuckoo*, a stage play by Alfred Laurent.

Summertime tells the story of Jane Hudson, a school secretary from Akron, Ohio, who saves up her money and finally fulfills her life-long dream of going to Venice. Once in Italy, the lonely spinster falls in love with an antiques dealer she believes to be single and is heartbroken when she learns that he is married - although separated. Torn between her desire for happiness and her fear of a relationship that has no future, Hudson continues the affair but knows she must return home to Ohio.

Thrilled with the part, and the character of Jane, Kate eagerly agreed and set out for Italy with her usual traveling companions, Collier and Wilbourn. Once in Venice, the women took a room in the Bauer Grünwald Hotel, the only one with air conditioning and modern conveniences. They did their best to acclimate themselves to the unpleasant smell of the city, caused by the polluted water in the canals.

The sight of a movie crew in Venice created quite a stir, and the wary Venetians gawked at Kate and gossiped about how bony and unattractive she was. She was indeed thinner after the bouts of dysentery she contracted in Africa, and her face was scarred from the surgery for the skin cancer. Some prudish Venetians complained that the movie featured an illicit love affair; others feared that the filming would interfere with the tourist trade.

The producers did their best to appease the people of the city and even promised the Catholic Church that Kate and her fellow actresses would not bare their arms or wear short skirts in and around holy places like the St. Mark's Basilica in the Piazza San Marco. They had to re-shoot a scene showing Kate outside the Basilica wearing a sleeveless dress, covering her up with a long-sleeved shirt and full skirt.

In one memorable scene, Jane is filming her paramour's antique shop when she accidentally falls into a canal. Afraid that the filthy water would further damage her skin and impair her health, Kate objected to filming the scene in the canal, but Lean, insisting the scene look realistic, partitioned off a section of the canal with plastic sheets and filled it with disinfectant. Looking at the foamy water, Kate said, "If you think I'm going into that, you're crazy."

Vincent Korda, the Hungarian art director, suggested they use wind machines to blow the foam down the canal. With the suds out of the way, Kate - covered head to toe with Vaseline for protection - did the take four times before Lean was satisfied. After each take, she was pulled out of the water by a gondolier, then she dried her hair and replaced her wet dress with an identical dry one before falling in again. "It tastes lousy . . . like a swimming pool in California with all that chlorine," she said.

Though her skin was undamaged by the contaminated water, she did contract conjunctivitis, causing her eyes to itch and tear, a condition that would plague her the rest of her life.

Collier's health also began to suffer during the trip, sending her and Wilbourn back to New York. In their absence, other friends came to visit, including Noël Coward, who stayed five days, and then Tracy. There was palpable tension between Kate and Tracy, who had been spending a lot of time with Grace Kelly in preparation for their upcoming film *Tribute to a Bad Man*. Kelly's well-known dalliances with married men, including Gary Cooper, Bing Crosby, and Clark Gable – not to mention Tracy's own philandering – gave Kate ample reason for concern.

Kate was lonely and felt isolated from the cast and crew but knew she was responsible; the film crew assumed that she "had madly exciting things to do" and left her on her own, but she said later, "It's my own fault entirely. I am rather a sharp person. I have a sharp face and a sharp voice . . . It puts people off, I suppose."

When it was completed, *Summertime* ran afoul of censors and had to be edited; Hollywood's Production Code Administration particularly objected to the scene in which Jane and her Italian lover consummate their relationship. But the film was favorably reviewed when it was released in June of 1955, and Lean later called it his favorite of all his movies. Kate was nominated for yet another Oscar for Best Actress, though the winner was Anna Magnani for *The Rose Tattoo*.

Many years later, BBC Channel 4 reviewer Laura Bushell said, "Hepburn made a career out of playing vibrant heroines with a vulnerable side and it's her portrayal of Jane's insecurity and loneliness that give the film its substance . . . *Summertime*'s notions of dating etiquette and holiday romance have dated greatly . . . but as a coming-of-age story it remains touching. As a showcase for Katharine Hepburn, it is superb."

Kate's career, however, was entering an uncertain period. Now in her late forties, she found herself less in demand for the romantic parts she used to play. "Being an actor is such a humiliating experience," she said later. "You are selling yourself to the public, your face, your personality . . . As you get older, it becomes more humiliating because you've got less to sell."

Kate was depending less on her looks and more on her talent. As an actress, she had developed true proficiency in her performances, an ability to set her personality aside to create a believable character in her own image. Whether that was enough to make her happy in her own life, when she wasn't pretending to be someone else, was a far more complicated proposition.

18
"IF THIS WAS MEANT TO BE A TRAVESTY, IT IS"

On her way home from Italy after filming *Summertime*, Kate stopped in London and visited with Ruth Gordon, who was rehearsing for the part of Dolly Levi in the London production of *The Matchmaker*, a Thornton Wilder play that would later be adapted to film as the hit musical *Hello, Dolly*. Kate also paid a visit to Michael Benthall, her director for *The Millionairess* and *As You Like It*, and Robert Helpmann, her co-star *in The Millionairess*, who were preparing a trilogy of Shakespearean plays for a tour that summer in Australia.

Benthall and Helpmann asked Kate to join them on tour and play the three female leads: Katharine in *The Taming of the Shrew*, Isabella in *Measure for Measure* and Portia in *The Merchant of Venice*. Excited to return to the stage, Kate accepted immediately and went back to New York to prepare.

With her Shakespearean instructor unavailable - Constance Collier's health was deteriorating - Kate enlisted speech coach Alfred Dixon to help prepare her for the parts. Dixon's coaching methods were strange: In one of his exercises, Kate recalled later, she had to "make a mooing noise with lips closed, starting very low on the scale, gradually rising higher and higher and then slowly all the way down again, until at last you had to stop for lack of breath. The result resembled a loud, long air-raid warning emitted by a cow, repeated over and over again."

But Kate – worried that the laryngitis she suffered in *The Millionairess* would return – thought the exercise was brilliant, "the best loosener-upper in the world." Dixon's most counterintuitive advice was to never breathe deeply, but only inhale slightly when necessary. This prevented Kate's voice from cracking, giving her confidence for the difficult work ahead.

In April 1955, Kate was devastated to learn that Constance Collier had died in Manhattan. It left a big hole in her life: Collier had been a great friend, traveling companion, and coach, who had helped her immeasurably in her development as an actress, especially with demanding Shakespearean roles. It was a lonely time for Kate: Her friendships with Harding and Luddy had waned, as had her relationship with Tracy, who was still rumored to be pursuing Grace Kelly as he had Joan Fontaine. But in hard times, Kate knew that she was stronger than Tracy, who wallowed in self-pity and took his misery out on everyone around him.

Tracy viewed Kate's decision to go on the Australian tour as a personal attack on him. The day she left, May 5, he began to drink heavily. Shooting for *Tribute to a Bad Man* was scheduled to begin on June 1 in the Rocky Mountains, but Grace Kelly had backed out of the production and was replaced by a volatile Greek actress, Irene Papas. Additionally, the script was weak and the director, Robert Wise, was an unknown entity.

Though Wise would go on to make two of the most popular films of the 1960s - *West Side Story* and *The Sound of Music* - in 1955, he didn't have enough of a resume to impress Tracy, who arrived on location six days late, offering no explanation, and disappeared again two days later. With the star AWOL, there was panic on the set, and the producers and the director called Kate in Australia. A week later, Tracy resurfaced, only to complain that he couldn't stand the altitude - 8,000 feet above sea level - and insisted they film at a different location.

Howard Strickland, MGM's head of publicity and one of Tracy's few remaining friends at the studio, rushed to Colorado to help with negotiations. But Tracy wasn't interested. On June 25, studio executives fired Tracy and replaced him with James Cagney. A few weeks later, MGM terminated Tracy's contract.

Kate heard the bad news all the way in Australia: Tracy's alcoholism had done him in. Tracy called her himself, but there was nothing to be done.

Kate's tour in Australia was not going well either. The first nine weeks, with limited runs in Sydney and Brisbane, had been successful, but Melbourne did not like her. In a review of *Measure for Measure* printed on the front page a major Melbourne paper, one critic wrote, "I have no idea why Miss Hepburn chose to come to Melbourne, except that it was quite obvious her career must be over as a motion picture star." The Australians were not fond of Kate's films - only *The African Queen* had scored points at the Australian box-office. Meanwhile, with no air-conditioning in the theaters, Kate was sweltering in heavy costumes in 100-degree heat.

The one thing she did enjoy about the trip was the natural beauty of the land, and the "great shallow blue lakes [near Adelaide], surrounded by glistening white sand, black and white branches of trees sticking up out of the water and birds of every kind and description everywhere." She was fascinated by the lyrebird, which danced "like an Indian warrior about to go into battle."

When Kate returned to Hollywood after the Australian tour ended in November of 1955, she headed straight for Tracy's corner and stayed there. Despite all the talk that his career was over, he received an Oscar nomination that year for his performance in *Bad Day at Black Rock*, which John O'Hara of *Collier's* magazine had called "one of the finest motion pictures ever made."

Kate was more protective of Tracy than ever. "I suppose I had to prove something - to myself," she said later. "I felt I had reached out as an actress and felt more fulfilled. And so I wanted to reach out to Spence. I knew that he had to help himself, but I also knew that I could help him too - once I had fortified myself."

Over the last few years, Kate and Tracy had lived apart more often than together – but now, as his health declined, she wanted them to merge their lives as much as possible. She curbed her smoking to help him do the same and vowed not to leave him by himself anymore since that's often when the problems started. Tracy was now so ill, with a weak heart and a severely damaged liver from so much drinking, that his friends didn't think he had much time left. Kate did all she could to help, from watching his diet to making sure he got some exercise. When Tracy flew to Europe to make *The Mountain* with Paramount, she went with him.

The film, about a plane crash in the Alps, was shot in high altitudes at Chamonix, France, which was hard on Tracy's heart and lungs. Though she stayed out of his way on the set, she otherwise rarely left him alone.

Phyllis Wilbourn, whom Kate hired as an assistant after the death of Collier, came with Kate wherever she went. Wilbourn's relationship with Tracy was sketchy; she wasn't used to his barbs and confrontational manner, and he wasn't used to having her underfoot. To taunt her, he learned to mimic her, finding, as Garson Kanin noted, "the precise tone and pitch of her voice, the lovely lilt of her speech, the best of her upper-class British accent." When the mood struck him, Kanin said, Tracy would reply to Wilbourn's questions in her own voice, causing her to blush and stammer.

Well aware of Tracy's cruel streak, Kate appreciated Wilbourn's perseverance and did her best to make amends. "She is a totally selfless person, working for a totally selfish person," Kate said later. Her relationship with Wilbourn would be among the most enduring of her life, lasting into their old age. "She can do everything, which through the years has been wildly handy for me," Kate said. "She is a very good cook. She can talk to anyone - from the president to the doorman. She never takes a vacation. She backs me up. And she is - what should I say? - she is *there* to help me - to keep me company - to let me be alone - to do things for other people which I should be doing for other people . . . She's unique. She's an angel."

If Tracy did not care much for Wilbourn, she was in good company. He didn't like many of Kate's friends - he thought Harding was extremely spoiled – though he did enjoy Irene Selznick, who often went swimming with Kate when she was in California – which often meant breaking into other people's property. "Mind you, nothing as convenient as the pool at George's [Cukor]," Irene said. "Kate would bring masses of towels, a huge lunch, and we'd make a day of it . . . We'd swim our way across town, from one pool to another, until we reached the surf at Malibu. We gave our patronage to friends and strangers alike, showing up uninvited, unexpected, but we assumed welcome . . . An empty house and a sparkling pool had the effect on us of a formal invitation."

After Irene sold her house in 1953, she and Kate would stop in "to see how the house was doing" and once gained entry through a pantry door that had been left open. In this respect, Kate still hadn't grown up. Even in her late forties, she was still trespassing, just as she did as a mischievous child and in her rowdy early Hollywood years with Harding. "We felt like Tom Sawyer and Huck Finn," Irene said. "For two people so passionate about privacy, this was a hell of a thing to do. We knew better, but somehow felt entitled."

One day, checking out the upstairs bedrooms of Irene's former home, they heard a woman's voice downstairs, sounding terrified. Kate, chagrined, called out, "We'll be right down. It's all right, I assure you." Seeing the shocked look on the woman's face, Kate apologized profusely as the woman led them to the front door. It's a wonder they were not arrested.

Late in 1955, with Kate and Tracy both back in Hollywood, Kate agreed to star in Paramount Studio's *The Rainmaker*, playing a Depression-era woman who lives with her father and brothers on a Kansas cattle ranch. *The Rainmaker*, written and adapted to the screen by N. Richard Nash, was directed by Joseph Anthony. The title character, a con man who comes to town promising to end a long drought, was played by the hot young actor Burt Lancaster, who just two years earlier had made the iconic scene of smooching with Deborah Kerr on a Hawaiian beach as the surf crashes around them in *From Here to Eternity*. Kate's scenes with Lancaster were much less racy, but she appreciated the fact that she could wear a cotton shirtdress or pants for most of the shooting.

While the film was the first Anthony had directed, his proficiency as a screenwriter, playwright, actor, and dancer infused *The Rainmaker* with an ethereal quality Kate had never experienced, allowing her to shine in a graceful and subdued performance. (Anthony disliked actors who over-acted; once, he instructed an actress he was directing on stage, "Don't just do something. Stand there!")

As in *Summertime*, Kate was playing a lonely woman em-powered by a romantic affair, which seemed to be a new niche for her. "With Lizzie Curry [*The Rainmaker*] and Jane Hudson [*Summertime*] and Rosie Sayer [*The African Queen*] - I was playing me," she said later. "It wasn't difficult for me to play those women, because I'm the maiden aunt." *The Rainmaker* earned Kate an Oscar nomination for the second year in a row, her seventh overall.

Kate finished the film in time for the holidays and went home to Fenwick for Christmas with Tracy in tow. The re-lationship between her father and Tracy was still stilted and awkward – the two men had similar temperaments and nei-ther approved of the other's influence over Kate – but some progress was being made: Dr. Hepburn had finally stopped expecting Tracy to marry his forty-eight-year-old daughter.

In January of 1956, Kate and Tracy headed to London, where Kate was to film a cold war comedy, *The Iron Petti-coat,* at Pinewood Studios. Originally titled *Not for Money,* based on a story by producer Harry Saltzman, the screen-play was written by Ben Hecht, one of Hollywood's greatest screenwriters (author of *The Front Page, Spellbound,* and *Notorious,* among others). Hecht had Kate in mind to play the female lead, Vinka Kovelenko, a captain in the Russian Air Force who lands a Russian jet in West German territory and is taken prisoner.

Hecht wanted Cary Grant to play the male lead, Capt. Chuck Lockwood, who is ordered to sell the Soviet aviatrix on all that is good about America and convince her to defect. But Grant was unavailable, so Bob Hope stepped in. Hope saw a golden opportunity to escape the United States at a time when his reputation as a family man was being tarnished by the publication of a tell-all book by a former lover, Barbara Payton.

The film's creators were hoping to capitalize on the success of a movie with a similar theme, the 1939 Greta Garbo-Melvyn Douglas comedy, *Ninotchka*. But Hope threw a wrench into things by turning the script over to his own gag writers, as was his usual practice, and they changed Hope's role from a debonair leading man to his usual wise-cracking comic self.

Worse, many of Kate's best scenes were cut, ruining her aspirations to create a Garbo-like role. Privately, she called Hope "the biggest egomaniac with whom I have ever worked in my entire life" and characterized the film as "a cheap vaudeville act" with her stuck in the role of the "stooge."

Aside from the palpable hostility on the set, the conjunctivitis Kate had picked up from her dip in Venice's Grand Canal was giving her trouble. In a conversation with *Evening Standard* reporter Thomas Wiseman, Kate said, "I used to get by in films on my eyes and my teeth. For this film I think I might have to manage on my teeth."

Kate carried on stoically, doing her best despite her abbreviated part, the frequent tearing of her eyes, and a co-star she did not care for. Director Ralph Thomas appreciated Kate's cooperation: "She never lost her spirit, but it was very difficult for her to perform with someone whose stock in trade was telling funny stories." Later, Kate said that Hope thought her sense of humor was basically "zilch."

The Iron Petticoat came out in England in June of 1956, but when Metro-Goldwyn-Mayer released it in the American market in December, Hope – whose production company controlled the US rights – had cut twelve minutes from it. In a full-page ad in *The Hollywood Reporter*, Hecht accused Hope of "blowtorching" Kate's role and offered Kate and her fans an apology.

"Miss Hepburn was removed from it by 50 percent," Hecht told journalist Mike Wallace in a 1958 interview. "I got irritated and took my name off it – it had nothing to do with the movie I wrote." Hope replied with an open letter apologizing that Hecht had a hit on his hands and hoped they would keep up corresponding in public; his ad was signed "Bob 'Blowtorch' Hope."

It was certainly an exaggeration to call the movie a hit – but thanks to low production costs, *The Iron Petticoat* actually turned a small profit. However, it was savaged by critics. "Miss Hepburn's Russian affectations and accent are simply horrible, and Mr. Hope's wistful efforts with feeble gags to hold his franchise as a funny man are downright sad," wrote Bosley Crowther in *The New York Times*. "The notion of these two characters falling rapturously, romantically in love is virtually revolting. If this was meant to be a travesty, it is."

Later, Kate said it was the worst movie she had ever made, adding that she couldn't even bring herself to watch the final product.

Horrified by the experience, Kate tried to put the mess behind her and, for a long while, simply refused to talk about it. Tracy's career, meanwhile, took a turn for the better when he was considered to star in the film adaptation of Ernest Hemingway's *The Old Man and the Sea*.

Kate's former beau Leland Hayward, who had produced successful stage productions of *South Pacific* and *Oklahoma!*, desperately wanted Tracy to play the part of Santiago, the aging Cuban fisherman who battles a giant marlin in the waters of the Gulf Stream. Considering Tracy's health problems and the challenges of shooting on location, Kate was concerned, but Hayward argued that this could be the role of his lifetime. Hayward still had to convince Hemingway, who had his doubts about Tracy, and find a film company willing to take on such an ambitious project with such an unpredictable actor.

To prove the film had commercial appeal, Hayward suggested Tracy and a child actor tour the country doing readings from the book. Hemingway approved, but Tracy refused. Hayward then proposed making a documentary using "local people on a local ocean with a local boat" which Tracy would narrate. Tracy agreed.

To secure financing, Hayward assured Warner Brothers that Tracy had already committed to play the part, a bit of skullduggery that caused Tracy to threaten to back out when he caught wind of it. To convince Hemingway that Tracy was the right man for the job, Hayward flew with Tracy to Florida to meet the author in person. Remarkably, Tracy stayed sober for the trip, so much so that Hemingway thought he was a teetotaler. Hemingway was also impressed that Tracy was an early riser, getting up at six-thirty each morning, while Hayward slept until noon.

Hemingway took Tracy to the little port of Cojímar, Cuba, a fishing village west of Havana, which was being considered as a shooting location. Tracy even got a glimpse of the old fisherman that the main character was based upon: Anselmo Hernandez was asleep in his shack after fishing all night.

The trip went well, Warner Brothers put Peter Viertel to work on the screenplay of *The Old Man and the Sea* and agreed to distribute the film with Tracy in the lead role.

Kate flew with Tracy on his return trip to Havana for the filming of *The Old Man and the Sea*, scheduled to begin in April 1956, with Fred Zinnemann directing. They were given a spacious villa with servants.

The initial plan was to use a stunt double to shoot scenes of the Old Man battling the giant marlin, but Zinnemann didn't want to use a double, and no one could find a giant marlin. Many fishing expeditions were launched – some with Hemingway on board – hoping to get footage for the film, but no one managed to hook a fish anywhere near as big as the 1,000-pound Marlin the script called for.

By this time, Hemingway's high opinion of Tracy had sunk. The actor had gained thirty pounds when he stopped drinking, and now, distraught by Zinnemann's attitude toward him and the difficulties of filming, he was drinking again. Hemingway said he hoped to make it through the spring without killing anyone, including himself.

After four months, hardly any footage had been shot, and Tracy was restless in his luxury villa, complaining that he had little to do. It was also rumored that Zinnemann and Hayward were sparring over Viertel's script – which was completely faithful to Hemingway's novella – with Hayward refusing to make changes that Zinnemann sought. With the production in limbo, Hayward finally fired Zinnemann and shelved *The Old Man and the Sea* until he could find another director.

Faced with an unexpected hiatus, Kate and Tracy returned to California, where they agreed to star in William Marchant's *Desk Set*, a comedy about women working in a television station reference library who are dismayed to learn that they may be replaced by a computer. Kate played Bunny Watson, the network's chief researcher, and Tracy played the engineer who brings in the computer that will ultimately take her job.

While the film gave moviegoers a chance to see Hepburn and Tracy reunited, *Desk Set* was neither a critical success nor a hit at the box office. Bosley Crowther wrote in *The New York Times* that the stars "lope through this trifling charade like a couple of old timers, who enjoy reminiscing with simple routines. Mr. Tracy is masculine and stubborn, Miss Hepburn is feminine and glib. The play is inconsequential."

Tracy, back in his milieu, regained enough strength to tackle the rigors of *The Old Man and the Sea* once *Desk Set* was completed. Production of *The Old Man and the Sea* was scheduled to resume in August 1956, with new director

John Sturges at the helm, but tropical storms in Cuba made shooting on location impossible.

Forsaking Cuba for California, the producers filled an oversized tank with 750,000 gallons of water and stocked it with gargantuan - albeit fake - marlin that matched the ones in Earnest Hemingway's imagination, and shot the rest of the film at the Warner Brothers studios.

The beginning of 1957 marked a painful interlude in both Kate's and Tracy's lives: On January 14, Humphrey Bogart lost his battle with cancer. On their last visit with Bogie, who managed to smile and joke despite his pain, Kate gave him a kiss, and Tracy shook his hand. "Goodbye, Spence," Bogart said in parting - something he had never said before; he always said "good night" or "see you." Tracy told Kate, "Bogie's going to die." Two days later, he did.

Kate turned fifty that year and looked her best since *The African Queen*. Tracy, only seven years older, had gray-white hair, a face lined with crevices, and a thickening midsection. While Tracy was considering retiring, Kate had no such plans.

"Most actors worry that each job will be their last," the author Scott A. Berg wrote in his memoir, *Kate Remembered*. "Spencer Tracy's deteriorating health offered good reason for him to believe as much. In his mid-fifties, he increasingly spoke of retirement, repeatedly saying, `I really don't need this anymore.' Intent upon looking after him, Kate knew such idleness would surely hasten his deterioration. She believed more than ever that work - the harder the better - was the essence of life."

Kate took her own advice. When she wasn't offered any films that sparked her interest, she decided to return to the theater in Stratford, Connecticut, with the American Shakespeare Theatre, playing Portia in *The Merchant of Venice*, and Beatrice in *Much Ado About Nothing*. She was the only major Hollywood star of her day willing to take the risk of performing Shakespeare in front of live audiences, night after night.

Rejecting more comfortable lodgings, she opted to stay in an old fisherman's shack, where she slept on the screened-in porch. The house had once been owned by a woman who sold bait, which became obvious to Kate when people came to the door asking for worms. "Sorry not today," Kate would reply, "Would you like some coffee?" It was an invigorating abode for Kate, who spent her mornings swimming in the chilly river and her afternoons racing a motorboat up and down the coast, "getting drenched by the water and reveling in it."

As Portia in *Merchant of Venice*, she and Morris Carnovsky, who played Shylock, were in only one scene together, and the critics loved him more than her. Walter Kerr of *The New York Times* wrote, "Miss Hepburn is a highly giddy adolescent who has been reading far too many novels . . . I wish I knew what she had in mind for Shakespeare's quick-witted maiden." In his review, the critic John Gassner wrote, "If there was a better Shylock than Carnovsky's in the entire stage history of *The Merchant of Venice*, it is not apparent to me from my personal experience or my reading."

Rehearsals for *Much Ado About Nothing* were a disaster. Kate despised her co-star, Alfred Drake, and the feeling was mutual. During one rehearsal, Kate deliberately disrupted Drake's performance, then laughed as he stormed off the stage.

Afterward, John Houseman, the company's artistic director, followed Kate to her dressing room, where she announced she was "weary but exhilarated - like an athlete after a sports contest in which she felt herself the winner." When Houseman approached Drake, Drake tendered his resignation. "I reminded him that he had a contract," Houseman recalled. "He declared that he refused to work with the bitch." Houseman eventually persuaded him to stay, and after Kate promised to behave herself, the two remained civil for the duration of the play.

Houseman noted that Constance Collier's coaching had led Kate to chew the scenery at times. In *Much Ado About Nothing*, he complained, she played a pivotal scene like a "grand tragedy - raging, kicking hassocks around, and howling like a banshee. It was hysterical, insincere, embarrassing and utterly unbelievable, but it shook up the audience and confirmed her star status."

For her portrayal of Beatrice in *Much Ado About Nothing*, Kate received unexpected praise from critic Brooks Atkinson, her nemesis at *The New York Times*. Atkinson called her performance "not only shrewd but fresh and joyous and admirably suited to the personality of [its] leading lady," adding that "Miss Hepburn is an extraordinary star, an actress who commands an audience with glamor and personal magnetism. She is beautiful, debonair, piquant, with a modern personality."

Kate had hoped that Tracy would join her during her theatrical run in Connecticut, but he always had an excuse not to come: He was reshooting some scenes for *The Old Man and the Sea* or was held up for one reason or another. Once, she drove to Idlewild Airport in New York to pick him up only to receive word that he had somehow got lost on the way to Burbank and missed his plane.

That fall, Kate went on tour with *Much Ado About Nothing*, driving to each city with Phyllis Wilbourn and Bernard Gersten, the company's executive stage manager, taking food along for picnics and stopping - at Kate's insistence - to take hikes in the woods.

Concluding the tour, Kate went to Hollywood and turned her attention back to Tracy, who was ill once again and depressed. She encouraged him to make *The Last Hurrah*, based on the novel by Edwin O'Connor. Tracy would star as Frank Skeffington, a Boston-Irish politician; John Ford, who had not seen Kate seen since their affair in the 1930s, would direct.

Kate delighted in seeing Tracy's spark and creativity re-surface while making the film, but Tracy had his mind on retirement. "I've joked about retiring but this could be the picture," he told one reporter. "I'm superstitious - you know that's part of being Irish - and I'm back with John Ford again . . . I feel this is the proper place for me to end. Even the title is prophetic."

The Last Hurrah, released in the fall of 1958 only weeks after the long-delayed debut of *The Old Man and the Sea*, received excellent reviews, leaving Tracy to rethink his plans of retiring.

More than most people, actors are constantly being reminded of their age, based on the parts they are offered and the roles they play. By now, Tracy had become one of America's favorite old men. Kate was right behind him, though she was aging far more gracefully as she prepared to play, for the first time in her life, an old woman.

19

"HE CLOSED HIS EYES - HE WAS GONE - JUST GONE"

Katherine Hepburn had never shared top billing with any film actress in her life. But in June of 1959, there she was, a screen legend, preparing to play alongside a rising star named Elizabeth Taylor because she was hungry for the chance to appear in *Suddenly Last Summer*, the film based on the play by the great Tennessee Williams.

"I felt Tennessee Williams was the greatest living playwright at the time - brilliant and full of poetry," Kate said later. "And I knew it would be a challenge to perform many of his speeches. But I thought he was a truly tragic figure, and this play showed that. I remember reading it and thinking this man keeps going farther and farther 'out there,' and one day he won't be able to come back."

Kate also thought her old friend, George Cukor, might direct; that the film would be not as graphic and disturbing as the play; that shooting would be done in Hollywood. None of that turned out to be true - the producer nodding yes to all her terms was Sam Spiegel, the same fast-talker who had gotten *The African Queen* off the ground with similar deceptions.

In that case, everyone could look back and laugh about Spiegel's ruses because *The African Queen* was such a success. But *Suddenly Last Summer* was a different beast altogether, a trauma from beginning to end, marked by on-set turmoil and clashing artistic visions.

Betraying his promises, Spiegel moved the production from Hollywood to England to lower production costs. The script was not toned down – if anything, it was even more graphic than the play, featuring homosexuality, cannibalism, and incest; Gore Vidal, the famously provocative author and literary personality had adapted it. Instead of hiring Cukor – who was contracted to direct *Let's Make Love* with Marilyn Monroe – Spiegel settled on Joe Mankiewicz, who was already in Kate's doghouse for committing what she considered an act of betrayal nearly a decade earlier.

Back in 1950, when Kate was in Los Angeles on tour with *As You Like It*, she had left a pair of tickets at the box office for Mankiewicz and had asked him to come backstage after the performance. He did, and was kept waiting for a long time, along with Kate's many other visitors, while she primped. When she finally let the guests into her dressing room, she talked nonstop – the very picture of a self-involved movie star – as people wandered in and out. Tracy, clearly agitated by the scene, poured himself a drink, to Kate's evident displeasure. Mankiewicz had soaked it all up and included the scene, almost exactly, in *All About Eve*, his classic film starring Bette Davis as an aging Broadway star. Angry that her privacy had been violated, Kate avoided Mankiewicz until they were thrown together for the new Tennessee Williams film.

Kate's role was Violet Venable, a wealthy Southern matriarch who schemes to lobotomize her niece, Catherine, to hide the truth surrounding her son's death and sexual deviance. Elizabeth Taylor plays the emotionally traumatized Catherine, who is being treated by neurosurgeon Montgomery Clift, who tries to determine if the young woman is a candidate for such a drastic procedure. As he attempts to discover the truth behind the young woman's trauma, Cliff's character falls in love with Catherine. He gives her a truth serum, leading her to disclose horrors.

When Kate arrived in London with Wilbourn, she battled with Mankiewicz constantly over how she should play the role. Kate thought a character as evil as Violet would have to be clinically insane, but Mankiewicz disagreed. He considered Violet arrogant and eccentric but also cunning. His compromise with Kate was that he would film a scene both her way and his, but ultimately, he would choose the take he wanted. As he recalled, "Kate wanted very much to direct herself. This is a battle I don't think a director can ever afford to lose . . . I insisted on the performance being played my way."

Kate also abhorred the salty language in the script, and could barely bring herself to speak some of her character's lines. When she expressed her revulsion to Mankiewicz, he responded, "That's the play and that's what we have to do."

Kate was not Mankiewicz's only problem. Clift, who had been badly injured in a car accident two years earlier, consistently arrived on the set under the influence of alcohol or pills and could only film for minutes at a time. Mankiewicz had hired him at the insistence of Taylor, who had been friends with Clift since 1951 when they had co-starred in *A Place in the Sun*.

Against his better judgment, Mankiewicz chose not to fire Clift for his behavior, but Spiegel wanted him gone after watching his first few takes. Taylor's response was brusque: "Over my dead body." To further complicate matters, Mankiewicz appeared to be infatuated with Taylor, who brought her fourth husband, Eddie Fisher, to the set daily. The British film crew was so horrified by Taylor's incessant profanity on the set that Mankiewicz had to ask Fisher to tell her to stop.

Kate tried her best to help Clift, who couldn't remember his lines and "washed down his codeine pills with brandy." She invited him to stay at her cottage for a weekend in an attempt to dry him out and talk some sense into him. In the end, she said, "none of my arguments did any good. I thought he was weak. Simpatico but weak."

Taylor was the last to arrive on the set every day. "There's nothing more frustrating than wanting to work and not being able to," Kate said later. "It's the rudeness I minded, keeping people waiting when they're all ready to go. Not just the other actors, but the crew . . . and the people paying the bills." Kate thought Taylor "preferred being a movie star to being an actress," but also considered Taylor "a brilliant actress, truly brilliant" – especially in her recent performance as Maggie the Cat in the film version of Williams's *Cat on a Hot Tin Roof*, opposite Paul Newman.

Amid all the off-screen drama, Kate was concerned about how she would be depicted in the movie; for the first time in her career, she was playing an old woman – and that put her in a vulnerable position. As Mankiewicz put it, "When [Mrs. Venable] spoke of her son, we had her look as young and beautiful as was possible, which with Kate was then very possible [with the aid of diffusion lenses]," he said. "At the end . . . we shot her hands after Catherine had told the truth. I wanted them to look like an old woman's hands. Kate didn't like that close-up . . ."

Kate hadn't minded that diffusion lenses were not used to soften her features in *The African Queen*, which was a decidedly unglamorous part. But here she felt she was deliberately being rendered hideous by Mankiewicz without her knowledge or permission, which hurt her vanity as well as her pride.

"I don't think Joe really liked actors," Kate said later. "He felt quite superior to them, and I think got great pleasure out of demeaning them."

On the last day of filming, Kate asked Mankiewicz, "So that's it? I'm finished?"

"You're finished," Mankiewicz said. "And you're marvelous. It's just great."

"But you're sure you're finished with me? You don't need any close-ups or reshoots?"

"I'm sure," he said. "Your work is finished here."

After confirming one more time that she was truly finished, she said, "Well, then, goodbye," and – right in front of the cast and crew – spat squarely in his face and stormed off the set. (Mankiewicz confirmed the story but said she spat at his feet). Kate then marched to Sam Spiegel's office and spat at him, too.

"When I disapprove of something, it's the only thing I can think of to do," she later explained. "It's a rather rude gesture, but at least it's clear what you mean."

Despite its graphic nature, *Suddenly Last Summer* was given special dispensation by Hollywood censors operating under the Motion Picture Production Code because the gay character of Violet's son Sebastian was so odious. "Since the film illustrates the horrors of such a lifestyle, it can be considered moral in theme even though it deals with sexual perversion," the Production Code Administration said. Critics applauded the film for its direct treatment of subjects previously considered taboo, and both Kate and Taylor received Oscar nominations for Best Actress, though neither won.

Williams loved Kate's performance. "She makes dialogue sound better than it is by a matchless beauty and clarity of diction and by a fineness of intelligence and sensibility that illuminates every shade of a meaning in every line she speaks," the playwright said. "She invests every scene - each bit - with the intuition of an artist born into her art."

But the film itself, Williams told *The Village Voice* in 1973, strayed so far from his original play that it "made [him] throw up." Vidal criticized alterations of his script by Mankiewicz. The director, meanwhile, brought the blame game full circle by describing Williams's play as "badly constructed . . . based on the most elementary Freudian psychology."

"The entire production was a nightmare - from day one," Kate said later – and reportedly refused to see the film when it came out in December of 1959.

When filming was concluded, Kate was relieved to return to the States and Tracy. They had been a couple for nearly twenty years now, and their relationship was at last acknowledged by the press, albeit discreetly. Writers alluded to Tracy as "Miss Hepburn's longtime friend."

"What would have happened to Spence [without Kate] is a dark thought," said an unnamed friend of Tracy's in 1960, as quoted in *Katharine Hepburn: A Remarkable Woman* by Anne Edwards. "He was thrashing about, unhappy, and she put his talent in focus so he could understand it. He's a queer bird with his own way of doing things, and it took a brilliant girl just to begin to see inside him."

In the summer of 1960, with Tracy's health relatively stable, Kate returned to Connecticut to the American Shakespeare Theatre to play Cleopatra in *Antony and Cleopatra*, and Viola in *Twelfth Night*. Kate and co-star Robert Ryan, who had starred with Tracy in *Bad Day at Black Rock*, and whose liberal mindset she admired, got along well during *Antony and Cleopatra*, and Kate earned some of her best stage reviews since *The Philadelphia Story*.

Discussing what American actors can bring to The Bard's plays, she told *Newsweek* reporter Calvin Tomkins, "There's something about the great American actor that's like a clipper ship in action, a sort of heart's directness. Spencer has it. He could do Shylock or Lear, or Macbeth - we could do Macbeth together." Of American playwrights, she said, too many were full of darkness and no light. "Shakespeare took into consideration the violence, the waywardness of man, but he also gave him the sun and moon and stars, and his own dreams," she said.

When Tennessee Williams asked Kate to star in his new play, *The Night of the Iguana* – he reportedly wrote the part of the lusty hotel manager Maxine Faulk with her in mind – she thought about it carefully but ultimately turned him down. The subject matter, which includes the statutory rape of a sixteen-year-old girl, was even less appealing to her than that of *Suddenly Last Summer*, and the part went to Bette Davis when it was staged on Broadway in 1961. Kate also wanted to spend time with Tracy in California as he shot his next film, *Inherit the Wind*.

Inherit the Wind was a fictionalized account of the 1925 Scopes "Monkey" Trial, in which an attorney defends a small-town high-school teacher who was put on trial for teaching the theory of evolution to his students in violation of state law. Kate admired Stanley Kramer, the film's director, and spent time on the set, watching, knitting, and occasionally offering her opinions. Tracy wasn't drinking, but he was irritable and impatient, glaring "at cameraman Ernest Laszlo when asked for another take," Kate said.

Kramer, who had worked with luminaries such as Marlon Brando and Humphrey Bogart, was in awe of Tracy's acting abilities. Tracy "thought and listened better than anyone in the history of motion pictures," Kramer said. "A silent close-up of Spencer Tracy said it all."

Kate agreed: "Spencer Tracy is a star of real quality," she wrote in her memoir. "He is an actor's star. He is a people's star. His quality is clear and direct. Ask a question - get an answer. No pause - no fancy thinking - a simple answer. He speaks. He listens. He is not wordy. He is not overemotional. He is simple and totally honest. He makes you believe what he is saying."

Kate continued to put her own career on hold for Tracy, following him to Hawaii, where he filmed *The Devil at Four O'Clock* with Frank Sinatra. Sinatra, a box-office powerhouse at the time, gave Tracy top billing, deeming him "the greatest actor in Hollywood."

During filming, Kate studied some still photographs taken of Tracy and director Mervyn LeRoy on the set. Kate was again impressed by Tracy's presence. "Spence, these are wonderful character studies," she told him. "Kate," Tracy replied, "those aren't character studies, they're just pictures of an old man. The truth is I'm old . . . so old that everyone has changed . . . Not just the movie business but the whole country." Though Tracy was feeling better – not drinking or smoking and living a quieter life thanks to Kate – at sixty-one, he did, indeed, look like an old man.

Kate and Tracy were spending most of their free time together now, though for decorum's sake, they kept two hotel suites when traveling and never went out in public together. Friends visited them in small groups, which Tracy preferred. Kate still did the cooking, cleaning, and driving. One evening when friends were over, she encroached on his masculine territory by throwing a large log on the fire. Tracy told her never to do that again in front of company. She didn't argue. That's just the way Tracy was.

Kate was acutely aware of her status as Tracy's partner and still not troubled by his relationship with his wife – or the fact that he saw Louise often and remained close to her. Their son John had divorced, which worried Tracy, but he was proud that their daughter Susie had become an accomplished photographer and musician.

With the exception of her stint performing Shakespeare in Stratford in 1960, in the three-year period from 1959 until the end of 1961, Kate adapted her schedule to suit Tracy's. She even flew with him to Germany in early 1961 when he filmed *Judgment at Nuremberg*, a project he almost backed out of because of his failing health.

Five days before shooting was set to begin, Tracy vacillated at the check-in gate at New York's Idlewild Airport, worrying about how the flight might affect his breathing and whether filming might prove too difficult for him. After a brief tête-à-tête, Kate kissed his cheek, and they boarded the plane together. When they arrived in Germany, Kate avoided the press at their hotel by exiting their car a couple blocks away and walking to the hotel's service entrance by herself.

Judgment at Nuremberg, directed by Kramer, centered on the 1948 hearings held in occupied Germany, where Americans put high-ranking Nazis on trial for their "crimes against humanity." Tracy, as the chief judge on the military tribunal, delivers one of the film's more poignant lines: "This, then, is what we stand for: truth, justice, and the value of a single human being." Tracy was proud of the film, which he considered the most important he had ever made, and his fervor infected his cast mates, including Burt Lancaster, Montgomery Clift, and Maximilian Schell, who won an Oscar for Best Actor.

The pinnacle of Tracy's performance was a thirteen-minute and forty-two-second speech, which he delivered in one take as two cameras rolled. Later, Kate said she had pressed hard for him to accept the role largely so he could be the one delivering those lines. "I couldn't bear the thought of watching somebody else in that part," Kate said. "Who else could have done it?"

Shortly after Tracy finished *Judgment at Nuremberg*, Kate was offered the one of the greatest, most challenging roles for any actress: Mary Tyrone, the morphine-addicted mother in *Long Day's Journey into Night*, Eugene O'Neill's classic semi-autobiographical play about a dysfunctional, decaying family. This would not be an adaptation, but a straight filmed version of O'Neill's play. Kate accepted immediately.

Ely Landau was producing *Long Day's Journey*, which had won a Pulitzer Prize and a Tony Award after it was staged on Broadway in 1956. Kate hoped to convince Landau to hire Tracy to play her character's husband, James Tyrone, Sr., so she invited him to breakfast at Tracy's place the next morning.

"It was extraordinary to watch her with Spence," Landau later said. "She was a totally different person. She turned really submissive - it's the only word I can use - and hardly opened her mouth, other than introducing us. She smiled, laughed at everything he said - which, by the way, was quite justified. He was the most charming man I've ever met."

Despite Landau's sincere invitation - "I don't have to tell you what it would mean to have you," he said - Tracy turned him down, and the part went to the acclaimed British stage actor Ralph Richardson. After the rigors of filming *Judgment at Nuremberg,* Tracy was simply worn down and worn out.

It turned out to be a wise decision; the working conditions for *Long Day's Journey into Night* were arduous. The director was Sidney Lumet, who had recently been nominated for an Academy Award for his first film, *Twelve Angry Men*, and would later be nominated again for *Dog Day Afternoon* (1975), *Network* (1976) and *The Verdict* (1982). For *Long Day's Journey into Night*, the cast rehearsed for three weeks in the fall of 1961 in New York, at reduced wages. When it came time to film, Lumet rushed through production, shooting the exterior scenes at an old Victorian house in the Bronx, then indoor scenes at the Production Center Studio in lower Manhattan, all in only thirty-seven days. Lumet called his crash-course approach "filmed theater." Whatever it was, everyone reaped the benefits.

Kate played the part of Mary Tyrone with gritty realism, refusing flattering filters or diffusive lighting, and at one point groveling on the floor. She was enchanted by O'Neill's masterwork. "O'Neill's knowledge of people, and his analysis of that couple, was really thrilling," she recalled later. "I just had to think and to concentrate and to read the lines. I felt entirely supported by the words. What an experience! I'll never forget it."

Many critics felt Kate's performance was her best ever. Arthur Knight of *The Saturday Review* marveled, "Her transformations are extraordinary as, in recollection, she suffuses her tense and aging face with a coquettish youthfulness or, in the larger pattern of the play, changes from a nervous, ailing but loving mother into a half-demented harridan. Her final scene, which contains some of O'Neill's most beautiful writing, is in every way masterful."

Calling Kate "the Divine Hepburn," Pauline Kael, film critic for *The New Yorker*, said of her transformation, "From being perhaps America's most beautiful comedienne of the thirties and forties," Kate has "become our greatest tragedienne."

"Kate believed her work in *Long Day's Journey into Night* was the best she ever did on screen," wrote A. Scott Berg in his book, *Kate Remembered*. "It was one of the few performances I ever heard her brag about - for both taking it on and pulling it off. Once, when a mutual friend of ours was raving about the performance Constance Cummings gave in the same role in a television production of the play, Kate listened politely for a few minutes of his gushing, then said, 'All right, that's quite enough.'"

The performance earned Kate an Academy Award nomination and the 1962 Cannes Film Festival award for best actress, once again making her a hot commodity in Hollywood. But there was no time for her to consider film offers: As she was finishing work on *Long Day's Journey into Night*, both Tracy and her father became gravely ill.

Tracy, in California, suffered a severe attack of emphysema. In West Hartford, Dr. Hepburn, eighty-two years old, was having a series of health problems, including a burst gall bladder.

"Dad would never complain about how he felt," Kate recalled later. "He simply *would not* say that he was suffering. Actually, [my brother] Bob said that he must have been in a terrible state. They discovered that he had a burst gall bladder. It had been full of stones and of course his abdomen was full of stones and of bile, too. Hard as a rock. He was gradually being poisoned. Bob said that the pain must have been really excruciating - not a word from Dad. He found moaning about one's health totally disgusting."

Dr. Hepburn underwent an operation but, according to Kate, "His blood pressure went down too far and it finally affected his ability to think and to talk." His wife Santa, a nurse, was taking care of him but couldn't do it alone, so Kate sent her assistant, Wilbourn, to help out.

Tending to the two most important people in her life was

grueling for Kate. When filming in New York, she would drive to Connecticut and spend late Friday and most of the day Saturday with her father, then fly back to California Saturday night to see Tracy and get back to New York for filming on Monday. When she finished filming *Long Day's Journey into Night*, she flew from California back to Connecticut every week.

Eventually, Dr. Hepburn needed a prostate operation; Kate's brother, Dr. Bob Hepburn, a urologist like his father, volunteered for the task. "It wasn't customary to operate on a close relative, but Bob thought that he could do it best," Kate said. "It was his specialty. So he did it. Bob said Dad at this time acted as though he were quietly studying his own demise - never a word of complaint. He just endured or he'd catch Bob's eye and would smile or wink at him."

In November of 1962, Kate flew to Hartford and found that her father had moved down to the first floor, to the study. "He seemed happy, as always, but much weaker," she recalled. "One morning Bob and I were eating breakfast in the dining room across the hall. We went in to see how Dad was and he seemed to be just quietly leaving this world. He smiled - he looked at us and he slowly stopped breathing. His chin fell. He closed his eyes - he was gone - just gone."

As she coped with her father's death, Kate seemed grateful that his suffering was over – and that she had been blessed with such a remarkable father. To Leland Hayward, she wrote: "Dad had a stink of a time for nine months. He said, 'thank God it was me and not your mother.' He heaved a sigh and was gone with a little sigh . . . How lucky I have been to have been handed such a remarkable pair in the great shuffle."

At fifty-five, Kate had lost both her parents – the people who had instilled in her the grit, courage, sharp mind, and the discipline and independence that had made her so unique, as a woman and an actress. Her relationship with her extraordinary parents and her deep attachment to her family homes in Connecticut were an inextricable part of her heritage and her emotional makeup.

"Such a remarkable man Dad had been," she recalled. "So strong. So definite. So tough and funny. He'll never be forgotten . . . Such a powerhouse coming to the end of the trail."

Kate struggled more with her mother's death than her father's, perhaps because hers was unexpected, or perhaps because she went first. With her father gone, the reverence and respect she had reserved for him would now fall entirely on Tracy, who in some ways had always been a father figure to her. Kate would always perceive his angry outbursts, which she called "smashing downs," as discipline – and to her, discipline meant love. As she often said, her sharp words with her own friends were spoken only because she cared.

After Thanksgiving, Kate flew back to California to be with Tracy, armed with a new determination to help him live a full, productive life for as long as possible. He was her best friend, and no sacrifice was too great. She would gladly forego everything she had, and everything she was, to keep Tracy with her as long as she could.

20
"THERE WAS A SOUND OF A CUP SMASHING TO THE FLOOR - THEN CLUMP - A LOUD CLUMP"

By the early 1960s, the media was becoming less considerate of Kate and Tracy's privacy. The couple technically lived separately – Kate rented a hillside home in Beverly Hills – but she spent most of her time at the cottage on George Cukor's property that Tracy had rented for many years. Nobody was fooled by the arrangement. An article in the January 1962 edition of *Look* magazine exposed Tracy's alcoholism and his longtime estrangement from Louise, describing his relationship with Kate as "something more than frequent co-stars."

Despite their separation, Tracy visited Louise for several hours each week, and she was appreciative of his continuing financial support of both her and her causes. In 1956, the *New York Journal-American* called Mrs. Spencer Tracy "one of the great women of the American progress, in the humanitarian tradition of Clara Barton and Jane Addams."

The saintly reputation of Louise was never tarnished, at least in the eyes of the public. Close friends said there was never another man in her life besides Tracy, and she continued to be forgiving about his infidelity – which was undoubtedly aided by great quantities of denial. The only social events she attended were fundraisers for the John Tracy Clinic, or other occasions when she was presented with an award. The Tracys continued to be photographed together until 1962, usually in publicity shots for the clinic, and Tracy's name remained on the clinic's letterhead.

Though Tracy's days as a leading man were over, he was still considered a living legend and treated like a god when he arrived on movie sets. Actor David Niven called him "The Pope" and whatever dictates he uttered were faithfully obeyed.

Kate's care of Tracy was so meticulous that whenever she was not available to cook for him, she'd leave him food in a basket at his door. She stocked his refrigerator with milk, which he drank on the rocks as if it were a cocktail, and she allowed him one beer a day, which his doctor said he couldn't live without.

Tracy wasn't well enough for the cold swims Kate once insisted on, but they still took slow walks together through the hills, flew kites, painted, listened to music, and read to each other. "Spence always loved his dime novels, his mysteries, but he began reading some big, serious novels too," Kate said later. "Even poetry. Yeats. He liked jazz but was listening to classical music. Beethoven symphonies. Schumann."

In the spring of 1963, after eighteen months under Kate's watchful eye, Tracy was much healthier. Stanley Kramer and Abe Lastfogel, Tracy's long-time agent, urged Kate to persuade him to play in Kramer's next film, the loopy comedy *It's a Mad, Mad, Mad, Mad World*, to be shot in the desert not far from Los Angeles, which doctors said would have a positive effect on Tracy's emphysema.

Tracy would only have to stay a few weeks and have little actual screen time, but would still receive top billing over the many show-business legends appearing in the film, including Milton Berle, Sid Caesar, Ethel Merman, Jimmy Durante, and Mickey Rooney. Kramer also promised to limit Tracy's workdays to six hours.

It's a Mad, Mad, Mad, Mad World featured Tracy as a police captain trying to recover a stolen fortune. Bosley Crowther of *The New York Times* wrote: "While the mad seekers are tearing toward the money in their various ways . . . Mr. Tracy sits there in wise complacence . . . And then, by a ruse I dare not tell you, he shows how treacherous his morality is."

When filming was finished, Tracy swore again that he was retiring, but Kate and Kramer were the only ones who believed him. Kramer recalled, "During the filming of *Mad World* . . . Spencer Tracy was in poorer health than I could remember. He had bad color and no stamina whatever. But then, even though this lack of energy showed, I think he had his best time ever during the making of a film. The comedians worshipped him. Never before or since has a king had the court full of jesters who strove only to entertain him so that his majesty might say 'that was funny,' or just laugh or smile."

Kate was too worried about Tracy to get in on the fun. He could barely walk by the time they got home, and by early summer, he was spending most of his time in his cottage, going out on the terrace occasionally or shuffling to a shady spot under some giant elms. By July, he was feeling well enough to take a drive with Kate to the beach – but on their way to Malibu for a picnic, Tracy started gasping for breath.

As Kate pulled his Thunderbird into a gas station, Tracy passed out; after calling the fire department, she gave him mouth-to-mouth resuscitation until the EMTs arrived. Though the emergency crew suspected a heart attack, doctors at the hospital determined the cause was pulmonary edema, a build-up of fluid in his lungs. Kate stayed by his bed, leaving before Louise arrived; when he was discharged, she stayed at the cottage with him. Though he was home, he was still under the care of a private nurse, who set up an oxygen machine in the hall outside his bedroom.

Taking care of Tracy had a huge impact on Kate's career. The five-year period between *Long Day's Journey into Night* and *Guess Who's Coming to Dinner* in 1967 was by far the longest time between public performances since her career began in 1928. "I never talk about that period," Kate told A. Scott Berg in his book, *Kate Remembered*. "Over the years she did," Berg adds, "but only to reveal that it was an extremely quiet time in her life, sad but satisfying."

"We were just quite happy being quiet together, truth be told," she told Berg. "Not much to say about those years. We just loved each other. Nothing more to say."

During this time, another Hepburn arrived on the scene: Audrey, nominated for an Academy Award for her portrayal of Holly Golightly in the classic *Breakfast at Tiffany's*. Both Hepburns had to contend with rumors that they were related, but they were not – Audrey was born in Belgium. While the two actresses were never close, they did share a mutual admiration. When *My Fair Lady* was released in 1964, Kate and Tracy sent a letter to Audrey and Cukor, the film's director, that read, "You two certainly hit the nail on the head and took such a chance. You scared all your friends to death - a million congratulations. It's a real triumph." Kate was also known to affectionately refer to Audrey, twenty-two years her junior, as her "little daughter."

In September 1965, Tracy's health took a serious turn for the worse. He underwent a prostatectomy - the removal of his prostate gland - and afterward, suffered kidney failure and lapsed into a coma. Over the next six weeks, he fought for his life, his lungs and heart further weakened by the trauma.

By now, friends in Hollywood had heard that Tracy was deathly ill. George Cukor, Lastfogel, Kramer, Ruth Gordon and Garson Kanin feared that he might not have much time to live and stopped by frequently to visit and fill him in on the latest gossip.

Kramer, who continued to bring Tracy scripts in spite of his condition, also brought one for Kate. It was the screenplay for *Ship of Fools,* based on the novel of the same name by Katherine Anne Porter. Kramer hoped it would inspire her to play the part of Mary Treadwell, an aging divorcée in search of her lost youth. Kate declined, and Vivien Leigh, ill herself and recently divorced from Lawrence Olivier, accepted the role, which would be her last screen performance.

In the fall of 1966, Kramer, hoping that Tracy had improved enough to work again, told Kate about a new script he was excited about. *Guess Who's Coming to Dinner* was the story of Joanna Drayton, an affluent young white woman who brings John, her black fiancé, home to meet her parents. Oscar winner Sidney Poitier had signed on to play John, and Kramer wanted Kate and Tracy to play the girl's parents.

Kramer knew it was a risk; Tracy could easily die before they finished filming. Kate and Tracy, moved by Kramer's act of faith, immediately agreed, even before they had read the script. His spirits buoyed, Tracy showed further signs of improvement. Kate and Tracy put their salaries - $250,000 each - in escrow, and Kramer did the same, to indemnify Columbia Pictures from loss if Tracy were unable to complete the film.

Also richly rewarding for Kate was the chance to work with

her twenty-two-year-old niece, Katharine Houghton, whom she had suggested that Kramer hire to play the part of Joanna. The second child of Kate's sister Marion, Kathy had previously played a small part on Broadway in *A Very Rich Woman,* a comedy written by Kate's friends Ruth Gordon and Garson Kanin. "She's beautiful, and she definitely had a family resemblance," Kate said later. It was a big break for Kathy – her first film in a career that would blossom with leading roles in over sixty productions in Broadway, Off-Broadway, and regional theater, and ten films, including 2010's *The Last Airbender* directed by M. Night Shyamalan.

The night before filming was scheduled to begin in January of 1967, Tracy's emphysema flared up, and Kramer had to postpone production for a few days to allow Tracy to regain his strength. To lessen the stress, Kramer agreed to shoot Tracy's scenes between nine and twelve in the morning, when he was feeling his best; he also, if possible, used a stand-in for Tracy when the camera was on another actor.

Kate arrived early the first morning of shooting to look over the set and jokingly told the crew, "In case my niece drops dead from the excitement, I'm here and I know all her lines, too." When Kramer got there, she told him the fireplace looked fake and should be ripped out and replaced by a real one, then discussed lighting with a member of the crew and Kathy's accessories with a wardrobe supervisor.

Before the first shot was filmed, Kate peered through the camera and told Kramer the angle was wrong. Frustrated, Kramer threw up his hands and said, "I'll give you the whole thing." Kate annoyed him in other ways, too. "I was irritated by her fear over her so-called 'ugly neck,'" he said.

"She wore scarves and high collars, and 'played low,'" sitting down or kneeling in scenes so people wouldn't see her neck."

But Kramer considered Kate one of the most creative artists he'd ever worked with. "She thinks like a director," he said. She was also in perpetual motion. "Work, work, work," the director noted. "She can work until everybody drops."

On days they were scheduled to shoot, Kate drove to Tracy's house at 5:00 a.m. to rehearse with him until it was time to head to the studio. When Tracy completed a scene and was satisfied with it, Kramer recalled, he'd yell to cameraman Sam Leavitt, "Did you get that, Sam?"

Kathy Houghton shared her Aunt Kate's work ethic as well as her aversion to the press; to Kramer's dismay, she avoided publicity whenever possible. "The publicity guys would want to take stills of her, and she'd say, 'I don't want to do that kind of publicity.' We had a Vogue layout all ready to go . . . and she nixed it," Kramer said. "My publicity man, George Glass, had aggravation all the time."

Kate was uncharacteristically cooperative with the press during filming, giving Jack Hamilton, a senior editor for *Look* magazine, permission to interview her on the set. "People say the story's a shocker," she said of the film's controversial storyline. "Even anybody with a pint-sized brain knows the day is soon coming when interracial marriages won't be funny, or surprising or anything else. It will be just: 'There it is.' It's a defenseless position, to judge people by their color."

Kate's uncommon openness with the press likely stemmed

from her awareness that *Guess Who's Coming to Dinner* would probably be Tracy's last film. Tracy knew it, too. Four days before the end of the shoot, he put an arm around Kramer and said, "You know, I read the script again last night, and if I were to die on the way home tonight, you can still release the picture with what you've got."

Still, he refused to go quietly. When Kate, sitting in the director's chair with her feet up, fed him lines from a poignant scene, he railed at her, "We can begin when you put your goddamn feet down and sit like a lady!"

Kate obeyed, then fed him the line again. In this scene, after listening to Joanna and John plead their case to marry, Tracy's character turns to his wife and says, "If what they feel for each other is even half what we felt, then that is everything." Kate fought back her tears.

Tracy was too ill to attend the wrap party when production finished in late May, but he did call Garson Kanin in New York and boasted - with obvious relief - that he had finished the picture. At the party, Kramer stood up and proposed a toast. "To Spencer Tracy, the greatest of all motion picture personalities."

When *Guess Who's Coming to Dinner* opened in theaters in December 1967 – the eighty-fourth film of Tracy's career and Kate's thirty-fifth – it was well received by the public and was nominated for ten Academy Awards. Kate received her tenth Academy Award nomination for Best Actress and finally won, beating out Anne Bancroft (*The Graduate*), Faye Dunaway (*Bonnie and Clyde*), Dame Edith Evans (*The Whisperers*), and Audrey Hepburn (*Wait Until Dark*). It was Kate's first Oscar since her Best Actress award for *Morning*

Glory, more than three decades earlier.

Though critics praised the performances of both Kate and Tracy, they were not as receptive to the storyline. As one critic wrote, "the race issue is prettified and pre-guaranteed a happy solution here because of the extraordinary character of this black man, and the built-in liberal stance of the parents, especially since Poitier represents the quintessentially respectable and unthreatening black, and Tracy and Hepburn represent the settled, establishmentarian liberals who can win over any case and make the nastiest world safe for love and ideals."

Poitier disagreed. "People said I was cast as the stereotype of the intellectual black man with no flaws," he later noted. "They said I should have played a garage mechanic, or someone like that, brought home to this wealthy San Francisco family by the daughter and presented as a candidate for marriage.

"Well, this objection has absolutely no historical sense. In 1967, it was utterly impossible to do an in-depth interracial love story, to treat the issue in dead earnestness, head on. No producer, no director could get the money, nor would theaters in America back it. But Kramer made people look at the issue for the first time . . . He treated the theme with humor . . . delicately . . . humanly . . . lovingly . . . *Guess Who's Coming to Dinner* is a totally revolutionary movie, and this is what so many critics failed to see. For the very first time, the characters in a story about racism are people with minds of their own, who after deliberations in a civilized manner, and after their own private reflections, come to a conclusion - the only sensible conclusion that people could come to in a situation like this!"

Whether or not America was ready for the film, the movie-going public and critics were ready to see Tracy and Hepburn together again. Penelope Mortimer of the *London Observer* noted that "while either [Tracy or Hepburn] or both are on screen, the most savage criticism [of the story] is replaced by gratitude . . . Miss Hepburn is, of course, unchanged and unchangeable. Anyone who feels as I do about this pair will go and see Guess *Who's Coming to Dinner* regardless of its fallacies and its hokum."

Just weeks after finishing *Guess Who's Coming to Dinner*, Kate and Tracy had their final, private scene. In her memoir, Kate wrote a letter to Tracy that described what happened in the early morning hours of June 10, 1967. They were both at Tracy's cottage on Cukor's estate. "You'd gone to sleep," she wrote. "When I thought that you were settled, I'd crept out of your room." This was their usual routine: Kate would stay with Tracy in his bedroom until he dozed off, then retire to her own bed in the maid's room off the kitchen. On Tracy's nightstand was a buzzer attached to a long wire that Kate carried with her at all times so he could summon her. But on this night, he didn't buzz.

"It was about 3:00 a.m.," she recalled. "You had wanted a cup of hot tea." Hearing him shuffle down the hallway, Kate got up to see if he needed help. She put on her slippers and went to the kitchen door. "Just as I was about to give it a push, there was a sound of a cup smashing to the floor - then clump - a loud clump. It was you falling to the floor. I was through the door. Yes - it was you. You were - just - dead. As if everything had stopped. Suddenly stopped. All at once. The End."

Kate crouched down and took him in her arms. "No life - no pulse - dead. Spence is dead. He is not alive anymore. He doesn't inhabit his body anymore. He is gone. His eyes are closed. It is tea spilled all over him. He never knew what happened . . ."

Kate sat there, wondering what to do. She called Wilbourn, then Ida the housekeeper, and Willie the gardener. They came over and helped her put Tracy's body back into his bed. Kate drew up the covers and lit candles. Later, the coroner determined that Tracy had a heart attack.

"He looked so happy to be done with living, which for all his accomplishments had been a frightful burden to him," she recalled later. "One builds one's own jail. I never knew him, I think. And he is the only one who ever knew me - who was onto me. I think I was a comfort to him. I hope. Dear Friend."

Before calling Tracy's family, Kate and Wilbourn began moving Kate's belongings – clothes, personal items, everything – into her car. "Then I thought - God - God - Kath - what are you doing - you've lived with the man for almost thirty years," she recalled. "This is your home. Isn't it? It is part of you. These walls - this roof - this spot on the earth. I carried everything back into the house. You can't deny your life of thirty years."

Next, Kate called Tracy's doctor, the head of publicity at MGM – who would create a story for the public that Tracy was alone when he died, discovered by his housekeeper – and Cukor. Finally, she called Tracy's wife Louise and his children, John and Susie, and his brother Carroll. To each of them, she said the same thing. "Spence is dead."

When Tracy's family arrived, Kate offered them breakfast. "Eggs? Bacon? Toast? Fruit? Anything you – please eat . . ."

Louise went down the hall to Tracy's bedroom carrying her cup of coffee. "Well, she was in a peculiar spot - no doubt about that," Kate recalled. "She could never bear to admit failure. Now he was dead. And he would never come back. She had dreamed - hoped - imagined that he would. But now all those hopes had died with him. This strange woman - me - had obviously been with him when he died. And he is mine - oh - oh - oh . . ."

When the undertakers arrived, Kate began picking out something for Tracy to wear. "What suit? Oh, the old gray pants and the brown tweed - the old one –"

"But he's my husband," Louise said. "I should pick out the . . ."

"Oh, Louise - what difference does it make?" Kate snapped.

A few days later, Kate called Louise and said, "You know, Louise, you and I can be friends. You knew him at the be-ginning, I at the end - or we can just pretend that - I might be a help with the kids."

"Well, yes," she said. "But you see, I thought you were only a rumor . . ."

Kate was dumbfounded. "After nearly thirty years?" she thought. "A rumor? What could be the answer to that?" For a few minutes, she tried to imagine how Louise could be so naïve, so full of denial – unless she was simply trying to be hurtful. "It was a deep and fundamental wound - deeply set - never to be budged," Kate concluded. "Almost thirty years Spence and I had known each other - through good and bad times. Some rumor. And by never admitting that I existed - she remained - the wife - and she sent out Christmas cards. Spence - the guilty one. She - the sufferer . . . I had not broken up their marriage. That happened long before I arrived on the scene."

It was only after Tracy died that Kate realized the price everyone paid by not acknowledging the truth. "I think now that I took the easy road," she said later. "It is better to straighten things out. Then everyone - and in this case Susie and Johnny - would have been able to know their father with me. It would have been better. But it would have had to be pushed by Louise - the loser in the situation. Yet it would, I believe, have been ennobling to her. And supremely honest. And it would have made it easy for him to do - what would in this case have been the direct and simple thing for him to do. Then he could have had the best of both worlds. And if he had felt that it was her idea, his guilt would have been removed.

"Oh yes - but if she'd done that she would have had to have been a saint. Well, yes. But what's wrong with being a saint? Too much to ask, I agree. Louise was in a hopeless situation. And as for me - I was complacent. I didn't push for action. I just left it up to him. And he was paralyzed.

"I must say it taught me a lesson - one must figure out how much you care about this or that. Then put up a fight. Or don't. Do you love someone? If you love someone, and the person gives every evidence of wishing to part and you know really that it is finished - let the person go! Do yourself a favor. Be noble. It has a better lasting effect than hanging on and constantly reminding yourself and the other that your life together has been a disaster. And it is honest. And it is going forward. The status quo in a bad marriage is not a productive state. The new relationship may open many doors beneficial to everyone concerned. That solidified failure is so sterile."

At Tracy's wake, Kate waited until everyone had left before entering. "I'm sorry, Miss Hepburn, the coffin is closed," she was told. "Mrs. Carroll Tracy told me to close it. I . . . shall I . . ."

"No - no - leave it . . . it doesn't really matter, does it," she said. "I just had a few little tokens - but it doesn't matter. Leave it. I'll stay just a minute."

The man walked away. "I would have liked to have seen his face once more - but what was the difference - yesterday - today - tomorrow . . . He was gone," she said later. "I wonder if they found my little painting of flowers I put under his feet. I don't think so. And it doesn't matter - things. Never fight about things. That's what Dad and Mother said. Things don't matter. And they don't and he's now safe from harm."

Kate thought it best not to attend the funeral that took place the next day at a Catholic church in Hollywood, where pallbearers included Cukor, Kramer, Frank Sinatra, James Stewart, and John Ford. Then she had second thoughts. "Well, I got to thinking about Spence's last trip through the town and I said to Phyllis, 'Let's go down to [the undertaker] Cunningham & Walsh and see the old boy take off.' We went. We peeked. No one was there, just the hearse. So we drove up into the driveway."

"May we help?" they asked.

"Why not?" the men replied.

"So we helped lift Spence into his spot in the wagon. Closed the door and off they went and off we went after them. His cortège. Down Melrose, then left on Vermont; then we could see the church. They went on toward it. We stopped. Goodbye, friend - here's where we leave you . . . And we turned and went back home."

21

"THE WIDOW WHO COULDN'T MOURN"

When she learned that Spencer Tracy had died, Kate's old friend Laura Harding flew to Hollywood from New York to comfort her. Two days after the funeral, they went back East with Phyllis Wilbourn. "Kate was the widow who couldn't mourn for obvious reasons," said her friend, the actor Peter O'Toole. At least not in public. Her private grieving took place in the sanctuary where Kate always retreated in times of crisis – Fenwick.

The Hepburn family's ocean-side retreat in Old Saybrook, Connecticut, was always full of life in summer. The house was filled with the voices of Kate's sisters and brothers and her nieces and nephews as they dashed through the rooms and down to the waterfront where "Aunt Kat" walked each morning before plunging into the cold Atlantic waters. Sixty years old now, she still played games with the children, running three-legged races or groping around blindfolded in blind man's bluff.

But after two weeks, Kate needed to be around her peers. So she and Wilbourn traveled to the affluent island community of Martha's Vineyard, 160 miles up the coast, to visit Ruth Gordon and Garson Kanin, who were staying at a hotel in Edgartown. Kate liked it so much she got a room at the hotel, too, and continued her daily morning walks and cold ocean swims. "It was pretty and we would drive out here and there to wonderful beaches and little towns," she recalled. As the days passed, she began thinking about the only thing that ever helped heal the most painful sorrows of her life: Going back to work.

What Kate didn't realize was that much of Hollywood privately thought of Kate as his widow. Louise, as Tracy's legal widow and executor of his estate, would receive $500,000 and the ranch they owned together. But in the minds of many, Katharine Hepburn was Tracy's true partner in life and some press coverage in the days after his funeral acknowledged that perception.

Kate cared little about what the public thought about her and Tracy; her main objective was to get back on a movie set. While she was at Martha's Vineyard, in August of 1967, O'Toole sent her the script for *The Lion in Winter*, a twelfth-century drama based on the convoluted and tortuous relationship between King Henry II (O'Toole) and his estranged wife, Eleanor of Aquitaine (Kate).

Kate and O'Toole had become friends eight years earlier, when she appeared at his dressing room to congratulate him after his performance in London in *The Long and the Short and the Tall*. At the time, he was a twenty-seven-year-old stage actor who had yet to appear in his breakout film, *Lawrence of Arabia* (1962) or *Becket* (1964, when he also played King Henry II), both of which earned him Oscar nominations.

After Tracy died, he said later in a televised interview, "I heard that she was in Martha's Vineyard and a script came my way called *Lion in Winter*. I thought, I'm going to send it to Kate, and see what happens. I had no high hopes at all." Soon afterward, "The phone rang in my house in London and I picked it up and a voice said, `Do it before I die,` and it was Kate. That fast, like that."

"What was fascinating about the play" that the film was based upon, Kate said later, "was its modernness. This wasn't about pomp and circumstance but about a family, a wife trying to protect her dignity and a mother protecting her children."

She became even more excited about the project after seeing *Dutchman*, a film made by Anthony Harvey, the director O'Toole wanted, based on an Amiri Baraka play about a sinister white woman who stabs a black man on a New York subway train. That might not have seemed like the best audition for a grand costume drama, but Kate considered Harvey's work "absolutely riveting. It grabbed you by the throat. Exactly the approach that our material needed. Not that glossy old MGM stuff, but cold people living in cold castles." When she finally met Harvey, they hit it off immediately and developed what would become an extremely close, lifelong friendship.

Kate was ecstatic to be working again. Acting was not only her bread and butter but, it seemed, her very reason for being. Few women had navigated life in Hollywood as successfully or with as much longevity.

O'Toole wasn't the only one sending her film scripts. She also accepted the leading role in a satirical comedy-drama, *The Madwoman of Chaillot*, at the behest of Ely Landau, producer of *Long Day's Journey into Night*. Landau agreed that shooting for *Madwoman* could wait until *Lion in Winter* wrapped up the following spring.

In late October of 1967, with two projects lined up – both to be filmed in Europe – Kate spent a week in Paris before heading to London to rehearse *Lion in Winter* with Harvey, O'Toole, and a host of talented English actors, including Anthony Hopkins, Nigel Terry, John Castle, Timothy Dalton, and Jane Merrow.

The younger actors were in awe of Kate, especially Hopkins in his very first film role. "To start my film career with those two [Hepburn and O'Toole] was quite an event," Hopkins said later. "I'm never nervous as an actor, that's a waste of time. So I wasn't nervous of her, but I managed to get my cloak caught in the door and I fell over a few cables because obviously I was, deep down, a bit in awe of her."

Harvey, who at the time had only made one small-budget film, gushed, "working with [Miss Hepburn] is like going to Paris at the age of seventeen and finding everything is the way you thought it would be."

During rehearsals, Kate was as bossy and impatient as ever. Later, O'Toole gave a television interviewer a dead-on impersonation of Kate's behavior on the set, complete with her distinctive vocal mannerisms: "I will give you sixty seconds in which you are to be word perfect and I will not give you another minute, pig. I have come here now at 10 o'clock in the morning and I am perfectly ready to work. Where is everybody?" O'Toole laughed. "Told everybody off. Delightful woman. The best of America."

Known for his own tyrannical behavior on the set, O'Toole admitted that Kate ruled the roost. "She is terrifying. It is sheer masochism working with her. She has been sent by some dark fate to nag and torment me." Later, Kate said O'Toole was wild and rambunctious, "sometimes utterly impossible, a real Irishman - too much charm and too much liquor. But I was used to that. And what an actor! Great voice. Great performance. Great fun."

At one point, Kate invited a reporter to observe rehearsals, where she got into character as Eleanor – laughing, shouting and once surprising the rest of the cast by crying real tears. Director Harvey said, "If we'd had a camera, and everyone had been in costume, we could have filmed it and released it."

After three weeks of rehearsals, Kate and Wilbourn and the cast set off for County Wicklow, just south of Dublin, Ireland, where interior scenes were shot in a replica of a twelfth-century castle. Later, they also shot in Wales and France.

Even in Ireland in the winter, Kate swam twice a day in the frigid Irish Sea. "Why on earth would you do a thing like that?" O'Toole asked. "It's the shock," Kate responded, "so horrible that it makes you feel great afterwards." She spent the rest of her free time walking the hills of County Wicklow. She picked up pieces of broken glass from the ruins of a Georgian mansion to send home to make a chandelier.

Shooting for *The Lion in Winter* wrapped up in the spring of 1968, and the film was released in October. Not only was it a commercial success – the twelfth highest-grossing film of the year – but critics raved. One reviewer called Kate's performance "triumphant . . . an aging beauty who can look her image in the eye, a sophisticate whose shrewdness is matched only by her humor."

Getting deeply immersed in the making of a great film did wonders for Kate's spirits, and she was excited to travel to southeastern France for her next project – *The Madwoman of Chaillot* at the Studios de la Victorine.

At first, Kate was not interested in the part of Aurelia, an eccentric French countess working with her equally eccentric friends to prevent corporate industrialists from digging up the streets of Paris in search of oil. "I don't understand all this complicated stuff," she protested. But Landau was relentless, John Huston was slated to direct, and she would get to work with a stellar international cast, including Dame Edith Evans, Yul Brynner, Charles Boyer, Giulietta Masina, Margaret Leighton, and John Gavin.

Kate and Wilbourn moved into an old house in the village of Beaulieu-sur-Mer on St. Jean-Cap-Ferrat in Nice. Kate swam in the warmer waters of the Mediterranean and rode a bicycle to the village's shops and sidewalk cafes clad in an old red sweater of Tracy's, slacks, and tennis shoes. She went to bed at eight-thirty every night, regardless of whether or not she was scheduled to work the next morning. Evans, her co-star in *Madwoman*, accused Kate of sleeping her life away. "It's true. I don't go out much," Kate told her. "But when I do, I decide I don't miss much."

Kate still ate a hearty breakfast, steak and fresh fruit for lunch, then snacked on chocolate throughout the day. When she was at work at the Studios de la Victorine, she would climb a ladder to reach the cherries on the trees behind the executive offices, then tell the workmen, "Hide the ladder so no one'll get the big ones."

Just eighteen days before shooting started, Kate was disappointed to learn that her old pal Huston – with whom she had bonded so well in *African Queen* – had backed out of the project because of creative differences with Landau. He was replaced by Bryan Forbes, one of England's top directors, who later would become widely known for his film *The Stepford Wives* (1975).

Despite the enormous reservoir of talent on hand, the film script – based on the celebrated French poetic satire *La Folle de Chaillot* by Jean Giraudoux – proved difficult to master. "John was no fool," Kate said of Huston's abandoning this surreal, allegorical tale of a countess who holds a mock trial and lures greedy capitalist villains into a bottomless pit by telling them of an oil reserve beneath her house. "The big problem," she said, "is that material like this plays better on a stage than on screen, which requires something more literal. I mean, you have to photograph something. And I think it's difficult for a movie audience to accept an entire film that is so abstract and stylized."

The actors also had trouble figuring out how to play their parts and speak the lines, which Kate called "terribly artificial." Flummoxed, some of the actresses resorted to impersonating Evans, the acclaimed British actress who played Aurelia's friend Josephine, the trial judge. Kate found Evans's diction "terribly amusing . . . but I don't think she knew what she was doing any more than we did. It was really quite hopeless."

Reviewers agreed when the film was released in October of 1969. Vincent Canby of *The New York Times* called the story, even in its original form as a stage play, "an incredibly precious theatrical conceit," adding that "when the film does depart from the original, it does so in all the wrong ways." As for Hepburn's performance, he wrote, "Miss Hepburn's madwoman is as sentimental (and therefore, as redundant) as her mannerism of gently clenching her perfect teeth, looking into the middle distance and weeping through her tears."

The failure of *The Madwoman of Chaillot* disappointed Kate because she agreed with Giraudoux's social commentary. "I think *The Madwoman of Chaillot* has more relevance today than it did twenty years ago," she said. "The world has gone cuckoo. We're still dominated by greed, and that's what Giraudoux was talking about."

While in Nice, Kate had an opportunity to process some of her grief over Tracy's death: The Academy of Motion Picture Arts and Sciences asked her to film a short introduction for the awards ceremony's montage of Oscar-winning performances, which included a clip of Tracy as the Portuguese fisherman in *Captains Courageous*. Kate's segment was a poignant moment in the ceremony, particularly since Tracy's family was in the audience to accept the award for Tracy if he were to win for *Guess Who's Coming to Dinner* – which would have given him three Best Actor awards, the most ever at the time (today, Daniel Day-Lewis is the only actor with three).

Everyone who loved Tracy was disappointed when Rod Steiger took home the award that night for *In the Heat of the Night*, but Kate felt Tracy had been vindicated somewhat when she won for Best Actress. "Well, I suspect my award was really given to the two of us," she said.

"Much of what I know about acting I learned from Spencer Tracy," she said in Nice, after learning that she had won. She called Tracy a "sturdy oak buffeted by the wind - a throwback to an age of rugged heroism . . . that vanishing American, the self-made man. He was what we imagined our grandfathers to be." Days later, she told the British journalist Alexander Walker, "I had twenty-five years of perfect companionship with this man among men. He had been a rock, a protector. There are very few great actors. Spencer was one. I'm not in his class."

As always, Kate did not attend the Academy Awards ceremony. Her feelings about the Oscars have always been complicated. When she was given her very first nomination – for *Morning Glory* in 1934 – she felt she had been nominated for the wrong film. While *Morning Glory* was "tricked up, charming, mugging," she later told writer A. Scott Berg, her other film that came out the same year, *Little Women*, was far better – "what I call the main-course performance, not the desert."

Convinced that she could not possibly win for *Morning Glory* – she was, after all, only twenty-six and new to Hollywood – she skipped the ceremony, hosted by Will Rogers and held at the Ambassador Hotel on March 16, 1934. Later, when told she had won, Kate said she was tempted to release a statement saying she did not believe in awards - "or some asinine answer like that."

In truth, she later admitted, "mine was really bogus humility, because I was genuinely thrilled to win." After her first nomination, Kate vowed never to attend the Academy Awards ceremony, a promise she was not proud of because the real reason she skipped the event, she admitted to Berg, was that she could not handle losing.

"I think it is very noble for the people who go and lose," she said, "and I think it is very ignoble of me to be unwilling to go and lose." Growing up in the highly competitive Hepburn family, winning was everything. "I can't think of a single, logical defense of someone who occupies a position in the industry that they refuse to go to the biggest celebration that that industry has to offer. I think it's unpardonable, but I do it . . . I have no defense."

For years, visitors to Kate's homes reported seeing her Oscar statuettes and plaques proudly displayed. But she seemed to have changed her tune later in life. When Berg asked Kate in 1982 about her trophies, she said that she had given them to a museum in the Empire State Building. "I mean, if I don't go to the ceremony," she said, "I can't very well put them on my mantelpiece, can I? I simply have no right to."

So in April of 1968, with her usual mixed feelings, Kate cabled an acceptance speech from Nice that thanked the Academy and praised William Rose, who wrote the script for *Guess Who's Coming to Dinner*. "Rose wrote about a normal middle aged unspectacular unglamorous creature with a good brain and a warm heart who's doing the best she can to do the decent thing in a difficult situation. In other words she was a good wife. Our most unsung and important heroine. I'm glad she's coming back in style. I modeled her after my mother. Thanks again. They don't usually give these things to the old girls you know."

Even after winning for *Guess Who's Coming to Dinner*, she still lost the Best Actress award more often – eight times – than anybody in the history of the Oscars. (Her record was later broken by Meryl Streep, who has been nominated fifteen times but won only twice). But she would eventually rack up two more wins – for *The Lion in Winter* (1969) and *On Golden Pond* (1982) – to give her four statuettes in her career, which still stands as a record for the most Best Actress awards ever given to a single performer.

In the spring of 1969, when Kate won for *Lion in Winter*, she was watching the Academy Awards in Irene Selznick's apartment in New York (she still did not have a television of her own). At the ceremony, Ingrid Bergman surprised the audience by announcing an extremely rare outcome – Kate and Barbra Streisand had tied for Best Actress - Streisand for *Funny Girl*. It was the first time two actors had tied for an Oscar since 1932. "Hello, gorgeous," Streisand said to laughter as she accepted the statuette. *Lion in Winter* director Anthony Harvey accepted the award on Kate's behalf.

Ruth Gordon, now seventy-two, also received an Oscar that year, for Best Supporting Actress for *Rosemary's Baby*. Gordon had already won an Oscar for co-writing the screenplay for *Adam's Rib,* but this was her first acting award in a film career that dated back to 1940. So she could have been speaking for her close friend Kate, watching on television, when she half-joked, half-groused about the delay in being recognized for the full measure of her greatness: "I don't know why it took so long."

22
"I PRAYED –
SOMEONE HELP ME –
AND OUT I WENT"

Before Kate left for Europe in October of 1967 to film *The Lion in Winter*, her good friend, theater producer Irene Selznick, approached her with an audacious proposal: Would she be interested in playing the French fashion designer Coco Chanel in a Broadway musical planned for the following year?

The idea of Katharine Hepburn starring in a musical was comical. Kate laughed out loud when Selznick first mentioned it. She had never attended a Broadway musical, never mind perform in one. She considered herself utterly without musical talent and, in her memoir, tells the story of a friend, Marcia Davenport, who asked if that was really her voice heard singing in the woods in *Little Women*.

"Yes - yes, Marcia, it was," Kate replied.

"Well, I think that you should do something about it," her friend snapped.

Raising the stakes was the fact that *Coco* would not just be any musical. It was being written by none other than Alan Jay Lerner, who had won an Oscar for his screenplay for *An American in Paris* and, with composer Frederick Loewe, had established one of the great songwriting teams ever, creators of classic tunes like the celebrated score to *My Fair Lady*.

Rosalind Russell had originally been cast as Coco Chanel – her husband, the producer Frederick Brisson, envisioned the project as a vehicle for her – but she had to turn down the role because of arthritis. After Kate stopped laughing at the idea of warbling on stage, she began to seriously consider the offer – after all, she had always been fearless and relished a challenge. And this would be a challenge of

Herculean proportions. The only tunes she felt comfortable with, she said, were hymns – like the chorus of "Onward Christian Soldiers" that she sang in *The African Queen*. "But I can be loud," she said, "and I figured if Rex Harrison could star in a musical, so could I."

For ten days in New York, Kate prepared for her audition by studying with the composer and arranger Roger Edens, MGM's music coach, who had worked with stars such as Judy Garland and Ethel Merman. "Roger was an extraordinary man," Kate recalled later. "He helped people who could do it to make the song interesting, fascinating - whatever."

But Kate struggled. "Roger was not easy to please," she said. "Now, I was quite aware that to him I was not even one step up from a *dud*. Sometimes that cold look in his eye froze my soul. And by the same token, if I by some wild chance pleased him, I drove home full of joy." Remarkably, after many hours of working together, Edens concluded that Kate's voice had potential after all.

Kate arrived at her audition – actually a dinner party in Selznick's suite at the Pierre Hotel - wearing pants, sandals, a turtleneck, and layers of sweaters. Wanting to get the singing over with first, she sipped tea by the grand piano and waited for the guests to arrive, including Lerner and Brisson. With Edens accompanying her on the piano, Kate put down her tea and sang a bit of Cole Porter's "Thank You So Much, Mrs. Lowsborough – Goodby," then a tune from Lerner and Loewe's *Camelot* and another Porter song, "Miss Otis Regrets."

To Kate's surprise, Lerner was suitably impressed and agreed that she could pull it off. "She's remarkably musical," he said later. "Unlike most actors who forget to act when they sing, she was always acting." Kate found the situation terribly amusing. She called Stanley Kramer when she got home to Turtle Bay and said, "They seemed to like me. They must be desperate."

The plan was for *Coco* rehearsals to begin sometime after Kate had finished *The Madwoman of Chaillot* in the spring of 1968. But there was a slight problem. Lerner had assured Coco Chanel that his highly fictionalized book would cover only the early years of her life and career in the 1920s and 30s. Since Kate was already in her early sixties, Lerner and composer André Previn had to completely revamp both book and score to focus on her later years. Revisions were still far from finished when *Madwoman* finished shooting, so the show was postponed for an entire season, until the fall of 1969.

With lots of time on her hands, Kate became involved in what appeared to be her first post-Tracy affair, with William Rose, who, ironically enough, had written two of Tracy's final films: *It's a Mad, Mad, Mad, Mad World* (with his then-wife Tania Rose) and *Guess Who's Coming to Dinner*.

Like Tracy, Rose drank too much and appeared in desperate need of saving. He was in the middle of a divorce and had told London's *Sunday Express*, "I'm rich, fat, burned out, and I'm looking for someone to come with me in my claret-coloured Maserati to Italy next month. I've rented a villa in Portofino and I want to be there for my fifty-first birthday at the end of August."

"I was very worried about Willie, who was drinking much too much every day," Kate said later. "I thought that he was desperately lonely. He kept talking about a Maserati - a car he wanted to pick up in Italy." Kate suggested they travel together to get the Maserati Rose had just purchased, saying it sounded like a fun adventure.

In her memoir, Kate devotes page after page to their trip, in screenplay style, with dialogue that often sounds like a Samuel Beckett play as they flirt, argue, get lost, stop at hotels, and finally pick up the car and bring it to a boat to be shipped back the United States. "And I wondered what I was doing here," she writes. "What did I want? What did he want? I concluded that we were both absolutely desperate - belonging nowhere - dawn till dusk - and no one giving a rap."

Once again, Kate found herself with a brilliant, complicated man who did not feel good about himself. "He had been hurt and hurt badly," she wrote. "But when? He had been very well thought of always as a writer . . . And it is a curse that he doesn't get any joy from it - any confidence . . . And as a woman who has been trained to make people - children, parents, audiences, to say nothing of the opposite sex - feel good about themselves, it is a great challenge to meet someone like Willie."

As she prepared for her role in *Coco*, Kate traveled to Paris to meet the legendary Coco Chanel in person. She was terrified to meet the famous icon, now in her mid-eighties, who had founded the Chanel brand and redefined what fashion meant for women ever since the post-World War I era. "I had worn the same clothes for forty years, literally, even the shoes," Kate said. "I thought, 'If I don't like her, it will be an agony.' Alan Lerner said, 'Don't be silly, you'll like her.'"

Lerner was right. After meeting Chanel in her Paris apartment atop her salon, Kate said, "We had a delicious lunch and she - after a carefully delayed great entrance - was enchanting." Following lunch, she and Alan watched Chanel's fashion show from the stairs leading down to the salon. Kate had trouble communicating with Chanel because her French was poor, but she left her a souvenir from *The African Queen* - an African brass medallion - along with a note.

When Chanel went back to her apartment and found the medallion, Kate said, "She was like a little girl, she was so tremendously pleased by discovering the gift. I liked her at once, she was amusing, tough in a good sense, and fun. She got to me. The essence of her style was simplicity. Exactly what I appreciate most."

Chanel liked Kate as well, but she was horrified that a woman of Kate's age would be playing her. "Why, she must be close to sixty!" she said. But Lerner held firm.

Back in New York, Kate began working with music coaches Susan Seton and Lynn Masters. Edens, who had coached her so adroitly in preparation for her audition, died unexpectedly before the show went into rehearsals. So Seton stepped in to help her learn and interpret each song. Alfred Dixon, the vocal coach who had saved her from disaster in *The Millionairess*, had also passed away, so his former assistant, Masters, took over. She taught Kate how to project her voice - and protect it - so she'd be able to make it through eight performances a week.

For months, Kate worked hard to master "the whole concept of that sound coming up from way down below by the diaphragm and traveling through that relaxed tunnel - well, not tunnel - shaft really, then into my head," she recalled later. "Head tones" Seton called them. "Feel the vibrations?" she asked. "Yes, yes," Kate said. "Head, not throat. Bypass the throat. Forget the throat. The chest bones, top of skull. That I could do."

With a budget of nearly $900,000, *Coco* was, at the time, the most expensive show in Broadway history. In late September of 1969, Kate showed up for rehearsals at the Mark Hellinger Theatre wearing sandals, baggy beige pants, a white T-shirt, and a black, high-necked sweater. Lerner commented, "She has twenty pairs of beige slacks, white shirts, and black sweaters. When she gets up in the morning, she knows what she's going to wear. She never considers what she's going to have for dinner, because her cook knows she eats simply (a steak, potato, and salad). All the decisions that exhaust the normal person, she has eliminated."

Kate, as usual, arrived at rehearsals first and left last, learning everyone else's lines as well as her own. But *Coco* was truly a one-woman show: Kate was on stage for all but twelve minutes of the show's two-and-a-half hours. Jerry Adler, *Coco*'s stage manager, told a *Time* reporter, "She leaves the younger folks for dead at the end of the day. When she's not in a scene, she perches on a staircase munching things - packets of meat and cheese and fruit she has brought from home - listening and watching the onstage action over and over."

But *Coco* was a troubled production from the start. While the lyrics were among the best Lerner ever wrote, many felt the music of André Previn was derivative and uninspired. And Kate was unhappy with the cast, which she later called "pretty mediocre" with the exception of George Rose, who played Coco's friend and manager Louis Greff. "With all the actors in New York," she said, "it always amazes me how difficult it is to find a few with real talent."

Perhaps most troublesome, director Michael Benthall – who had directed her so well in *The Millionairess* and four Shakespeare plays – appeared to be over his head in such a mammoth, complex musical production. The set itself was sometimes dangerous; when a giant, movable turntable she was standing on malfunctioned, Kate, some twenty feet off the ground, had to jump four feet across a chasm created when a set piece didn't come together correctly. Benthall had problems with other elements of the production as well, like the part when characters from Coco's past appeared on large screens in filmed segments.

The grand finale of the play was a fashion show featuring Chanel designs from 1918 to 1959. The complicated set design was contrary to the simplicity and straightforwardness of Chanel's style – and, like the play itself, lacked the simple sophistication Chanel's admirers had come to revere.

Eventually, Benthall was pushed to the sidelines and the show's talented young choreographer, Michael Bennett, stepped in as director. Bennett would later win seven Tony awards in a spectacular career that included the mega-hit musical *A Chorus Line*. "Bold and brash and full of his own ideas, he clashed constantly with Lerner and [Hepburn]," wrote A. Scott Berg in *Kate Remembered*, "both of whom, he felt, had somehow turned the show from the life of Chanel into that of Katharine Hepburn."

But the musical was also fertile ground for the creative

minds involved. One night at dinner, discussing her frustrations with the play, Kate exploded to Lerner, "Who the devil cares what a woman wears!" Lerner snapped to attention. "Kate, that's a good lyric," he said, and used it. He also used Kate as inspiration for a lyric by quoting one of her sayings, "one is as one does."

Despite the difficulties, Kate had fallen in love with the character she was playing. "I've felt all along that Coco and I were alike," she said. "Two females who have never been intimidated by the world, who never shifted our stripes to conform to public opinion. She is practical, vulnerable and a fighter. She's not afraid to put herself on the chopping block. She's taken some real body blows. And her capacity for survival is what fascinates me. You know, I'd play this part for free. Because that's me, Coco, on the chopping block now."

The December 18, 1969, premiere of *Coco* was a much-hyped, much-anticipated social event. But, as *Time* magazine wrote, it was "a disastrous party . . . Dramatically, the champagne was flat, the hors d'oeuvres tasted of sawdust and the small talk on- and off–stage sagged into yawns." Nonetheless, Kate's performance earned rave reviews; Clive Barnes of *The New York Times* wrote, "She growls out the most ordinary lines as if they were pearls of great price, gems of wit, nuggets of wisdom. She grins and she is enchanting. She prowls gloweringly down to the footlights, mutters a word for ordure in an idiomatically terse fashion, and remains devastatingly charming."

As for her musical ability, Barnes noted, "Her singing voice is unique - a neat mixture of faith, love and laryngitis, unforgettable, unbelievable and delightful." He capped off his love letter to Kate with: "Dear Miss Hepburn - perhaps they should have made a musical of your life rather than a dress designer. They say some beauty is ageless - yours is timeless."

Those nearest and dearest to Kate – her loyal ex-husband Luddy, her friends Laura Harding, Ruth Gordon, and Garson Kanin, Lauren Bacall, Sue Seton, and Irene Selznick – all turned out in force to show their support and attend the opening night after-party. Most of them were dressed to the nines. Ever the non-conformist, Kate wore her usual beige pants and black sweater. The real Coco Chanel, still miffed that her younger self was not being portrayed onstage, refused to attend the show, even on opening night.

From day one, the show was a hit, with big crowds showing up nightly. And yet Kate was petrified. "If I could describe to you the terror - the sinking inadequacy - the blank horror which I felt every night before I went on," she said later. "Like playing tennis without a racquet. Or, say, with a racquet with no strings - impotence - and pretense - Katie sings - Well, to me it was a great example of Katie *doesn't* sing."

She was ever-mindful of the audience, praying that she could live up to their expectations. "They were out there sitting - waiting - and they'd paid a big price for those tickets and they had a right to the best and here I was about to go forth - armed with a squeak. A mouse posing as a lion. I got my face on - fixed my hair - the shoes - the costume - the hat - then I sat, heart pounding . . . Relax - relax - they don't expect you to be Callas . . . No, no, you don't get it - *I* expect *me* to be Callas - otherwise why am I here? I prayed - I wept

- I did my exercises - I prayed - someone help me - and out I went. Please, God . . ."

Fearless – or at least pretending to be – she barreled on-stage. "And do you know what?" she said. "Love came across the footlights. And in waves and hugs . . ."

It was almost as if she could feel what the audience was thinking: "That's all right, Katie - so you can't sing but we get it - we hear you - we feel - we know you."

Kate and her fans, it turned out, were having the adventure together, which gave her the courage to continue. "And so together we worked it out," she said. "And I got a little better - enough better so that I didn't die. And I continued work-ing with Sue Seton. And Coco was a great character and Lynn Masters came every night for weeks to warm me up. And I relied on what I could do, and so I went on . . ."

Despite the weakness of the play, and even if Kate's perfor-mance barely resembled the actual person of Coco Chanel, Katharine Hepburn's movie-star personality, talent, and popularity - as well as the respect she had earned over the course of her forty-year career - drew full houses every night for seven-and-a-half months. Later, she said it was the first time in her entire career that she felt the public was not against her but truly loved her. That, of course, had always been the goal, ever since she had decided, as a young wom-an, that she would be a big star.

Outside the theater, opposition to the Vietnam War was turning the country upside down and Kate – the child of liberal activists – felt she needed to address it. In May of 1970, a few days after four students at Kent State University were killed by Ohio National Guard troops during an anti-war demonstration, she gave a short post-performance speech. "You may call them rebels or rabble rousers or anything you please," she said. "Nevertheless they were our kids and our responsibility."

By August, large crowds were still jamming the theater, but Kate was ready to stop. She was replaced by Danielle Darrieux, the famous French singer and movie star. Darrieux performed well – but for American audiences, the production just wasn't the same without Kate. *Coco* closed two months later.

Most performers would be eager for time off after such a grueling, eight-shows-a-week schedule. Not Kate. Two weeks after stepping off the stage, she headed for Spain with Wilbourn to film *The Trojan Women*, co-starring Vanessa Redgrave, Irene Papas, and Geneviève Bujold. The director would be Michael Cacoyannis, a Greek filmmaker whose 1963 off-Broadway production of *The Trojan Women* had been well-received by the critics. When a reporter asked Kate why she elected to make a Euripides drama written in 415 B.C., she simply said, "I've never done Greek Tragedy, and before my time runs out, I'd like to have done everything."

In the tiny town of Atienza, Spain, where *The Trojan Women* was being filmed, Kate moved into a little house overlooking rustic fields intended to represent the landscape of ancient Troy. Off set, she wore sandals, khakis, a black shirt, and a wide-brimmed straw hat to protect her from the sun. After the rigors of *Coco*, she was even thinner than usual but had lost none of her vigor or nerve.

Kate, of course, had her own opinions about how to play Hecuba, the aging queen of Troy, which led to disputes with Cacoyannis, who already had his hands full with his other demanding actors. Cacoyannis did not appreciate Kate's nosing around the set and suggesting that her way of playing scenes was superior to his; not only was he Greek, but he had directed the show in New York and had written the screenplay.

The director's inability to persuade Kate to do things his way, and the inconsistent accents of his stars, resulted in an awkward final product. Despite some compelling moments, in the end, distribution of the film was limited, and the public's reception was lukewarm. Kate was unfazed by *The Trojan Women*'s lack of success; she had done her Greek tragedy and was on her way back to New York to rehearse for a national tour of *Coco*.

After all her intense preparations, the chance to reprise her portrayal of Coco Chanel was too tempting to pass up. And keeping busy remained her best antidote to the grief she still felt over the death of Tracy. The day *Coco* opened in Cleveland on January 11, 1971, Kate learned that the real Coco Chanel had died the previous day in Paris. After receiving a standing ovation for her performance, Kate tearfully discussed Chanel's death. "Miss Chanel was a remarkable woman with a fine mind and a fine heart and the driving inspiration behind my performance," Kate said. "She is not with us anymore, but I hope that someplace she may be listening."

In Los Angeles, the play's producers had placed in her contract a stipulation that she not repeat a profane ad-lib that she had used to great effect during the show's original New York run. It happened during a climactic moment when the audience wonders whether Coco's latest collection has been a hit or not. Kate walks down to the front of the stage and sums it all up with one word: "Shit!" – the most concise, emphatic explanation imaginable. Invariably, the audience roared with laughter.

Kate signed the contract and, as the Los Angeles dates neared, tried different approaches but discovered that nothing else drew the same reaction. So she wrote to Edwin Lester of the Los Angeles Civic Light Opera Association asking for permission to reinstate it. "In an era of literature and cinema and theater where every other expression is a four letter word - it is - let's face it - curiously head in the sand to prohibit the use of the least offensive of these expressions," she said.

Charmed by the letter, Lester replied that her inquiry "was sufficient for us to acquiesce, particularly if acquiescence would make you happy." He added, "Let me tell you how much we are looking forward to your visit with us, even though you bring that naughty word along with you."

Touring was exhausting for Kate, but she was contractually obligated to keep it up, and her appreciative audiences kept her going. As she crisscrossed the country for six months, loyal fans trailed Kate from one town to the next, just to be in her presence. One young man claimed he hitchhiked to every city on the *Coco* tour, surviving solely on peanut butter sandwiches, just to catch a glimpse of her. He never spoke to her or sent a note - he just wanted to watch.

In February 1971, the touring company played the Bushnell

Auditorium in Hartford, Kate's hometown. Kate stayed with her father's elderly widow, Madelaine "Santa" Hepburn, on the night of the show, which turned out to be a disaster; Hartford was buried under several feet of snow, and there was a mechanical failure on the set. The reviews were horrible. To top it off, the temporary chauffeur Kate had hired – fifty-five-year-old Luella G. West – broke into the Hepburns' Bloomfield Avenue home.

Kate immediately fired her, but when she returned to the house with Wilbourn, Santa, and Kate's regular chauffeur, Charles Newhill, they found West hiding inside a closet with a hammer in her hand. Kate and Newhill struggled with her while Wilbourn called the police.

During the scuffle, West bit Kate's index finger nearly off before disappearing out the front door. "The finger hung by a thread," Kate said. "Phyllis got me to a doctor. I was in agony. Next day, I had to go on for a matinee in a splint. My brother Robert, who's a doctor, found a Dr. Watson, a wonderful man, who grafted it back on." Despite the pain, she never missed a performance.

Kate did not press charges again West. This was fortunate for the assailant because, as West's lawyer was quoted as saying, "Attacking Katharine Hepburn in Hartford is like attacking the judge before sentencing."

The *Coco* tour ended in June at the Ahmanson Theatre in Los Angeles. Now Kate was at loose ends again – and Hollywood was a town that, since Tracy's death, held many painful memories. As if seeking closure, she paid a visit to the bungalow on George Cukor's estate, which had been left basically the same since Tracy's death four years earlier: A model of an antique sailing ship was still above the fireplace, as were some of Kate's artwork and Tracy's black leather chair. Cukor suggested she stay to see if she might find some solace there.

23

"I'VE BEEN ABSOLUTELY PETRIFIED ALL MY LIFE"

In the fall of 1971, Kate was dismayed to learn that Garson Kanin had written an exposé of her relationship with Tracy. She felt deeply betrayed by the book, *Tracy and Hepburn: An Intimate Memoir*, which she said put "a great strain on our friendship."

"Katharine Hepburn has created, with diligence and intention, a world of her own, and she lives in it happily ever after," Kanin wrote. "She is its Empress, its leading citizen, and the most common of its commoners . . . When you enter her world you are expected to observe its strictures and you do so without question. You eat a cooked fruit with every meat dish; you arrive on time and leave as early as possible (say, on her third yawn); you do not gossip; you agree with every one of her many opinions and approve each of her numerous plans; you do not get drunk no matter how much you drink; you love her dog, Lobo; you applaud the efforts or output or creations of all her friends (whether they or their works are known to you or not); you do not complain (you may, however, rail); you say nothing that may not be repeated; you refrain from lies, dissemblances, and exaggerations; you omit discussions of your physical state, symptoms, or ailments (unless preparatory to asking her advice); you take her advice; you do not use obscene, coarse, or lewd expressions."

Kate was shocked that her old friend – knowing how deeply private she and Tracy were – would write such a book. She refused to speak to Kanin for years.

When Christmas arrived in 1971, Kate returned to the safety and comfort of the Hepburn family home in West Hartford, as usual. But what would normally be a happy occasion was instead filled with sadness: The family was gathering at 201 Bloomfield Avenue for the last time. Santa Hepburn, the seventy-year-old widow of Kate's father, had decided the house was too big and lonely for just one person and was moving in with her sister.

In his will, Dr. Hepburn had bequeathed equal shares of the property to Santa, Kate, and her brother Robert, who was Dr. Hepburn's executor. After talking it over, the three agreed to give the Hepburn house to the University of Hartford. Kate and Robert arranged for the university to buy Santa's share for $82,000, then donated their shares to the university.

"So it was over - life at 201," Kate recalled later. "Clean it up - move out - and give it to Hartford University. The moving out was quite a job, a very, very sad job for all of us - it was the end of our beginning."

Kate traveled back to Hollywood to revise a film script George Cukor had given her. Graham Greene's novel, *Travels with My Aunt,* was a series of anecdotes about a young man and his eccentric, seventy-something aunt, that he planned to adapt to a film. At first, Kate didn't think it could make a successful transition to the screen – but after many re-readings of the book, she began to imagine ways it might work. She decided to rewrite it herself. Over a span of eight months, she labored over the screenplay, often putting in sixteen-hour days. Shortly before filming was scheduled to begin, she sent it to MGM president James Aubrey.

Aubrey was not impressed with her work, believing the script lacked charm. He wanted the movie to show flashbacks of Greene's aunt as a younger woman, which meant that a younger actress would be needed to play the role.

"Well, you know I'm not going to be able to shoot that script [of yours]," he told Kate over the phone. "I think . . . and Metro thinks . . . and I agree with them, that we should put it aside for a time."

"You mean I'm fired?" Kate barked. Aubrey didn't answer and hung up. The next day, Kate was given her notice for refusing to work. "I would never refuse to work ten days before a picture was scheduled to start," she protested. "I would consider that an outrage. And I said, 'Go ahead and say I'm fired. It's all right with me.'"

Within ten days, MGM had signed the noted Shakespearean actress and Oscar-winner Maggie Smith to play the part and began shooting. "I thought of suing them because I don't feel things like that should be allowed to happen," Kate said. "The script was practically all mine. Cut to hash, but practically all mine . . . I was never paid a cent . . ." When it was released in December of 1972, *Travels with My Aunt* received mixed reviews. *The New York Times* called it "lucid, controlled and graceful" while *TV Guide* said the screen-play adaptation "was not entirely successful." But it was nominated for Best Picture by the Golden Globe and Smith was nominated for both an Academy Award and a Golden Globe for Best Actress.

Wrung out from the fight over *Travels with My Aunt*, Kate had to face more grim news: John Ford was dying of cancer. Ford's wife, Mary, knew of her husband's affair with Kate in 1937 but still allowed Kate to visit him in Palm Desert, California – an especially generous gesture given that her husband continued to have strong feelings for Kate long after their affair ended.

"Tracy complained that he had never known a woman who kept so many of her old flames ignited - aflicker if not in full blaze - as Hepburn," A. Scott Berg noted, citing Luddy's continued presence, Leland Hayward checking in often with career advice, and her continuing friendship with the director George Stevens. As for Ford, Berg said, "almost until the end of his life, John Ford spoke of retiring to Ireland, taking Kate with him."

Ford's health had deteriorated rapidly in the early 1970s; he suffered a broken hip, which put him in a wheelchair, and was now being treated for cancer. Kate hated seeing him so miserable, but the two chatted for hours until he grew too tired to speak. He died the following year, on August 31, 1973.

At the time, Kate was suffering health problems of her own, including arthritis in her hip, an early indication of the palsy that she would battle for the rest of her life. Soon, she would have surgery to treat the condition. Her head and hands shook a little now, and her voice had started to quaver. Other than smoking, she had always practiced healthy habits to ward off aging and illness and was still otherwise fit. In coming years, she would take special care to control her movements and alter the phrasing of her voice to minimize the shakiness.

In 1972, Ely Landau – who had produced *Long Day's Journey into Night* – contacted Kate at Fenwick. He wanted her to consider joining the cast of a film version of Edward Albee's 1967 Pulitzer-Prize winning play, *A Delicate Balance*, to be shot in England for his new venture, the American

Film Theatre.

Kate wasn't enamored with the character she would be playing – an upper-class woman named Agnes, who shares a comfortable suburban home with her husband Tobias and her alcoholic sister Claire. She was also confused by the script. "I knew that Albee was considered 'the great white hope' of the American theater," she said later, "but I had absolutely no idea what that play was about."

Ultimately, she was convinced to make the film by the wonderful company she would keep: Her old friend Joseph Cotten, who had shared the stage with her in *The Philadelphia Story*, would co-star, as would Paul Scofield, still considered one of the greatest Shakespearean actors of all time. The director would be Tony Richardson, who, at age twenty-four, had brashly invited Kate to tea during the London run of *The Millionairess*.

Richardson thought it was odd that Kate disliked her character because he thought she and Agnes shared many characteristics. "There's a lot of that same kind of inflexible, authoritarian quality in her," he said, "She suited the part terribly well, the obsession with the home - the New England background - all very 'Kate.'"

After filming began outside London, it dawned on Kate that Albee's play was about self-protection. This she understood deeply, all the more so after her privacy was violated by the Kanin memoir. "I think we are all enormously self-protective," she said. "I identified with these people who resented the intruders in their privacy, and I think that's what made me, after not wanting to do it at all, finally decide to go ahead. I'm a very private person. Here were these people, miserable though they might be, and they wanted to keep their 'shell' intact."

As with most productions, there were problems. The house they were shooting in was so small that it was difficult for the cameras and equipment to move around; Kim Stanley, who was playing Agnes's alcoholic sister, had to quit for health reasons, replaced by Kate Reid. "Katharine Hepburn threatened to quit because Kim Stanley was not memorizing her lines, and was improvising all over the place," Albee said later, a clash Reid heard about. "By the time Kate [Reid] landed in London, she knew the first half of the play." Kate, meanwhile, argued with her director about most of her scenes, as usual.

A Delicate Balance was the first installment of Landau's American Film Theatre series that ran between 1973 and 1975. Like his *Long Day's Journey into Night* a decade earlier, these were not adaptations but filmed versions of stage plays that remained faithful to the original script. The Albee play was shown in 500 theaters in 400 cities, with admission based on subscription to the entire series. Critics were split about its merits. Roger Ebert of the *Chicago Sun-Times* praised this "fine, tough, lacerating production" with a cast that "could hardly be better," but *TV Guide* called it "unfortunately stiff, dull, and extremely stagy."

Once she had finished *A Delicate Balance*, Kate, enjoying her time in London, decided to move ahead with a project, by another famed playwright, that had been gestating for years. Producer David Susskind had long wanted to make a television version of Tennessee Williams's *The Glass Menagerie* and desperately wanted Kate to play Amanda

Wingfield, the aging matriarch. He had started to pester her about taking the role as early as 1965, but Kate steadfastly maintained that the part would always be Laurette Taylor's after she created it so indelibly in the original Broadway run of 1945.

Kate was not the only one in awe of Taylor's legendary portrayal of the fading Southern belle. In the 2004 documentary *Broadway: The Golden Age, by the Legends Who Were There*, several stage veterans rank Taylor's performance as the most memorable of their entire lives. "She was like Spence," Kate said of Taylor. "This was her life. She could do it. She knew how in her bones . . . No agony of preparation - like the Method - no constipation. They were born able to show you - tell you - make you feel - arrest you - make you watch."

Susskind asked Kate again in 1967, and she refused again, even though he pointed out that several other actresses had played the role since Taylor. Insisting that she was too old to learn how to film for television – then considered artistically inferior to the big screen – Kate continued to refuse his offer, and Susskind backed off. But he kept after her. Finally, in 1972, she agreed.

Kate had asked Susskind to hire a director she could trust, and he chose her friend Anthony Harvey, who had directed her so beautifully in *The Lion in Winter*. Kate worked hard on her Southern accent and constructed the character based on memories of her father's Virginia family, which, like the Wingfield clan, had seen its share of hard times.

The Glass Menagerie had long been a favorite play of Kate's because it revealed "more about what a lack of money can do to human beings than any play I know." Kate also considered Amanda the "most tenderly observed, the most accessible woman . . . [Tennessee Williams] ever created."

Kate's portrayal wasn't as glamorous as other actresses who had played the part, partly because she accentuated the defeated aspect of the meddling mother who is desperately worried for her family and their future.

Filming for television was not as difficult as she had feared; in fact, she now saw it as a way to broaden her horizons and increase the roles and projects available to her. When the show aired in December of 1973, critics were impressed. John J. O'Connor of *The New York Times* wrote, "Miss Hepburn's Amanda is a wonderfully effective blend of Southern gentility and fierce determination, but occasionally, only occasionally, she is overly dominated by another personality, that of a strong-willed, intensely mannered actress named Katharine Hepburn. Any reservations about this *Glass Menagerie* are relatively slight," he continued. "It is a special TV event, demanding attention."

Before the film aired, Dick Cavett invited Kate to appear on his television talk show, never dreaming that she might say yes. "The common wisdom is that no one will ever get Katharine Hepburn in front of a television camera – and it was gospel," he said later. "Her privacy was practically enforced by the military. It was total."

But Kate's friends Irene Selznick and Lauren Bacall urged her to do it, and she knew it would be good publicity for both *The Glass Menagerie* and *A Delicate Balance,* scheduled to air within a week of each other in December of 1973. So she agreed. "Getting her was really a kind of miracle," Cavett said. "It was a challenge and Hepburn likes a challenge, and she likes something new and likes to conquer things."

What she agreed to, however, was only to come to the studio to check things out – the cameras, lights, chairs, the décor, and, of course, Cavett himself. Kate arrived at the ABC sound stage early, with Wilbourn by her side. Cavett rushed out to greet her, instructing the director and camera crew to get ready to shoot.

Kate was nervous, but not shy: She switched chairs with Cavett and asked the crew to fix the wobbling table in front of her - "and nobody answers!" she yelled. Then she swapped the wobbly table for the one beside her so she could put her feet up. She loudly – and repeatedly – complained about the color of the carpet ("Put a rug over it! I'll bring one!") and gave her opinion on other ways to improve the looks of the set ("Whose idea was this?" she said of the color scheme. "Make it all one color!"). Cavett, wearing white tennis shoes, white pants, and no suitcoat, fidgeted, trying not to look worried. Finally, she said, "Let's just go ahead and do the interview now."

Without preamble, Kate launched into the story of her life, from her childhood and family in Hartford to her early years of fame, laughing and flitting from one subject to another. "My brother," she said, "told me not to appear on this show. He said, 'They'll find out you're a bore.'"

She was anything but, disarmingly confessing to her insecurities. "I've been absolutely petrified all my life," she said. "I look at the thing and just hope I'm going to drop dead before it happens. How I ever opened in *Coco* I don't know."

Relaxed and unguarded, she laughed about Dorothy Parker's famous remark that "She ran the gamut of emotion from A to B" while appearing in *The Lake* – which Kate called "the most petrifying experience I've ever had." She confessed to not attending the Oscars because she was "too gutless" and "afraid I wouldn't win it." Comparing her own acting to Tracy's, she said, "I was aware of a certain sort of cheapness in what I did because my concentration was not anywhere near as good as his. He and Laurette Taylor I think had the greatest – they were remarkable."

She even speculated about why she was the object of so much public fascination. "I think the reason people have an affection for me now is that . . . I must have lived a life that a lot of women think would be a nice life to have lived. They think it's dignified but they think it's free . . . I've done what I've wanted to."

As the interview wound down, Cavett said, "I hate to say this but we've come to the end of the time we have tonight."

"You mean I'm finished? I can go?" Kate said. "Thanks very much. I've had a lovely time. Bye-bye!" With the haste of someone who just remembered that she had left the stove on, she suddenly hopped up and bolted off the set – apparently unaware that this was only the first part of a two-part interview to be aired on successive nights.

"But can't you wait till I say goodnight?" Cavett called after her.

"No," she said before disappearing behind the curtain. "You say goodnight. Goodnight!"

Leaving so abruptly seemed so spontaneous and so Kate –

until Cavett revealed later that the two of them had planned the whole thing as a joke.

When it aired in October of 1973, Kate's appearance on the show created a flurry of excitement in Hollywood – and the rest of Los Angeles, too. People yelled at Kate from buses and open windows, Cavett said, delighted with the interview and Kate's candor. A group of college students who encountered her began chanting, "Hey Kate, you were great!"

During the interview, Cavett had asked Kate if she regretted never making a film with Lawrence Olivier. "Well, neither one of us is dead yet," she said.

Later – apparently in response to the interview – George Cukor sent her the script for *Love Among the Ruins*, a television movie he was directing for ABC, and asked if Kate would star in it with Olivier. She was still recovering from surgery to treat the osteoarthritis in her hip but couldn't pass it up – and six months later was shooting in London.

Love Among the Ruins was a romantic comedy/drama about an aging London theater actress, Jessica Medicott, who is sued for breach of promise by her much younger ex-fiancé – after promising to marry him, she changed her mind. Olivier plays Sir Arthur Granville-Jones, a famous London barrister Medicott has hired to represent her – and whom Medicott had seduced and abandoned forty years earlier. Unbeknownst to her, he is still in love with her. The actress claims she does not remember Granville-Jones, but throughout the course of the legal dispute, she falls in love with him anyway.

Olivier was delighted with their collaboration and was

surprised that Kate was not the diva he was expecting. She was professional and hardworking, he said, more an actress than a star, something he had never fully understood. Kate, meanwhile, was thrilled to be working with Cukor for the first time since he had directed her and Tracy in *Pat and Mike* twenty years before. Cukor took great pains to make her lovely for the film, providing her flattering costumes with high necks and soft lace and elegant hats that framed her face.

When *Love Among the Ruins* premiered on ABC in March of 1975, both Kate and Olivier won Emmy awards for out-standing lead actress and actor in a special. Cukor won for directing, and the film itself won an Emmy for outstanding special program.

Later, Kate described Olivier as "a first-rate actor" but "a second-rate person" because of a gargantuan ego that made him undermine his then-wife, Vivien Leigh, with whom Kate had been friendly. "Larry always wanted to be a big movie star," Kate said, "and while he was considered the greatest actor on the stage, he was never in the first rank as a star in the movies. Then Vivien comes along and gets Scar-lett O'Hara. Wins the Academy Award. Biggest picture ever made. Suddenly Larry says, 'Oh darling, we really must get you out of Hollywood now. Let's go off and do Shakespeare together.' Now Vivien could do anything, but he was clearly trying to keep her in her place, which was billed beneath him."

Years later, Kate said, Olivier did the same thing after Leigh played Blanche DuBois in *A Streetcar Named Desire*. "And she's brilliant," Kate recalled. "Wins the Academy Award.

Most talked-about movie of the year. And suddenly Larry says, 'Oh darling, we really must get you out of Hollywood now. Let's go off and do Shakespeare together.'" Plus, there was the well-documented physical abuse. During a tour of New Zealand in the late 1940s, Leigh could not find her shoes and refused to go onstage without them. Olivier became enraged, cursed at her and slapped her in front of cast and crew. "Small man," said Kate. "Giant actor. Very small man."

With *Love Among The Ruins*, it became clear that Kate's foray into television was no longer an experiment – it was becoming a new career. Starting in 1973, when she turned sixty-six, she would make more television movies than big-screen films, weaving her singular personality ever more deeply into the fabric of American popular culture.

As she was entering a new medium, Kate finally made amends with a much older one – the motion-picture industry that she had spent more than four decades conquering. On April 2, 1974, she made her first and only appearance at the Academy Awards – to present the Irving G. Thalberg Memorial Award to Lawrence Weingarten, a producer and longtime friend.

After being nominated for Best Actress eleven times and winning three times (both records at the time), Katharine Hepburn finally showed up at the industry's biggest party. She was rewarded with a standing ovation, her peers grateful for the chance to finally show how they felt about her. Kate was moved and humbled. "I'm living proof," she said, "that a person can wait forty-one years to be unselfish."

24

"SHE'S TOUGH. CHRIST! SHE WANTS TO DO EVERYTHING!"

After completing *Love Among the Ruins*, Kate stayed in New York for three weeks with Phyllis Wilbourn before heading back to California, where she was slated to co-star with John Wayne in *Rooster Cogburn*, a sequel to his Academy Award-winning *True Grit*. Kate and Wayne were born two weeks apart, in May of 1907, had a good friend in common in the director John Ford, and both had been huge stars for decades – but, remarkably, had never met. The attraction was immediate. At their first meeting, Kate told him, "I was born to be your leading lady, Duke. Twenty-five years too late."

It's deeply ironic that Katharine Hepburn, the ultra-liberal protofeminist who inspired generations of women to independence and assertiveness, would swoon for the politically conservative John Wayne, the ultimate macho he-man. But swoon she did. "Good humor, I should say, and a sharp wit," is how she described him in her memoir. "Dangerous when roused. His shoulders are broad - very. His chest massive - very. When I leaned against him (which I did as often as possible, I must confess - I am reduced to such innocent pleasures), thrilling. It was like leaning against a great tree. His hands so big. Mine, which are big too, seemed to disappear. Good legs. No seat. A man's body. Rare in these gay times."

When it came to politics, Wayne was a hard-core conservative who would have sent Kate's mother into apoplectic fits. He was also the former president of the Motion Picture Alliance for the Preservation of American Ideals, which Kate had spoken out against during the McCarthy era, and a staunch supporter of America's involvement in Vietnam.

How could Kate be attracted to such a man? They were friends – not lovers – who, despite their political differences, were both disgusted by the cultural changes going on around them, especially the shifts in gender roles and relationships between the sexes. When she spoke of Wayne, Kate sounded like one of his legions of fans who yearned for a simpler America that no longer existed – perhaps never did.

"John Wayne is the hero of the thirties and forties and most of the fifties," she said. "Before the creeps came creeping in. Before, in the sixties, the male hero slid right down into the valley of the weak and the misunderstood. Before the women began dropping any pretense to virginity into the gutter. With a disregard for truth which is indeed pathetic. And unisex was born. The hair grew long and the pride grew short. And we were off to the anti-hero and-heroine."

Wayne treated women with respect both on and off screen, especially the ones he called "good women." Kate was one of the good ones, he said: "She's so feminine - she's a man's woman. Imagine how she must have been at age 25 or 30 . . . how lucky a man would have been to have found her."

He told a reporter on the set of *Rooster Cogburn*, "I love her. You should have seen her up on those mountain locations. She can't ride a hobby horse. But she climbed right up on those horses and gave 'em hell . . . And in one scene she jumped into a kayak and shoved off into a raging river. Yes, sir, she's tough. Christ! She wants to do everything! She can't ride worth a damn and I gotta keep reining my horse in so she can keep up. But I'd hate to think of what this goddamned picture would be without her."

Even in her sixties, Kate was still doing her own stunts. "I haven't waited all these years to do a cowboy picture with Wayne to give up a single moment now," she insisted. Kate hadn't ridden a horse in decades, and her hip surgery was only a year behind her, but she wanted no special privileges. Wayne understood her pride and aversion to pity; he had had a lung removed because of cancer but refused to let it slow his pace. The aging stars invigorated each other, though they may have been a bit much for their director, Stuart Millar.

Kate's character, spinster Eula Goodnight, was reminiscent of Rose Sayer in *The African Queen*. Wayne's *Rooster Cogburn*, a hard-drinking former U.S. Marshal seeking to redeem himself and regain his badge, grudgingly takes Eula with him to find the men who murdered her father. He eventually warms to her, though unlike *The African Queen*, their characters don't fall in love and marry in the end.

Wayne gave permission for the press to be on the set, which made Kate so uncomfortable that on the last day of shooting, she had to redo the final scene several times. When they finally wrapped, Kate was stunned when Wayne removed the eye patch he had worn for the part, took her in his arms, and kissed her passionately on the mouth. She stood dumbfounded for a moment, glancing around at the strangers on the set, then made a quick exit. Wayne lit a cigar and then spit on the sound stage floor. "Damn!" he shouted. "There's a woman!"

She came back later to celebrate with the cast and crew, this time receiving a bear hug from Wayne. "What a wonderful experience," she said, beaming up at her co-star.

Rooster Cogburn was released in October 1975 and was a box office success, the twenty-fifth top-grossing film of the year. Vincent Canby of *The New York Times* called the film "a high-class example of the low Hollywood art of recycling," but movie-goers didn't care. Like Canby, they were just happy to watch "a cheerful, throwaway Western, featuring two stars of the grand tradition who respond to each other with a verve that makes the years disappear."

In June of 1974, Kate returned to Hartford to narrate a documentary produced by her brother-in-law, Ellsworth Grant. *Resolved to Be Free*, sponsored by the Society for Savings and the State Bicentennial Commission, spotlighted Connecticut's role in the Revolutionary War and was offered free of charge to schools. In one of the film's more stirring moments, Kate utters William Prescott's famous words from the 1775 Battle of Breed's Hill: "Men, you are all marksmen - don't one of you fire until you see the whites of their eyes!"

When she returned to New York, Kate found that Broadway composer Stephen Sondheim had moved in next door. Before long, his all-night piano playing began to grate on her nerves. One night in 1974, as he was working on the score for the film *A Little Night Music*, Kate, clad only in her pajamas, climbed the fence between their gardens and pressed her face against the glass of his music room window. "I must have looked like an old witch," Kate said. "He had another young man with him, and they had drinks in their hands, and all of a sudden they both looked at me and absolutely froze. I just stood there. Seconds passed. They just stared at me. I stared at them. I disappeared. Afterwards - silence."

When the stage beckoned again, Kate heeded and signed

on to star in a twelve-week Broadway run of *A Matter of Gravity*. The play was written by the British author Enid Bagnold, whose 1935 novel *National Velvet* was made into a successful 1944 movie starring Elizabeth Taylor and Mickey Rooney. At eighty-six, Bagnold became fast friends with Kate. "Enid is quite extraordinary," Kate said. "My God, imagine writing a play at her age!"

Kate wasn't convinced she was the best fit for the part of the eccentric dowager Mrs. Basil, who begins to question her atheism after watching Dubois, her new cook-housekeeper, perform a miracle by levitating into the air. But Kate's admiration for Bagnold – and her stubborn refusal to back down from a challenge – overcame her hesitation. She even agreed to do a six-month national tour after the Broadway run. "I always feel that if something is difficult - as the theater has always been for me - it must be good for me to do it."

There were aspects of Mrs. Basil that Kate identified with – including her atheism – and, in spite of her initial reluctance, she energetically threw herself into the role, to the delight of her audiences, who flocked to the theater. When the play opened in Philadelphia, she got a chance to catch up with Luddy, who, at seventy-seven and in poor health, had moved back into his family home on the Philadelphia Main Line. The show then moved on to Washington, New Haven, Boston, and Toronto. By the time it hit Broadway – opening on February 3, 1976, at the Broadhurst Theatre – it had already broken even, mostly thanks to Kate.

The New York Times's film critic Clive Barnes wrote, "I have rarely seen Miss Hepburn better even in the movies . . . her acting is now in the lambent heat of its Indian summer."

Barnes was less impressed with the play itself, calling *A Matter of Gravity* "probably too much matter, and too little art," but enjoyed Kate's performance so much that he went to see it again. The praise he heaped on Kate in his Sunday review in the Arts and Leisure section seemed to reflect the enduring influence that Spencer Tracy's simple and direct acting style had on her continuing development as an actress. Barnes wrote: "It's as though the feathery bravura and the challenging nasality and a chin held so high that one scarcely dares question the authenticity behind so much panache had all dissolved at last, had been absorbed into simplicity, had come home to roost and rest, leaving only a clear intention in the eye, an economy of gesture . . . and a directness of address . . . She isn't decorating, she means every bloody word of it . . . In her tartness and her melting laughter, Miss Hepburn is integrity incarnate, piercingly authentic."

In April, after nine weeks of the twelve-week run, Kate asked to be released from her contract so she could make her next film, after which she would continue with the national tour in the fall. The movie was *Olly Olly Oxen Free*, the story of a junkyard owner who enlists two boys to help her build a hot-air balloon. Kate had promised director Richard Colla that if he could get financing for the film, she'd accept the role - just so she could fly the balloon. By the summer of 1976, he had raised enough money, so Kate headed back to California to begin filming.

Kate knew that stunt-doubles were necessary but was un-happy with the man assigned to grab a rope on an escaping balloon in her stead – "That man doesn't look a thing like me at all," she protested. So she seized the rope herself, was lifted off the ground, and hung suspended in mid-air until crew members pulled her down.

For the finale of the film, she and the boys land the balloon on the concert stage of the Hollywood Bowl as the *1812 Overture* booms. Kate climbed out of the balloon in front of thousands of spectators and said, "This should prove to all of you that if you're silly enough you can do anything."

It was a great performance by Kate and her young co-stars, with spectacular scenes of the balloon in flight. But Colla was unable to get the film released because distribution companies were worried that Kate couldn't carry a low-budget movie on her own. It was finally released in Midwestern theaters two years later and in New York in 1981, but to little fanfare. *Olly Olly Oxen Free* would become Kate's lost film, with some enchanting footage never to be fully appreciated.

In October 1976, Kate began the six-month tour of *A Matter of Gravity*, which played in Denver, Vancouver, San Francisco, Los Angeles, San Diego, and Phoenix. In Los Angeles, staying at Cukor's old bungalow and working in the garden, she stepped in a hole and fractured her ankle in three places. But the injury didn't slow her down; she missed only two performances and played the rest of the tour in a wheelchair.

In the middle of one performance, when the flash of a camera interrupted her scene, Kate broke character and wheeled herself to the edge of the stage. "You're a pig," she told the photographer. "You have no consideration for the actors trying to concentrate during difficult scenes or for the people who paid good money to come here. Such a lack of consideration is an illness of our society." Then she wheeled back and picked up where she left off. The incident, foreshadowing confrontations stage actors would have later with audiences over ringing cell phones, received national attention.

In April 1976, while *A Matter of Gravity* was still running on Broadway, Kate received word that her old beau Howard Hughes had passed away at the age of seventy. By then, he had become the eccentric recluse of legend, with long hair, beard, and fingernails, weighing only ninety pounds and suffering from malnutrition. Hughes had displayed signs of mental illness, especially obsessive-compulsive disorder, since the 1930s and within a decade was surrounding himself with dozens of Kleenex boxes that he continuously stacked and re-arranged. He also wrote detailed memos to his aides with explicit instructions not to look at him nor speak to him unless spoken to.

When she got word that Hughes had died, Kate remembered the last time she saw him, in 1951, when he still owned RKO Studios. During one of their periodic phone calls, he had offered Kate free run of the studio's prop and furniture departments. One night, after most employees had gone home, she showed up at the RKO warehouse and was wandering down an aisle, examining some lamps and vases, when she heard a familiar voice calling her name.

A man dressed in khakis, a white shirt, and hat approached her holding a handkerchief close to his mouth to filter out the dust. It was Hughes. They hugged and chatted, then sat down – Kate on a plain wooden chair and Hughes on a gold-painted throne. "Howard," she laughed, "I see you haven't lost your flair for the dramatic."

Kate talked about her thriving career and her relationship with Tracy. "There was nothing terribly dramatic about the meeting," Kate recalled later, "except that it happened at all, and that by then he was clearly becoming this eccentric figure. He was going around the bend, politically speaking, and, I suppose, in other ways as well. Very anti-Communist." They were happy to see each other but, Kate said, "He seemed sad to me. I remember thinking there was something pathetic about the meeting, that he seemed so detached."

Hughes said Kate should tell the warehouse supervisor what she wanted, and it would be delivered in the morning. Then he left. They continued to speak on the phone from time to time, with dwindling frequency. During one of their last calls, Kate was in bed when Hughes called and asked her what time it was. She fumbled for her clock and mumbled, "Four o'clock." He replied, "Day or night?"

After *A Matter of Gravity* closed in March of 1977, Kate joined her extended family at Fenwick. The weather was bitter, but inside, Kate jovially entertained her nieces and nephews, cooking, laughing, and sharing her steadfast opinions. "Religion is a sop for the masses," she liked to say, and denied the existence of God, although she acknowledged that the teachings of Jesus Christ had merit. If she answered the telephone, her distinct voice could be heard saying, "Katharine Hepburn? She's not here. This is her sister."

In January 1978, George Cukor, now pushing eighty and lacking the stamina to make a major movie, suggested that he and Kate collaborate on a television version of Emlyn

Williams's *The Corn Is Green*. Kate liked the screenplay, describing the character of Miss Moffat as ". . . someone moving forward, not falling backward . . . someone at the wheel of their life instead of being dominated by excuses."

Moffat, a strong-minded Englishwoman who inherits a cottage in a Welsh mining village in the late 1800s, becomes dedicated to educating the town's boys, who are forced to work in the mines before they are ten because they can reach into crevices the men cannot. Miss Moffat has high hopes that one especially gifted boy will win a scholarship to Oxford, but when he gets a girl pregnant, he plans to forego his dreams. To salvage the situation, Miss Moffat agrees to care for the baby.

Kate made the arrangements for filming to begin - in Wales, for authenticity. "Couldn't be faked," she said. "Like *The African Queen* being done in Africa. You pick up the indefinable when you go to the source. Something different. Something that you can't just imagine. The air - the hills - the light - the mist - the soft, soft water. The language. Very odd. Hard to catch." A few weeks later, she and Cukor were rounding up a cast and crew in London. Within eight weeks, they were ready to shoot.

As Kate and Cukor selected the cast members, most of whom were younger and more beautiful, she thought, "Who's going to look at you . . . ?" Then she decided "Oh, hell, who cares. It's a great play . . . and it's life isn't it? You plow ahead and make a hit. And you plow on and someone passes you. Then someone passes them. Time levels."

Ethel Barrymore had established the role of Miss Moffat on Broadway in 1940, and five years later, Bette Davis played her on the big screen, but Kate worked hard to make this version her own.

Exterior shots for *The Corn Is Green* were filmed on a farm in the small Welsh village of YsybytyIfan, which included a stone farmhouse that served as Miss Moffat's home, and cattle barns in back that served as her school. In nearby Wrexham, Kate joined a group of sightseers on a tour of an operational coal mine. Descending 1,300 feet down into the darkness in a cage elevator, Kate chatted with miners drinking tea from their thermoses. As the elevator took them back to the surface, she heard one man begin to sing in "a beautiful tenor voice" as the others gradually joined in. She came back up covered in coal dust but remembered it as a "thrilling" experience.

When she wasn't filming, Kate stayed with Wilbourn in a 300-year-old cottage with a large fireplace made from three enormous blocks of slate excavated from nearby quarries. She kept to her usual routine, getting up daily at five to prepare herself a hearty breakfast of "fruit, eggs, bacon, chicken livers, toast, marmalade, coffee." After she'd eaten, she'd study the script for an hour, take a cold shower or bath, and go for a bike ride - all before seven. At night, she'd wash her hair, then let it dry while she ate dinner from a tray in front of the fire.

In one scene that called for Miss Moffat to ride an ancient bicycle up a steep hill, Kate was forced to swallow her pride and allow a double to stand in for her. "I was humiliated," she said. "Nearly had a stroke. But I just could not pump up that hill. Infuriating failure. I have always been able to do my own stuff. But my legs just could not push hard enough to keep that bike from a drunken wobble. They thought that I was silly to be so mad that she could and I couldn't. Yes, I suppose so. But, there it is. I still am mad. Damned old legs."

Kate was sad when filming was finished and she had to leave Wales. She had grown to love "the hills, valleys, skies, flowers, fields, stone farmhouses, barns, narrow roads lined with pink and purple foxgloves, [with] sheep roaming the hillsides." The cast and crew moved on to London to shoot the rest of the footage on a sound stage, but it was difficult to capture the spirit of the open countryside.

Reviewers complimented Kate's performance in *The Corn Is Green* when it was broadcast by CBS in January of 1979, and she was nominated for an Emmy award. But critics were unimpressed by the film itself, calling the story outdated, and the character of Miss Moffat unoriginal. Some blamed Cukor's direction, perhaps unaware that his health was failing.

When Cukor and Kate returned to the States, he told her he was unable to maintain his property and would have to sell it, along with Tracy's old bungalow. He suggested Kate buy it, but she didn't see many more Hollywood films in her future – and knew that it wouldn't be the same without Cukor there, anyway.

With heavy heart, she began packing up the cottage, stopping often to reminisce about her thirty years there, first with Tracy and then by herself. In her letter to Tracy, she wrote, "Strange to be going. I couldn't bear to leave the house after you died. I kept it - even the books on the oak table. I sit in your chair now. The books have never been moved. Silly, I suppose. I was trying to keep you there. Now we're both going."

Kate said goodbye to Tracy's favorite rocking chair that she found in the window of "an old wreck of a shop" on Olvera Street in Los Angeles. The Chinese owner said it wasn't for sale – it had belonged to his grandfather – but Kate kept coming back and finally wore him down; he sold it to her for a small fortune. She also said goodbye to her own red upholstered chair. "I moved it about according to the occasion," she wrote. "It seems heavier now. It wasn't then."

Kate said goodbye to Tracy's bedroom, into which she had moved after he died, with its view of an "old messy shapeless banana tree" outside the window. "I eat breakfast in bed very early and look right out across the patio at that silly tree," she wrote. "Doesn't even grow bananas."

Tracy's daughter Susie came by to take a few things: a crystal egg with her father's astrological sign; a first edition of *The Old Man and the Sea* that Hemingway had signed "Spencer from Papa"; a Christmas card from Field Marshal Bernard Montgomery showing him seated at a table with Winston Churchill; and a card from Stanley Kramer, the director of *Guess Who's Coming to Dinner*, that read, "May your music go on and on."

Kate kept a few things for herself, including a pretty corner cupboard her father had found for her in Cromwell, Connecticut. "It was pine - stood in the corner left of the fireplace," she wrote. "It will come back to Fenwick now with me."

On the day the furniture was to be loaded up and carried away – November 21, 1978 – it rained hard. Another chapter of her life was ending and, with so many of her friends falling ill or passing away, it was only natural for her to wonder how many chapters she had left. "It was a strange thing packing up that house," Kate wrote. "Now it's done. Bit by bit by bit, one removes one's self."

25

"A CRANKY OLD BROAD BUT A LOT OF FUN"

In July of 1979, the only man Kate ever married, Ludlow Ogden "Luddy" Smith, passed away at the age of eighty. To Kate, it seemed as though eons had passed since they were married in 1928, when both were still in their twenties, and then divorced in Mexico six years later. Their friendship cooled after Luddy married Elizabeth Albers in 1942 and had two children – but was re-kindled after Albers died in 1973.

In his seventies, Luddy was diagnosed with inoperable cancer. Kate invited him to Fenwick often, but eventually he became too sick to visit. So she went to see him at his home in Philadelphia. "I tried to do everything for Luddy that I possibly could," Kate said later, "knowing I could never re-pay him for all the support he had given me. Unimaginable - my life, had it not been for Luddy. He was heaven-sent."

When she wasn't visiting Luddy – and then mourning his passing – Kate was keeping herself occupied by attempting another of her improbable firsts: Making a record. That spring, she had received a letter from Ben Bagley, a New York record producer, asking if she would be willing to con-tribute a few tracks to an album of Cole Porter songs.

Bagley ran a small label, Painted Smiles, known for releas-ing idiosyncratic albums of celebrities - not all of them tal-ented singers – performing show tunes by iconic composers like Porter, Ira Gershwin, and Harold Arlen.

Surprised and intrigued by Bagley's invitation, Kate met with her friend and music coach Sue Seton, who had helped her get through *Coco* a decade earlier. "Somehow, as I stood there at Sue's piano, I thought I really did sound a bit bet-ter - or was it that I felt a bit better?" she recalled. "Or was it that Sue, who is an adorable and sensitive creature, was able to convince me that I was a bit better? I mean there was some actual sound there. Wasn't there? Was there?"

She scheduled an audition with Bagley and performed three songs - "Thank You So Much, Mrs. Lowsborough – Good-by"; "The Queen of Terre Haute"; and "A Woman's Career." Bagley liked her renditions so much that he brought her into the studio to record all three. They appeared on *Cole Porter Revisited, Vol. 4*, which also featured songs by Broadway veterans such as Blossom Dearie, Dolores Gray, and Helen Gallagher.

"Oh dear," Kate thought when she heard the recordings. "What is it that's not there - that just makes it not quite - certainly not arresting to listen to?"

Her singing, she thought, was similar to her painting. "It is thrilling to do. And you finish it and it looks devastating and you hang it on the wall. Then gradually you realize that you just can't keep looking at it. And finally you take it down and hang it in another room - one which you don't go into so often. And if anyone says, 'Those lilies, who painted that?' Thrilled, you say, 'I did.' But you know in your heart."

Despite her own spot-on assessment of her singing ability, she hungered for recognition. So one day she took the record to Fenwick and casually left it on the big round kitchen table with the Tiffany lamp hanging over it, knowing her musical brother Dick would see it. But the record just sat there all weekend, untouched.

Finally, on Sunday, Kate said to Dick, "Aren't you going to play the record?"

"What record?"

"That one - on the table."

"Oh - Cole Porter," Dick said. "I can't stand Cole Porter."

"Oh cruelty!" Kate thought. "Oh wounds of life! Crushed . . . I went out of the kitchen. What a goddamned bastard - how mean can you get."

Dick's friend Virginia Harrington overheard the conversation and put the record on the turntable in the study. Dick remained in the kitchen, ignoring it, but Kate stood in the hall and listened.

". . . and the truth came to me. Why are you so upset, Katharine? You are so upset because you can hear - and it just isn't - that's it. It just isn't. If you thought it was good, you wouldn't give a rap what Dick did or didn't do. But you know . . . And I laughed - at myself really, because I did know that my misery was really caused by the fact that I myself knew that again I had done it but *not* done it. Ah, life . . . Well, next time. Or should I say - next life."

Though her singing career was now officially over, Kate had certainly not given up on her film career. The question was whether the industry had given up on her, now that she was in her early seventies. Times in Hollywood were changing. Studios had moved to Los Angeles and its surrounds and were filming far more often in Europe and other exotic locales. Few of the luminaries who had graced the screen in Hollywood's heyday were still alive and working. After John Wayne's death in 1979, there were really only two: Katharine Hepburn and Henry Fonda.

Remarkably, the two had never met. The story of how they came to make one last great film together began with Henry Fonda's daughter Jane. She saw the stage play *On Golden Pond* by Ernest Thompson that opened on Broadway in February 1979. With Tom Aldredge and Frances Sternhagen playing the leads, it ran for 126 performances (and another 256 performances Off-Broadway). Moved by the story of an aging couple dealing with the husband's failing health, Jane purchased the rights to the drama so her father could play the role of the cantankerous Norman Thayer. Jane would portray his daughter. For Norman's wife, Ethel, there was really only one natural choice: the elderly but ageless Katharine Hepburn.

Despite the storied careers of Henry Fonda and Kate, it was doubtful that a film company would be willing to put up millions of dollars for a movie that centered on the health travails of two senior citizens. So Jane Fonda was the key. Even though her part in the film was small, she had been a big star since the 1960s and had the clout to raise the necessary funds and co-produce. With Jane pushing hard, Twentieth Century-Fox agreed to make the film, with Thompson adapting the screenplay from his own stage play.

After meeting Jane in New York, Kate went to California to visit with Henry Fonda and the film's director Mark Rydell, who had recently directed *The Rose* with Bette Midler. Extending her hand to Fonda, Kate said, "Well, it's about time."

Rydell and producer Bruce Gilbert were both concerned about their aging stars' health. Henry had a serious heart condition, and Kate's palsy was getting worse. Since the 1970s, she had shown symptoms of the disease – her head and hands shook and her voice quavered. It was barely noticeable at first, but now she found herself often shaking uncontrollably.

Deciding that her condition only made her character more believable, the producers scheduled shooting for June 1980. But in April, Kate dislocated her shoulder playing tennis with a friend and had to undergo surgery on her rotator cuff. Her recovery would take a minimum of three months, her doctors said, suggesting she wait even longer to make a movie.

"I knew the film was dependent on the Fonda part being lazy, and not working, and not wanting [or able] to do a lot of physical things," Kate recalled. "The wife, my part, had to carry all the luggage, do everything, and here I am with an arm that's really bad. Well, I tried to get out of the picture, but Fonda said, 'No, you'll be fine. You'll do it. We won't get anyone else.' He stuck to his guns and in July, 1980 [just two weeks late], we found ourselves on location in New Hampshire."

On the first day of shooting, in Laconia, New Hampshire, Kate arrived on the set and presented Fonda with a gift. "Now, Hepburn is a presence wherever she is," Fonda said. "In a room, she is the only one in it . . . she doesn't do anything to dominate, she just does and is . . . as people saw her . . . they sort of just melted in front of her . . . By the time she got to me, I was alone . . . She came up to me holding her outstretched, cupped hands in front of her. Something crumpled was inside those hands but I didn't know what it was. She came right up to me and stood there."

In her hands was a fishing cap. "I want you to have this,"

Kate said. "This was Spencer's favorite hat." Fonda is not normally one to show emotion, but at this gesture, he was moved to tears. He wore the hat not only in their first scene but throughout the film.

Like Kate, Jane Fonda was a smart, tough, independent woman who could handle herself and defend her opinions. Rydell was nervous about how the two women would get along. "After all, Jane is the big star of the eighties and Katharine [used to be] the big star," he said. "You had the sense in the first few days of two lionesses prowling the same ground."

Jane had trepidation of her own. "To work with her, and to work with my father, was a terrifying, waking-up-in-the-morning-wanting-to-throw-up kind of experience," Jane said. "But . . . when we went to rehearsals, I realized that she was as nervous as I was."

At times, Kate felt like she was in the middle of a family therapy session. "It was strange," she said later. "It seemed as though I was the mother Jane had fantasized having . . . and if her father and I could make everything all right in the movie, somehow things would be all right in her life. There was certainly a whole layer of drama going on in the scenes between her and Hank, and I think she came by to watch every scene he and I had together. There was a feeling of longing about her."

Kate enjoyed working with Henry. "Henry Fonda's not one to make new friends and neither am I, but we got along OK," she said. "He has his own world. He likes to sit and fish, I like to walk through the woods alone. We are quite similar. He doesn't waste time. No small talk. And I hate to have idiotic conversations." She appreciated that he never complained during long evenings in the cold or sitting in a boat with the sun beating down on his sensitive skin.

But Kate also sympathized with how hard it must have been for Jane to grow up with a father like Henry. "Hank Fonda was the hardest nut I ever tried to crack," Kate said. "But I didn't know any more about him after we had made the picture than I did at the beginning. Cold. Cold. Cold."

Henry Fonda, meanwhile, came away with considerable admiration for Kate. "You want to hear about Katharine Hepburn?" he said. "She swam every morning and after work. She'd have her dinner and go to sleep at eight o'clock, get up at three or four and study her lines . . . At the end of September, when it was bitter cold, they catapulted the fourteen-year-old boy and me into the water. The company was more nervous than I. They thought, 'This old son-of-a-bitch is going to have a heart attack,' but I fooled 'em. I had a wet suit on under my wardrobe. Katharine had to dive into the water, too, but she didn't even wear a wet suit."

Rydell, meanwhile, was deeply impressed with both actors. "They approached this material bravely," he said. "Here you have Henry Fonda and Katharine Hepburn in their seventies, dealing with material that has to do with the final years of one's life, and how do you face death and how do you support one another . . . it was quite a resonant experience."

After its release in December of 1981, *On Golden Pond* became the second-highest grossing film of the year, behind *Raiders of the Lost Ark*. Henry Fonda's performance as the dying Norman Thayer received the most attention, perhaps because people knew Fonda's own health was failing. "Mr.

Fonda gives one of the great performances of his long, truly distinguished career," wrote Vincent Canby of *The New York Times*. He was so moving, in fact, that he won his first Academy Award, for Best Actor. With her father bedridden, watching on television, Jane Fonda tearfully accepted the Oscar on his behalf. "My father would say typically that this is just luck," she said, "But I will try to assure him that there's no luck to it." Henry Fonda died a few months later.

Kate also received good reviews, though often in the context of Henry Fonda's performance. Canby wrote, "One of the most appealing things about her as an actress is the way she responds to - and is invigorated by - a strong co-star . . . she needs someone to support, challenge and interact with. Mr. Fonda is the best thing that's happened to her since Spencer Tracy and Humphrey Bogart." Others, however, thought her performance was overly sentimental, not realizing that her eyes were teary at certain moments because of her chronic eye condition.

Nevertheless, Kate also triumphed at the Academy Awards, winning for Best Actress. It was her fourth Best Actress Oscar, beating her own record of three (twelve actresses, including Ingrid Bergman, Elizabeth Taylor, and Bette Davis, have two). When Bruce Gilbert accepted the award on her behalf, he quoted Kate as saying, "a simple thank you will suffice." In his book on Hepburn, Homer Dickens summed up the conventional wisdom that the award was considered a sentimental win, "a tribute to her enduring career."

Thompson was so pleased with Kate's portrayal of Ethel Thayer that he suggested her next project could be a return to live theater. He asked her to perform in one of his plays,

West Side Waltz, the story of an aging concert pianist. She immediately accepted, but the role was a challenge; she needed to act as if she were playing the music being fed over the theater's sound system.

Her shoulder had started to heal, but toward the end of filming *On Golden Pond*, she walked into a glass door, and her pain was so severe that Rydell had to shoot around her for several days. Her shoulder was not damaged, but two fingers were numb. Playing the piano provided therapy, though the process was long, difficult, and frustrating.

West Side Waltz tells the story of Margaret Mary Elderdice, a seventy-something widow and former concert pianist living alone on Manhattan's West Side. Fighting to retain her independence, yet increasingly unable to walk, she reluctantly takes in a roommate to assist her, a prim and proper middle-aged violinist.

Kate enlisted musical comedy star Dorothy Loudon to play the role of the violinist and chose the same director/producer team she had worked with in *A Matter of Gravity*: the director Noël Willman and producers Roger Stevens and Robert Whitehead.

Onstage, Kate and Loudon would have to choreograph their movements to match the music being played by professionals offstage. The two rehearsed daily at Kate's house. "I don't think Vladimir Horowitz and Isaac Stern have anything to worry about," Loudon said. "Actually, Kate is very good but I'm developing two chins from trying to balance the violin."

On November 19, 1981, two weeks before *On Golden Pond* was released, *West Side Waltz* debuted on Broadway. New

York critics were enchanted with Kate's performance. Walter Kerr wrote in *The New York Times*: "I'm not sure that author Ernest Thompson realizes . . . what multiple small miracles Katharine Hepburn is bestowing upon his play . . . One mysterious thing she has learned to do is breathe unchallengeable life into lifeless lines. She does it, or seems to do it, by giving the most serious consideration to every syllable she utters. There may have been a time when she coasted on mannerisms, turned her rhythms into a form of rapid transit. That time is long gone."

By the spring of 1982, as Kate turned seventy-five, it was clear that she had no intentions of slowing down. A film legend who could still claim star billing, all she needed was the right story. She had been thinking about one in particular for a number of years – a screenplay written by the relatively unknown Martin Zweiback, who had left it on the back doorstep of Tracy's bungalow years before.

The play, called *The Ultimate Solution of Grace Quigley*, was a dark comedy about an old woman who engages a hit man to kill her and other aging friends who have lost their will to live. The controversial subject matter had previously prevented Zweiback from getting the play produced, but Kate nonetheless asked him to work to develop the story. In the summer of 1982, she managed to convince Anthony Harvey to direct the film - now shortened to *Grace Quigley* - and hired newcomer Nick Nolte to co-star and began to hunt for a producer.

That December, Kate and Phyllis Wilbourn went to Fenwick to spend the month with her brother Dick and his family. Despite record snowfalls and hazardous road conditions,

Kate insisted on driving herself into town to run errands. On December 13, with Wilbourn in the passenger seat, her vehicle skidded on the ice, spun out, and crashed into a utility pole, crushing the front end of the car. Emergency crews arrived and pulled both passengers out. Wilbourn suffered only minor injuries, but Kate's right foot was nearly severed.

Rather than heading for the closest hospital, Kate insisted on being taken to Hartford Hospital, an hour away, so the doctor who saved her finger could also save her foot. The surgeon immediately operated, but it wasn't clear for several days whether the surgery would be successful. Kate was released from the hospital on January 2 and went to convalesce at her sister Marion's house, wearing a cast up to her hip. She was in and out of the hospital for the next eight months, then spent six more in physical therapy.

When Kate had recovered well enough from her car accident to go back to playing tennis, she had what at first seemed like a chance encounter – but soon turned out to be anything but that. Kate was about to take a lesson at the Beverly Hills Hotel one day when she noticed a young woman approaching. "All of a sudden, almost following us, came a girl - blushing madly - the blush spreading over her face - up her neck - but she was determined."

The girl stopped to pet Kate's dog, a three-year-old mutt with big eyes and half of his tail missing.

"It's Lobo, isn't it?" the girl said.

"Yes," Kate said. "Yes, it's Lobo."

"Could it be? Yes it is," Kate thought. "Susie - it's Susie. Spence's daughter." Her mother, Louise Tracy, had died not long before, at age eighty-seven.

"He looks fine," the girl said.

"Yes, he's fine, Susie."

Suddenly, they both were at a loss for words. Silence.

"Look, Susie, if you would like to get to know me, that can be very easily arranged. You know where I live, and you know the telephone number. Any time . . ."

"So she called," Kate recalled. "And we became friends. Just like that."

As they got to know one another, Kate and Susie shared their memories of Tracy. "He would come home every Sunday and play tennis with us and tell wonderful stories," Susie recalled. "He was generous, funny - he loved to kid."

The two women agreed, however, that there was much about him they would never know. "He was also complex and extremely sensitive," Susie said. "You couldn't convey the depth of feeling he did on screen without knowing what pain was personally."

At such moments, Kate could feel that even though Tracy was long gone, his spirit was vividly present. And life was moving on, which for Kate always meant more film projects – just as it had for Tracy. Around this time, *Grace Quigley* was finally coming together. Two Israeli producers, Menahem Golan and Yoram Globus, agreed to finance the film through their production company, Cannon Films, which was known for bringing small films in under budget. They began filming in October 1983 in New York.

Kate did not tell Golan and Globus about her injury, which she hid extremely well. She avoided strenuous movement, but, as always, didn't ask for any special treatment. She arrived on the set first and volunteered her opinions when she thought it necessary. Her co-star Nick Nolte called her "a cranky old broad but a lot of fun."

Grace Quigley premiered at the Cannes Film Festival in May 1984. It was not well received; critics didn't find euthanasia terribly funny. "The two actors exude endearing, though smarmy personas that impart a light-hearted and whimsical tone to otherwise unpleasant subject matter," one wrote.

Kate was disappointed. She wanted to focus on "the abominable way we treat our elderly" and play down the sensitive subject of euthanasia.

"If people can just learn to laugh instead of being terrified at what the future holds for them, they will be better off," Kate said. "What release! To sleep is the greatest joy there is. If I were a burden to myself and I could leave my money to younger people who could really use it, I would feel it was my privilege to do what I could do."

After *Grace Quigley* was finished, Kate had more surgery on her ankle at Hartford Hospital and for several months was in a plaster cast up to her knee. As always, she tolerated the discomfort with more patience than anyone thought possible.

In August of 1986, Kate's sister Marion died suddenly of a heart attack at the age of sixty-eight. "This was a real shock to all of us," Kate recalled in her memoir. "We had felt that we would all just go on and on." Marion had authored seven books on Connecticut history and legend. She and her husband Ellsworth, also a historian and a former mayor of West Hartford, had three children, including the actress Katharine Houghton, and two grandchildren. "I miss Dad and Mother and Marion every day and every night of my life," Kate said.

Perhaps feeling the importance of leaving a legacy of community involvement, as her parents and Marion did, Kate became more socially active around this time. She lent her name to Planned Parenthood and permitted the organization to send out hundreds of thousands of mailings seeking donations. When anyone praised her efforts, she'd say, "I'm not in a class with my parents. They were real reformers and noble people who set out to improve the state of man and woman - black, white, diseased, whatever. Why, I'm just ordinarily polite. They fought all the diseases of the day. I've fought for Planned Parenthood, abortion and how to laugh at life if I can."

But Kate was an inspiration to more people than she realized. In a national survey conducted in the mid-1980s, 4,500 teenagers were asked who they would name as their modern-day heroes. Katharine Hepburn, the only woman on the list – which included Michael Jackson, Clint Eastwood, and the pope - ranked seventh (the Pope finished behind her at number eight). Little could she have imagined that her struggle to forge a career on her own terms would inspire generations of young people to do the same.

As Kate approached eighty, she became more open to participating in film retrospectives, like the documentary about Spencer Tracy that she agreed to narrate in 1986. *The Spen-*

cer Tracy Legacy: A Tribute by Katharine Hepburn, made by PBS and MGM Television, shows Kate taking the viewer on a journey through Tracy's life and career. It concluded with a scene "as wrenching as it is unexpected," in the words of critic John J. O'Connor of *The New York Times,* when Kate began reading the letter she wrote to Tracy long after his death. Her eyes welling with tears, she said, "living wasn't easy for you, was it?" She invoked his drinking problem and noted the paradox that "you couldn't enter your own life but you could be someone else."

At other moments, she seemed to be talking about herself as much as Tracy. During a tour of the MGM studio lot, she pointed out the dressing rooms of famous actors of that era – Tracy, Clark Gable, Bob Montgomery, Lionel Barrymore and, of course, Katharine Hepburn. "It's a thrilling, wonderful, romantic, delicious business to be in," she says, "but you learn that you may always be the cake, but you do not remain the frosting."

Pointing to a sign that revealed the structure had been renamed after a more recent star – "Stallone Building" – she acknowledged that her flavor of frosting was on its way out, firmly declaring, "That changes."

26
"RETIRE? WHAT'S THE POINT?"

Kate didn't know it at the time, but *Grace Quigley* would be the last time she appeared in a starring role on the big screen. For the next decade, as she entered her eighties, she would appear in a series of made-for-television movies and one final big-screen cameo. Despite the uneven quality of the films themselves, these projects fulfilled their basic purpose: keeping her working and invigorated.

Some of the movies turned out well. Kate was nominated for an Emmy for her performance in the 1986 romantic comedy *Mrs. Delafield Wants to Marry*, playing a widow who shocks her upper-class, Anglo-American family by falling in love with her Jewish doctor, unleashing the prejudices of both families.

Less successful was her 1988 comedy *Laura Lansing Slept Here*, about a rich and famous novelist who moves in with a suburban family to prove that she can still relate to ordinary people. John J. O'Connor of *The New York Times* dismissed the film as exaggerated, unbelievable, and contrived, but raved that "the special Hepburn spirit remains, gutsy and disarming as ever."

When she wasn't working, Kate still liked to entertain mostly at home, but her social circle began to change. While filming *On Golden Pond*, she had met the pop legend Michael Jackson, whom Jane Fonda had invited to the New Hampshire shoot and then abandoned, leaving him with nobody to talk to. So Kate befriended him. "He fascinated me," Kate said later. "He's an absolutely extraordinary creature. He's worked his entire life, entertaining professionally since he was three, and he's never lived a single moment, I mean not a moment, in the real world. He doesn't know how to do anything but write his songs and thrill an audience."

One morning in New Hampshire, she scolded Michael for not making his bed – then was shocked to learn that he didn't know how. "He had never made a bed in his life!" Kate said. "He's E.T.!"

When Michael was in New York, Kate went to his concerts and invited him to dinner. When he played Madison Square Garden in August of 1984 during his Victory Tour with his five brothers, he came over to Kate's place for a small dinner party that included her niece Katharine Houghton, the writer A. Scott Berg, and her new friend, the television journalist Cynthia McFadden.

"He was wearing sunglasses and a satiny blue uniform trimmed in gold braid," Berg recalled. "Onstage, it would probably look dazzling. Up close it looked flimsy and gaudy . . . At twenty-five, he had the demeanor of an extremely polite ten-year-old."

As she made new friends, Kate became disengaged from some of her old pals. Laura Harding lived a quiet life in her estate in New Jersey, which Kate found insufferably boring. And Irene Selznick, her friend for more than fifty years, felt Kate was "growing old disgracefully," she told Berg, by making television movies that were "horrible" and being photographed in public with her new young friends like Michael Jackson. Selznick seemed jealous of Kate's new crowd, which included the director Anthony Harvey and McFadden, who eventually became so close to Kate that she was named executor of her estate.

Kate met McFadden in the early 1980s through Kate's sister Marion, and they quickly became friends. McFadden was still in her twenties and getting her law degree at Columbia University; later, she would become a well-known network television correspondent and anchor. When McFadden got married to *Hartford Courant* publisher Michael Davies in 1989, Kate took the highly unusual step of hosting the wedding at her family's Fenwick home, even taking down the famous sign posted at the gate that said, "Please Go Away."

Kate was also friendly with the gossip columnist Liz Smith, whom she enjoyed tremendously "despite her being engaged in what [Kate] called 'a moronic profession,'" Berg wrote. But not all of these new friends got along. When Berg's book, *Kate Remembered*, was published in 2003, just twelve days after her death, McFadden was said to be upset by certain sections about her, and Smith called it "Self-promoting fakery . . . Hepburn would have despised it and his betrayal of her friendship." Berg insisted he had Kate's blessing to write the book: "Countless times she spoke of my writing a book about her, insisting only that it never be published during her lifetime."

Ultimately, however, Kate proved forgiving of friends who wrote about her. After two decades of not speaking to Garson Kanin after he published *Tracy and Hepburn: An Intimate Memoir*, she finally made up with him after Kanin's wife Ruth Gordon passed away in 1985. "Oh," she said after her reunion with Kanin, "I'm too old to be carrying grudges."

Perhaps tired of reading other people's versions of her fascinating life story, Kate took control of her own legacy in 1991 and published her memoir, *Me: Stories of My Life*. The book was something she had been toying with in her spare time, and she finally managed to get it done. "I was terrified to have somebody write a book about me after I was dead," she told a *Hartford Courant* reporter. Publisher Alfred A. Knopf paid $4.25 million for the rights to her story, which included the particulars of her thirty-year relationship with Tracy - although she omitted some intimate details - as well as her love affairs with Howard Hughes and Leland Hayward.

When she began work on the memoir, she considered it a tribute to her parents and to Spencer Tracy's talent. When asked why she had selected the title, she said: "I called the book *Me* because that's what it is all about. I'm totally selfish. A me-me-me person. I suppose that's what people will say, and I won't blame them."

In a remarkable turnaround that began with her Dick Cavett interview in 1973, this once-private woman had successfully made the transition to public treasure. *Me* was a huge success – staying on the bestseller lists for over a year – and Kate joked to friends that she had become an American institution, like the Flatiron Building or the Statue of Liberty. In 1993, she even appeared in an autobiographical television documentary, *Katharine Hepburn: All About Me*, made for the TNT cable network. "So this is about Katharine Hepburn, public, private. Can you tell which is which?" she began, then added, laughing, "Sometimes I wonder myself."

As Kate's legend grew, she continued acting in made-for-television movies like 1992's *The Man Upstairs*, playing an elderly woman who befriends an escaped convict she finds hiding in her attic (Ryan O'Neal). It was not exactly Eugene O'Neill or Tennessee Williams, but it kept her working, and she was nominated for a Golden Globe for Best Actress.

Now eighty-five, Kate still swam at Fenwick almost every weekend but confessed, "My bum ankle forces me to crawl over the rocks to get out of the water. Imagine the obituary: 'Actress drowning in six inches of water.'"

She also threw her energies into painting, though she was too ashamed of the paintings to sign them. She considered organizing an exhibition but decided instead to decorate the walls at Fenwick. She still shoveled snow in front of her townhouse in Manhattan; when neighbors expressed their concern, she'd say, "Well, someone's got to do it, don't they?"

But Kate was clearly slipping. By the spring of 1993, she had trouble explaining to her driver how to get to her sister Peg's home west of Hartford, a place she had visited countless times. When a friend said he would visit the next day, she was shocked when he arrived, having forgotten all about it.

Producers and writers still sent her scripts, but she found most of them awful - patronizing stories about "cute little old ladies - what a goddamned bore," she said. For years, she worked on her own screenplay, *Me and Phyllis,* that consisted of scenes of her life with Wilbourn that reaches its climax with the car crash they suffered together in 1982.

One night in her living room, Kate performed the entire script for Berg. "She captured the dialogue between the two of them in funny detail," he wrote later, "and she brought me close to tears a few times in revealing her gratitude for having had somebody so dear as Phyllis in her life. Beyond that, it was a strange piece of work that was meant to be a quasi-documentary . . . for a moment, I felt like William Holden stumbling into Norma Desmond's parlor in *Sunset Boulevard*."

Several producers showed an interest in the project, but Berg said they didn't seem very serious: "I think a few of them were just interested in spending time with her and shopping her name around town." Each deal eventually fell apart.

With time on her hands, Kate spent many hours reading her fan mail and answering some of it. She enjoyed this process but also found it disturbing. "If they're really inspired by what I've done with my life," she asked, "why don't they do something with theirs? Not just watch old movies." More upsetting was the hate mail, usually inspired by her pro-choice statements, and the occasional threat. When the hate mail quoted scripture, she snorted, "So much for 'God is Love!'"

Despite her age and bad foot, Kate found it difficult not to work. "Retire?" she would exclaim to friends who gently raised the subject. "What's the point? Actors shouldn't walk away from the audience as long as the audiences aren't walking away from them. As long as people are buying what I'm selling, I'm still selling."

Remarkably, producers and audiences kept buying. In 1994, the year she turned eighty-seven, she appeared in three separate films – which proved to be the final three of her career.

Two were made for television. In *This Can't Be Love,* she

and seventy-eight-year-old Anthony Quinn played two aging actors who reunite after breaking up fifty years earlier. Directed once again by her friend Anthony Harvey, the movie was considered less successful than her similar TV film, *Love Among the Ruins*, with Lawrence Olivier. "Not even Katharine Hepburn and Anthony Quinn can salvage the ordinary and predictable light romantic drama," wrote Ray Loynd in the *Los Angeles Times*. "What makes this story . . . so watchable is Hepburn and Quinn's beguiling ability to poke droll fun at their very *own* Hollywood legends and egos."

In *One Christmas*, based on a short story by Truman Capote, Kate plays a New Orleans grande dame in a story that centers mostly on the relationship between a con-artist father (Henry Winkler) and his estranged son. Though she was nominated for a Screen Actor's Guild Award, critics were not impressed. "Physically, Hepburn looks fine," wrote Loynd in the *Los Angeles Times*, "but her voice is sometimes inaudible and her casting is frankly more sentimental than productive." One of her lines from the film was so perfectly "Kate" that it could have served as her epitaph: "I've always lived my life exactly as I wanted," she said. "I wouldn't change a single thing. No regrets."

Kate's final big-screen appearance was a small part in Warren Beatty's *Love Affair*, a remake of the 1957 classic *An Affair to Remember* starring Cary Grant and Deborah Kerr. While *Love Affair* ended up being neither a critical nor commercial hit – it cost $60 million to make and grossed just $18 million domestically – the story of how Beatty talked her into it was, in many ways, more interesting than the film itself.

Beatty, who produced and co-wrote the film, wanted Kate to play Ginny, the elderly aunt of Beatty's ex-football player Mike Gambril, who falls in love with singer Terry McKay, played by Beatty's real-life wife, Annette Bening. The part was essentially a cameo – and Katharine Hepburn simply did not do cameos. With the exception of her scene in 1943's *Stage Door Canteen*, which she did only to support the war effort, and 1959's *Suddenly, Last Summer*, when she co-starred with Elizabeth Taylor – Kate had been the star of every film she ever appeared in. No bit parts or walk-on gags. And no commercials.

But Beatty was desperate to have her, asking friends to lobby her on his behalf, calling her, and sending her so many flowers that Kate complained her place looked like a funeral parlor. After flying to New York to meet with her in person, Beatty finally convinced her to accompany him back to Los Angeles on Warner Brothers Studio's private jet and stay in a large, secluded house that Beatty had rented just for her.

Despite all that, remarkably enough, Kate had still not agreed to do the picture and made Beatty promise she could fly home to New York any time she wanted. After a few days, Kate complained that she was getting tired of Los Angeles, didn't like the script, and wanted to go home. Beatty convinced her to stay. Determined to make the best of it, Kate showed up at the shoot, on time as always. On the soundstage, Berg said, "She looked great - more alert and alive than she had in months."

Reviews of the film – and Kate's role in it – were mixed. Janet Maslin of *The New York Times* said Kate was "ill served by this one, looks acutely uncomfortable . . ." But Roger Ebert said, "Hepburn's scenes steal, and almost stop, the show. She has been old for a long time (she is in her eighties) but this is the first time she has also looked small and frail. Yet the magnificent spirit is still there, and the romantic fire, and she's right for this eccentric old woman, living alone in unimaginable splendor, and feeling an instant connection with the young woman her nephew has brought home."

When she got back to New York, Kate had to deal not only with her own declining condition but with that of her longtime assistant, Phyllis Wilbourn. No one knew exactly how old Wilbourn was, but Kate later discovered that she was four years older than Kate. As time went on, Wilbourn appeared tired, forgetful, and confused, and Kate began to take care of her assistant more than the other way around. "Phyllis needs a Phyllis," Kate said, and hired people to look after her.

Kate slowed down, too. "Her energy ebbed," Berg recalled. "Sometimes she'd want dinner as early as five o'clock; and she'd clamber up the stairs to bed - literally using her hands and feet - by six, before the sun had set."

Kate also began drinking more. "Unconsciously, Kate was using the liquor as an anodyne - not only to kill the mildly depressing bouts of loneliness but also her physical pain, which I had long suspected was worse than she ever let on," Berg said. "Emotional situations - a sad scene in a movie, a touching story, a death - could bring her to tears; but only once did I see her cry because something physically hurt."

In April 1995, Wilbourn passed away. When Berg called to offer his condolences and ask what she died of, Kate snapped, "What's the difference? She stopped breathing, and she's dead. And that's that." On May 11 – what would have been Wilbourn's ninety-second birthday – Kate and some friends buried her ashes in a cemetery in West Hartford, among Hepburns. "During the brief ceremony at the grave, as rain came down," Berg recalled. "Kate suddenly dropped to her knees and sobbed."

In an eerie echo of the way the Hepburn children were forbidden from mentioning the name of Kate's brother Tom after he died, Berg said, "I never heard her raise Phyllis's name again."

In the late winter of 1996, Kate was hospitalized with pneumonia. Within a few days, she was transferred to Fenwick, which was outfitted with a hospital bed, oxygen tanks, and round-the-clock nurses. She recovered, but the tabloid press had a field day. *The National Enquirer* published a horrific photo of her on its cover, quoting her as saying, "Don't be sad - I'm going to join Spencer . . ."

After she turned ninety on May 12, 1997, Kate began to show signs of dementia. Conversations were difficult. "She seemed to understand what was being said," Berg recalled, "but she seemed to lack the strength to respond. Direct questions seldom elicited more than a few words, which sometimes seemed to be in response to something that had been asked earlier . . . or unasked at all."

Soon afterward, when Berg asked Kate if she knew who he was, she said, "No," but when he moved closer, he noticed a tear rolling down her left cheek.

In May of 1999, Berg returned to Fenwick and found Kate appearing almost child-like: "Her eyes seemed bigger and more expressive, lighting up at small things - positively childlike. She smiled a lot."

That day, conversation with Kate's siblings Peg and Bob turned to discussions of the death of their brother Tom, when he was just a teenager. "I looked over at Kate," said Berg, "who had turned away from us and stared instead toward the fire, her face wet with tears."

In May of 2003, an aggressive tumor was found in Kate's neck. The decision was made not to medically intervene. She died on June 29, in her beloved Fenwick home, at the age of ninety-six.

In one of his last conversations with Kate, just before she lost her capacity to speak, Berg was about to leave when she asked him, "Are you still loved?"

"Yes," Berg replied, "he was."

"Good," she said. "I've been loved, too."

EPILOGUE
"SHE MAY HAVE BEEN OUR GREATEST ACTRESS OF ALL"

In November of 1990, after attending the memorial service for her friend Irene Selznick, Kate said, "Don't ever have one of those for me."

Her thinking, as always, was clear and unsentimental: "She's dead, and nothing's going to bring her back. Better if everybody had stayed home and thought about her for a moment, then gone on with their lives. And that's all they should do when I die. And if anybody wants to do more than that, they can rent one of my movies."

In keeping with her wishes, no memorial service was held for Katharine Hepburn. But she could not prevent the powerful tributes and outpouring of affection that followed her passing, immediately and in the years since.

Two days after her death, on the evening of July 1, 2003, the lights on Broadway were dimmed. Televisions specials and special issues of magazines celebrating her life and career were rushed into production. The intersection of East 49th Street and 2nd Avenue in the Turtle Bay section of Manhattan was renamed "Katharine Hepburn Place." President George W. Bush called her "one of the nation's artistic treasures."

Despite her insistence that people get on with their lives after her death, it's hard to imagine that Kate would not have enjoyed the posthumous attention she has received. Her alma mater, Bryn Mawr College, created the Katharine Houghton Hepburn Center – dedicated to both Kate and her mother – and every year awards the Katharine Hepburn Medal that "recognizes women whose lives, work and contributions embody the intelligence, drive and independence of the four-time-Oscar-winning actress." In Old Saybrook,

Connecticut, the Katharine Hepburn Cultural Arts Center, which includes a performance space and a Katharine Hepburn museum, opened in 2009.

On her hundredth birthday, the National Portrait Gallery in Washington mounted an exhibition called *One Life: Kate, A Centennial Celebration*. She even got her own stamp as part of the United States Postal Service's "Legends of Hollywood" series.

As she requested, Kate's belongings were put up for auction at Sotheby's in New York. In 2004, the event raised $5.8 million, willed to Kate's family, which at the time of her death included her brother Bob, her sister Peg, four nieces, and nine nephews (her brother Dick died in 2000).

Before Kate died, her friend and biographer A. Scott Berg read Kate a magazine article he had written that read, "Katharine Hepburn inspires because she speaks directly to the heart in a most intelligent manner. The reason for her staying power is that for the last half century, she - above all - has provided a treasury of images which represent timeless human values: courage, independence, truth, idealism, and love. She is romance."

"Christ," Kate replied. "I'm not romance. That's Marilyn."

"No," Berg said, "Monroe is sex and an object of lust . . . and a victim. You told me that the times you met her, she always reminded you of a 'lonely leaf blowing in the wind.'"

"Garbo, then," she said.

"No," Berg responded. "I think she's mystery . . . and also a victim."

"Well, then, I don't understand what you mean."

Berg then reeled off a list of the characters Kate had played in an astonishing career that spanned sixty-six years and produced fifty-two films and thirty-three plays: "Eva Lovelace, Jo March, Terry Randall with their artistic yearnings," he said. "Alice Adams with her social aspirations; Linda Seton, Tracy Lord, Tess Harding, Pat Pemberton, Bunny Watson getting whacked over the head by love; Rosie Sayer, Jane Hudson, Lizzie Curry, all desperate for love; Mary Tyrone, Christina Drayton, Ethel Thayer, even Eleanor of Aquitaine, all remembering the early glory of their love.

"Don't you see," he said, "they're all dreamers, believers, adventurers, women of spirit who remain true to themselves but manage to change and grow and give to another person. That's what I mean by romance."

"Okay," she said. "I won't argue with you."

Throughout her career, Katharine Hepburn was consistently dogged by the question of whether she was a great actress. "The old question about whether she could *act* may not only not have an answer," wrote journalist Claudia Roth Pierpont in *The New Yorker* shortly after her death, "it may not be the right question."

Noting that Kate admitted she was too content with herself to rank among the really great actors – "too much the strong and happily unreflective product of her parents" – Pierpont wrote. "She overcame every obstacle - horror, failure, love, the endings of most of her movies - to provide us with a continually renewed image of the strength that such overcoming required.

"We held her close not because she could act but because of the insistent life that hummed through every taut and peremptory inch of her, and that we imagined to be as natural as breathing or winning for someone so easily, imperiously free. It was in making us believe in this that she may have been our greatest actress of all."